A convincing argument for understanding the total customer experience and must-reading for any manager concerned with growing demand. This book is full of important insights which are shared in a lucid, engaging way.

—Gerald Zaltman, The Joseph C. Wilson Professor of
Business Administration, Harvard Business School,
and author of *How Customers Think*

In today's business environment, one can pick being product-focused, marketing-focused or consumer-focused. If you choose to be consumer focused, this is the book to read. *Clued In* is experience management 2.0.

—Watts Wacker, FirstMatter LLC
and author of *The Visionary's Handbook:
Nine Paradoxes that will Shape the Future of Your Business*

A must-read for CEOs in business, industry, health care, service, or education because it has the power to totally re-direct a marketing or strategic plan to immediately provide a value-added experience for customers.

—Ronald A. Swanson, D. Ed., Chancellor
Brown College, St. Paul, MN

Lou Carbone is to customer experiences what Edward Demming was to the quality movement—a pioneer in developing and codifying a managerial discipline around an important but abstract value. For more than 15 years—long before "customer experience" became a recognized business priority—Carbone has been helping companies design and execute what he calls "experience blueprints." In this book, he goes beyond hype, analogies and bumper-sticker exhortations to offer managers a proven set of principles, tools and prescriptions for delivering a holistic and preference-creating value proposition.

—Stephan Haeckel, retired Director of Strategic Studies at
IBM's Advanced Business Institute, and author of *Adaptive Enterprise:
Creating and Leading Sense-And-Respond Organizations*

Carbone opens our eyes to the importance of experience in creating lasting relationships between companies and their customers. He gives us a framework to assess, design and implement the clues that sum up to preference, loyalty and profit. Companies that leave these clues to chance do so at their peril.

—Nick Agelidis, Director, Customer Service
Nissan North America Inc.

It's time we realize that value is held in the minds and hearts of our customers, and is based on the total experience they have with our companies. *Clued In* does a tremendous job of demonstrating how we make this a conscious and repeatable strategy.

Our companies create experiences for our customers every minute of every day. In *Clued In*, Lou Carbone guides us through the conscious creation of these experiences, and how they translate into value in the minds and hearts of our customers and ultimately for our companies.
—Chuck Feltz, President of Deluxe Financial Services

Lou Carbone and his collaborator, Steve Haeckel, invented customer experience management in a groundbreaking article in 1994. Carbone has amassed vast knowledge of this vital subject in over 15 years of practice.
—Dr. Leonard L. Berry, Distinguished Professor of Marketing, Texas A&M University, and author of *Discovering the Soul of Service*

Clued In provides a powerful look into the world of understanding experience management. The case examples and frameworks create a rich language and understanding of how to "clue in" to customer and employee experiences. The book paves a roadmap for leaders on how to get started in better designing and managing experiences. Lou's passion for experience management was contagious—I found myself inspired and even more energized about the experience management journey Lou helped us begin at Taco Bell.
—Emil J. Brolick, President and Chief Concept Officer, Taco Bell

Lou Carbone deeply understands customers' experiences through the management of clues. These insights, shared in *Clued In*, help the rest of us build consistent and practical experience management activities that deliver repeatable and effective results.
—Mike Long, President and COO
Arrow North American Computer Products

Finally . . . a book that doesn't just tell us why "customer experience" matters and of the impending disasters that may await us when we get it wrong, but instead gives us a step-by-step toolkit on how to get it right and make it a part of our management practices today.
—John C. Ryan, Chairman/CEO
John Ryan Companies, The Art and Science of Financial Retailing

Clued In

In an increasingly competitive world, it is quality of thinking that gives an edge—an idea that opens new doors, a technique that solves a problem, or an insight that simply helps make sense of it all.

We work with leading authors in the various arenas of business and finance to bring cutting-edge thinking and best learning practice to a global market.

It is our goal to create world-class print publications and electronic products that give readers knowledge and understanding which can then be applied, whether studying or at work.

To find out more about our business products, you can visit us at www.ft-ph.com

Clued In

How To Keep Customers
Coming Back Again and Again

Lewis P. Carbone

An Imprint of PEARSON EDUCATION
Upper Saddle River, NJ • New York • London • San Francisco • Toronto • Sydney
Tokyo • Singapore • Hong Kong • Cape Town • Madrid
Paris • Milan • Munich • Amsterdam

www.ft-ph.com

Library of Congress Cataloging-in-Publication Data available

Editorial/Production Supervision: *Kathleen M. Caren*
Cover Design Director: *Jerry Votta*
Cover Design: *Anthony Gemmellaro*
Interior Design: *Gail Cocker-Bogusz*
Manufacturing Manager: *Maura Zaldivar*
Executive Editor: *Tim Moore*
Editorial Assistant: *Richard Winkler*
Marketing Manager: *Martin Litkowski*

© 2004 Pearson Education, Inc.
Publishing as Financial Times Prentice Hall
Upper Saddle River, NJ 07458

Financial Times Prentice Hall offers excellent discounts on this book when ordered in quantity for bulk purchases or special sales. For more information, please contact: U.S. Corporate and Government Sales, 1-800-382-3419, corpsales@pearsontechgroup.com. For sales outside of the U.S., please contact: International Sales, 1-317-581-3793, international@pearsontechgroup.com.

Printed in the United States of America

First Printing

ISBN 0-13-101550-8

Pearson Education LTD.
Pearson Education Australia PTY, Limited
Pearson Education Singapore, Pte. Ltd.
Pearson Education North Asia Ltd.
Pearson Education Canada, Ltd.
Pearson Educación de Mexico, S.A. de C.V.
Pearson Education—Japan
Pearson Education Malaysia, Pte. Ltd.

FINANCIAL TIMES PRENTICE HALL BOOKS

For more information, please go to www.ft-ph.com

Business and Society

Douglas K. Smith
On Value and Values: Thinking Differently About We in an Age of Me

Current Events

Alan Elsner
Gates of Injustice: The Crisis in America's Prisons

John R. Talbott
Where America Went Wrong: And How to Regain Her Democratic Ideals

Economics

David Dranove
What's Your Life Worth? Health Care Rationing…Who Lives? Who Dies? Who Decides?

Entrepreneurship

Dr. Candida Brush, Dr. Nancy M. Carter, Dr. Elizabeth Gatewood, Dr. Patricia G. Greene, and Dr. Myra M. Hart
Clearing the Hurdles: Women Building High Growth Businesses

Oren Fuerst and Uri Geiger
From Concept to Wall Street: A Complete Guide to Entrepreneurship and Venture Capital

David Gladstone and Laura Gladstone
Venture Capital Handbook: An Entrepreneur's Guide to Raising Venture Capital, Revised and Updated

Thomas K. McKnight
Will It Fly? How to Know if Your New Business Idea Has Wings… Before You Take the Leap

Stephen Spinelli, Jr., Robert M. Rosenberg, and Sue Birley
Franchising: Pathway to Wealth Creation

Executive Skills

Cyndi Maxey and Jill Bremer
It's Your Move: Dealing Yourself the Best Cards in Life and Work

John Putzier
Weirdos in the Workplace

Finance

Aswath Damodaran
The Dark Side of Valuation: Valuing Old Tech, New Tech, and New Economy Companies

Kenneth R. Ferris and Barbara S. Pécherot Petitt
Valuation: Avoiding the Winner's Curse

International Business and Globalization

John C. Edmunds
  Brave New Wealthy World: Winning the Struggle for World Prosperity
Robert A. Isaak
  The Globalization Gap: How the Rich Get Richer and the Poor Get Left Further Behind
Johny K. Johansson
  In Your Face: How American Marketing Excess Fuels Anti-Americanism
Peter Marber
  Money Changes Everything: How Global Prosperity Is Reshaping Our Needs, Values, and Lifestyles
Fernando Robles, Françoise Simon, and Jerry Haar
  Winning Strategies for the New Latin Markets

Investments

Zvi Bodie and Michael J. Clowes
  Worry-Free Investing: A Safe Approach to Achieving Your Lifetime Goals
Michael Covel
  Trend Following: How Great Traders Make Millions in Up or Down Markets
Aswath Damodaran
  Investment Fables: Exposing the Myths of "Can't Miss" Investment Strategies
Harry Domash
  Fire Your Stock Analyst! Analyzing Stocks on Your Own
David Gladstone and Laura Gladstone
  Venture Capital Investing: The Complete Handbook for Investing in Businesses for Outstanding Profits
D. Quinn Mills
  Buy, Lie, and Sell High: How Investors Lost Out on Enron and the Internet Bubble
D. Quinn Mills
  Wheel, Deal, and Steal: Deceptive Accounting, Deceitful CEOs, and Ineffective Reforms
H. David Sherman, S. David Young, and Harris Collingwood
  Profits You Can Trust: Spotting & Surviving Accounting Landmines

Leadership

Jim Despain and Jane Bodman Converse
  And Dignity for All: Unlocking Greatness through Values-Based Leadership
Marshall Goldsmith, Cathy Greenberg, Alastair Robertson, and Maya Hu-Chan
  Global Leadership: The Next Generation

Management

Rob Austin and Lee Devin
  Artful Making: What Managers Need to Know About How Artists Work
J. Stewart Black and Hal B. Gregersen
  Leading Strategic Change: Breaking Through the Brain Barrier
David M. Carter and Darren Rovell
  On the Ball: What You Can Learn About Business from Sports Leaders
Charles J. Fombrun and Cees B.M. Van Riel
  Fame and Fortune: How Successful Companies Build Winning Reputations

This book is dedicated to my family,
and to all the people who work to create and
manage valuable experiences for others.

The following experience management terms, methods, competencies, and tools are trademarked or registered to Experience Engineering®, Inc.

Methodology

Experience Assessment™
Experience Audit™
Experience Design™
Experience Implementation™
Experience Stewardship™

General Terminology

Experience Engineering®
Total Experience Management®
EE® (Logo)
Experience Clue™
Humanic Clue™
Mechanic Clue™
Process Clue™
Functional Clue™
Signature Clue™
Brand Canyon™
Customer Preference Model™
Experience Preference Model™
Experience Motif™
Experience Ribbon™
Experience Sticktion™
Experience Design Criteria™
Experience Pathways™
Experience Value Management™
Psychological Pathways™
Preference Intensity™
Preference Index™

Experience Management Competencies

Clue Sensitivity™
Sensory Attentiveness™
Experience Research™
Experience Language Analysis™
Experience Education™
Experience Metrics™
Experience Communication™

Experience Management Tools

ClueGrid™
Clue Ideation™
ClueScan™
ClueScan Diary™
CallScan Guide™
BagCam™, CoatCam™, CustCam™, HatCam™, PagerCam™, TieCam™, WristCam™
Customer Experience Mystery Shop™
EE101™, 201, 301, 401
Experience Assessment Report™
Experience Audit Report™
Experience Based Curriculum™
Experience Blueprint™
Experience CluePrint™, CluePrints™
Experience Dynamics Lab™
Experience Intervention Interview™, EII™
Experience Reflection Interview™, ERI™
Experience Metrics™
Experience Motif Generation™
Experience Narrative™
Experience Optimization Workshop™
Experience Wayfinding™
Humanic Learning Framework™
Humanic Narrative™
PsychoPATH™
Sensory Motif Palette™, Motif Palette™

CONTENTS

INTRODUCTION

BALANCING WHAT CUSTOMERS VALUE WITH WHAT BUSINESSES VALUE

Every sound business is built around a simple proposition: It makes or does something so well that customers will pay for the value being created. Peter Drucker, perhaps the most significant management scholar of our time, reduces this proposition to two basic axioms: A business has to make money, and a business has to make customers.

It's not an either/or—the two are opposite faces of the same coin. If a business doesn't make customers, it won't survive to make money. If it doesn't make money, it won't survive to make customers. One form of value must connect with the other.

Although many people in business will find this proposition familiar, fewer have extended its reasoning to the logical conclusion—that the *customer* is the ultimate arbiter of the value an organization creates and delivers, not CEOs, CFOs, shareholders, or stakeholders. Though each can make important contributions to the health and success of the business, none of them will be around for the long run unless the business creates value for its customers.

In recent years, many businesses—many entire industries, in fact—seem to have lost their sense of balance in this regard. In trying to maximize the value of customers *to their businesses*, they appear to have lost sight of the need for their organizations to create value *for their customers*. The evidence is depressingly familiar:

- Airlines have systematically reduced the experience of flying to the feeling of being herded onto and off of an airborne cattle car (a form of experience that was ongoing long before September 11).
- Banks persistently charge account holders premium penalties for the most routine services. Periodically, some even try to nick customers

for the experience of talking to a real live teller. Or the customer endures a circuitous maze created by the call center instant voice response banter to get to a destination.

- Credit card companies have tried to continually create new ways to bump interest rates into double digits and add painful penalty charges, to boot—this in an economy where the interest rate charged to banks has been at or near record levels.

Reorienting Priorities

From your own experiences, you can no doubt expand and extend this list with examples from across the full spectrum of business to find companies of every size and industry engaged in dysfunctional value creation. As wide-ranging as your examples may be, however, they'll probably have one thing in common: In virtually every case, someone will have made a decision that emphasizes how the customer can create value for the company (the financial value of the customer's business) more than how the company can create value for the customer. In few of these cases will the desires of customers have been factored in, let alone viewed as a priority. Far from trying to find a balance between customer expectations and business realities, it's a truism today that many decisions are based on only one perspective of value—the company's.

The question of how to balance the value of the experience to the customer and the value of the customer to the company leads to an opportunity to "value engineer" the relationship between organizations and their customers, thereby making any market segment profitable.

I believe today's organizations have become extraordinarily vulnerable. By neglecting to factor in customer expectations and preferences consistently —by essentially disenfranchising the customer from the focal point of value creation—these businesses have abdicated their obligation to customers and themselves.

The result? With modern management fixated almost solely on the bottom line, the value proposition of far too many businesses has become increasingly one-sided: lots of emphasis on the company but little on enhancing the customer value. The overriding concern for maximizing short-term financial results now permeates business thinking from "mahogany row" to the front line. Even customers are prepared to concede to a rationalization that says "I guess that's what they have to do to stay in business."

As a consequence, I believe today's organizations have become extraordinarily vulnerable. By neglecting to consistently factor in customer expectations and preferences, they have essentially disenfranchised the customer from the determinations of value. These businesses have fundamentally abdicated their obligation to customers and themselves. What's more, sensing how little value such businesses place on their interests, customers today have become unpredictable free agents: increasingly disappointed, disgruntled, devalued, and ultimately disloyal.

The things businesses do to make money need to be balanced against an enhanced assessment of what it will take to make and keep customers in tomorrow's even more competitive global economy.

The point? Without the long-term loyalty of their best customers to provide stability, the foundations of countless businesses are essentially anchored in sand. Yet it appears that many executives and managers charged with running those businesses are unwilling or unable to deal with their vulnerability.

They literally don't have a clue.

This is not the preface to a soft-hearted call to disregard all the hard lessons learned in recent years on the make-money side of the house. Far from it: Indulging every customer request, no matter how fanciful or far-fetched, in the name of enhancing customer experiences is no more a formula for success than is relentless and unrestrained slashing of expenses. Competitive forces will continue to make it imperative to become ever better at taking care of the financial aspects of the business. If anything, the pressure on the make-money side is only going to continue to ratchet up.

But this is precisely why it's time to address the balance by rediscovering the make-customers side of the equation, which makes this a call to re-anchor the foundation of the business itself. It's time to get "clued in"—to develop a renewed and urgent sense of customer value creation—because the consequences of disregarding long-term customer preference and loyalty in the name of short-term cost reductions and cost-laden loyalty programs are both predictable and painful to contemplate.

The premise of the analysis in this book is deceptively simple: The things businesses do to make money need to be balanced against an enhanced assessment of what it will take to make and keep customers in tomorrow's even more competitive global economy. That means reconnecting— and in some cases, connecting for the first time—with customers as intimate participants, sometimes even partners, in theprocess of value-creation. Now more than ever, the value created for customers needs to be a central consideration in the short-term growth and long-term health of any business.

And experience is the key.

The Experience Differentiator

Within harsh financial realities, creating value for customers by providing distinctive experiential value is an exacting challenge. But it's far from insurmountable. Making money and making loyal customers are not mutually exclusive.

The essence of experience as a value proposition is as old as business itself. It isn't tied to or limited by geography, demographics, or economic forces. It applies whether an organization produces products, delivers services, or does a combination of both. It doesn't matter whether the customer is a consumer or another business.

The fact is, customers cannot *not* have an experience! They'll have one whether you want them to or not. The question is, How random or managed is the experience you are delivering?

Experience has always been both a bridge and a by-product when customers connect with organizations. But up to now, too many businesses have acted as though competitive advantage comes more from *individual* product and service attributes than from an ability to create a cohesive *total* experience within which products and/or services are key components. But as many businesses have known for a long time, the "whole" is worth far more in impacting customers than any of the individual parts.

To be sure, the customer's total experience—much of it unconscious and emotional, rather than coldly rational—has always been a component of the value proposition puzzle. But now, as product and service attributes become commoditized and evened out, experiential elements and their value are rapidly coming to the fore. The quality of the customer's total experience is being increasingly recognized as the new differentiator.

Although this might seem like a bit of a stretch to some, it has been the focal point of my own work for at least 20 years. And I've been writing about it for more than a decade. In 1994, I collaborated with Steve Haeckel, who was then chair of the board of trustees of the Marketing Science Institute, in a first article on the subject for *Marketing Management*, the quarterly business management publication of the American Marketing Association. In "Engineering Customer Experiences,"[1] we laid out the basic principles on which I built my consulting business, and it eventually has led me to write this book.

"Customers always get more than they bargain for," Steve and I wrote, "because a product or service always comes with an experience. By 'experience,' we mean the 'take-away' impression formed by people's encounters with products, services, and businesses—a perception produced when humans consolidate sensory information." [1]

In the article, we introduced the concept of experience "clues" as the manageable building blocks of an experience defined as sensory information, whether occurring by design or happenstance, that collectively influenced the experience value perceptions in the mind of the customer. We also identified the stakes involved: "Unmanaged, these clues may cancel each other out and leave no net impression on the customer, or worse, induce a strong net negative perception. But if systematically crafted into a positive net impression, the clues promote customer preference, which a company can leverage to differentiate otherwise commodity-like products and services." [1]

Other Voices

In a subsequent issue of *Marketing Management*, John Deighton, now the Harold M. Brierley Professor of Business Administration at the Harvard Business School, responded at some length:

> This article raises fascinating questions that deserve serious scholarly attention. Here are two practicing marketers who tell us that marketing can design our feelings for us and cite enough evidence to make the assertion at least intriguing. They are claiming powers for the art of marketing that are beyond the ken of most marketing theory, and I take that to be a rebuke to the state of theory.
>
> When marketing studies consumer choice, using the methods and models of economics, it is doomed never to see anything more subtle than an economist could have seen. This article is a call to look beyond choice to the consumption experience, where we may see phenomena that stimulate our curiosity and point the discipline in directions that no other social science is as well equipped to go. It is worth remembering that the first steam engine was built before the laws of thermodynamics had been written, and so it is said that physics owes more to the steam engine than the steam engine owes to physics.
>
> "Experience Engineering" is being proposed before we have much understanding of the relevant science, but it just might be the spur to creating that science. [2]

In the years since, evidence has grown steadily to indicate that both business thought leaders and pacesetting businesses are catching on. Steve Haeckel deserves some long-delayed credit for that. Creator of the sense-and-respond managerial model set forth in his book, *The Adaptive Enterprise* [3], retired director of strategic studies at IBM's Advanced Business Institute, and now president of Adaptive Business Designs of Pound Ridge, New York, he has been working with me for years to promote the idea that systematically managing the "whole customer experience" represents an unprecedented—and untapped—source of competitive advantage. And that is unavoidably every company's real value proposition.

Dr. Leonard Berry, noted author and distinguished professor of marketing at Texas A&M University, represents another noteworthy voice.

Len points out that creating the kind of service customers truly value is far more than a matter of the words used in marketing efforts. "The marketed brand contributes to brand meaning," he states in *Discovering the Soul of Service* [4], "but not as strongly as the customer's actual experience with the company."

The tangible attributes of a product or service have far less influence on consumer preference than the unconscious sensory and emotional elements derived from the total experience.

On the basis of his groundbreaking research into how the human brain functions—research that is yielding some of the most important concepts and powerful tools yet brought to the field of marketing management—Dr. Gerald Zaltman of the Harvard Business School's Mind of the Market Laboratory presents the case for experience management with mantra-like precision: The tangible attributes of a product or service have far less influence on consumer preference than the unconscious sensory and emotional elements *derived from the total experience.* [5]

A year before their book, *The Experience Economy: Work Is Theater & Every Business a Stage* [6], appeared, Joe Pine and James Gilmore wrote an article in the *Harvard Business Review* entitled "Welcome to the Experience Economy" [7], in which they laid out their own approach to the subject. Haeckel and I wrote a letter to the editor to second their notions, emphasizing that "companies cannot avoid giving their customers a total experience. But they can and do avoid managing its production. The vast majority of businesses deliver experiences without thinking about them." [8]

We went on to emphasize the critical importance of translating this insight into business practice, noting that "Almost no one uses a systematic way of designing high-value experiences and delivering them consistently. Systematically engineering such experiences requires new management principles, tools, methodologies, and techniques." [8]

Getting Clued In

The implications are enormous. Those "new management principles, tools, methodologies, and techniques" at last are becoming available and proving their worth. The body of research supporting the competitive value of managing the customer's total experience is both compelling and growing. And landmark advances in understanding how people—especially in their role as customers—think and make decisions promise to provide the necessary knowledge and insight to help businesses rewrite the rules of the value proposition around systems that design, manage, and leverage total experiences.

For nearly 10 years now, my firm, Minneapolis-based Experience Engineering, has been in the forefront of the transition. We have been working with forward-looking organizations to create, in effect, the first steam engines of the experiential world.

In the pages that follow, I will share what I know about that world where experience—not traditional forms of product and service quality—is the focal point of the value proposition. I'll do so openly, sharing lessons we've learned with clients from an array of industries. I've divided this exploration into two parts.

In Part 1, I'll build the case for managing experiences—the global perspective that can help you see the outlines of this profound transition as they have begun to become visible.

- In Chapter 1, you'll start off with an in-depth comparison case study of two organizations whose very different fortunes reflect the way they did or didn't manage experiences over decades.
- Chapter 2 traces the evolution of the value proposition, particularly in the post–World War II world, where product attributes and service quality started to become commodities and have led to the coming of experience as a value differentiator.
- Chapter 3 takes a look over the edge of the "Brand Canyon" to discuss the relationship between brand and experience management and to show how focusing on experiences necessarily changes the way businesses think of themselves and what they make and do.

- In Chapter 4, you'll see how experience value can be managed by exploring some basic tools and models that will help you understand the dynamics of experience and experiential value perception.
- Chapter 5 narrows the focus to clues—the essential building blocks of experiences—exploring both the functional and the emotional forces at work in the mind of the customer as they are encountered absorbed and registered.
- Chapter 6 demonstrates how the challenge of managing clues places a premium on the development of cohesive and sustainable experience management systems that can evolve and grow over time.

In Part 2, the actual practice of managing experiences and the specific disciplines that can energize a systematic approach to experience management are featured.

- Chapter 7 focuses on *assessing* and a richer understanding of experience as the core of the value proposition.
- Chapter 8 introduces the discipline of *auditing*, in which you will learn to take apart existing experiences and see them as your customers do to gain insight into critical needs and true preferences in the process.
- In Chapter 9, you'll see how to leverage the insights from assessing and auditing into *designing* the total experience by creating clues that can be managed to connect with customer desires and lead to long-term preference and loyalty.
- By Chapter 10, you'll be ready to move into *implementing* experience designs, weaving and orchestrating the strands of individual clues into a resilient system that resonates more consistently for customers because experience and the value created is at the core.
- Finally, Chapter 11 explores the transition to *stewarding*, in which efforts evolve into maintaining and evolving an experience management system that produces sustainable, effective ways to make money *because* of the way you are making customers.

Finally, I've included an *appendix* of useful tools that have been developed or identified from others in 20 years of building experience management systems.

Value You Can Act On

My goal is to prepare you for a transformation that has been in the works more than a decade but is just now beginning to gain visible power and momentum. This transformation bodes well for businesses that have the willingness, the ability, and in some senses the maturity to regain a sense of balance between making money and making customers for the future.

As experience steadily eclipses conventional product and service perspectives in the minds of your customers, it has the potential to transform the most basic assumptions on which you've operated.

In the pages that follow, you will be comprehensively clued in to the dimensions, managerial imperatives, and learning from early adopters of what I term the practice of experience management.

References

1. Lewis P. Carbone and Stephan H. Haeckel. "Engineering Customer Experiences," *Marketing Management,* Vol. 3, No. 3, page 1 (Winter 1994).

2. John Deighton. *Marketing Management,* Vol. 4, No. 1, page 2 (Summer 1995).

3. Stephan H. Haeckel. *The Adaptive Enterprise, Creating and Leading Sense-and-Respond Organizations* (Harvard Business Press, 1999).

4. Leonard L. Berry. *Discovering the Soul of Customer Service: The Nine Drivers of Sustainable Business Success* (New York: The Free Press, 1999, page 201).

5. Gerald Zaltman. *"How Customers Think: Essential Insights into the Mind of the Market"* (Harvard Business School Press, 2003).

6. B. Joseph Pine II and James Gilmore. *The Experience Economy: Work Is Theater & Every Business a Stage.* (Boston: Harvard Business School Press, 1999).

7. B. Joseph Pine II and James Gilmore. "Welcome to the Experience Economy." *Harvard Business Review* (July/August 1998).

8. Lewis P. Carbone and Stephan H. Haeckel. Letter to the editor. *Harvard Business Review* (Nov.–Dec. 1998).

Part 1

THE CASE FOR EXPERIENCE MANAGEMENT

1

ORANGE ROOFS AND THE MOUSE: A TALE OF TWO ICONS

Clued-in management focuses on the total experience as the customer value proposition. Before laying out the case for this powerful approach, it will be instructive to see just how dynamic a force experience can be to a company's bottom line and vitality. Consider two organizations—one once identified by orange roofs and the other known by mouse ears—and the effects which decades of effective and ineffective experience management had on their respective fortunes.

The Roots of Experience

Roll back the calendar to the 1950s. In terms of business strategy this qualifies as close to the dawn of recorded experience management history. Yes, businesses managed their business before then. And yes, customers had experiences before then. But in many cases, the experiences were considered incidental to transactions; customers weren't very experienced (or very demanding); and the degree of choice, depth of information involved, and speed of marketplace change were far less powerful factors than they are today.

Today's interactive marketplace—with its emphasis on robust, fast-response consumer products and services, increasingly with experience management elements woven throughout—was still a relatively unexplored phenomenon in the slower and simpler 1950s. It was a different economic time and place. Having survived the Great Depression and a world war, during which most people learned to make do with whatever they had, Americans were beginning to understand how improved technology and war-era production lessons could benefit the nation's civilian population.

A lot of the things that seem commonplace today were unknown or unimagined then:

- Cars were stored in sheds in the back yard or along an alley, and the typical family got along with just one.
- Meals were almost always eaten at home, not in restaurants, and chances were that Mom packed a lunch for Dad to take to work right along with the brown bags the kids would take to school.
- The neighbors kept track of each other over the party line: Two, three, sometimes more families shared the same telephone circuit, which involved a physical line that vanished into the wall behind the family's single—invariably black—rotary-dial telephone.
- Keeping up with the Joneses focused on which neighbor would be the first on the block to get a television set. Fewer than one home in ten had a TV when the decade began. Today, three homes in four have more than one set.
- Laying out the Interstate Highway System was one of the crowning "paper" achievements of the first Eisenhower administration (1956). And the primary purpose envisioned for it was to provide a reliable road network just in case the country needed to move military equipment around. Hence its original name—the *Defense* Highway System.
- Back in those days, a cartoonist from Kansas was just starting to scratch at the dirt in Orange County, California, hoping to create an experientially managed playground in which he'd feel comfortable letting his daughters wander and play.

It was a time of expanding experiential choices, and nowhere were those choices changing more rapidly than away from the home. As an entire nation began to travel more, locating safe and comfortable places to stay and eat could be daunting. When the family traveled, often the itinerary was usually arranged to stop at the homes of relatives to eat or spend the night. (As a boy growing up in Rhode Island in those years, I recall my family packing a picnic lunch for the 45-mile drive up to Boston for Red Sox baseball games.)

As they ventured farther from things familiar, intrepid travelers soon discovered that it was even difficult to find consistent, readable signs telling them how far it was to the next town. The locals all knew, and generally there weren't enough strangers passing through to justify the expense of creating and posting such otherwise unnecessary clues.

On a more practical level, finding the desired destination on the map was just the beginning. Once there, people had to find food and lodging. As America began to take to the road, locating safe and comfortable places to stay and eat became a vexing challenge.

Seeing Orange

In a matter of just a few years, an "orange roof" came to mean safety, cleanliness, and reliability when on the road. It meant Howard Johnson, the "Host of the Highway." In the 1950s, Howard Johnson *owned* the roadside franchise restaurant market and along with Holiday Inn, it was one of the dominant icons in the relatively new roadside "motor hotel" (hence, *motel*) business, as well.

In many locations, the company parked its motor lodges adjacent to its restaurants so that road-numbed families far from home could find both a familiar, reliable place to eat and spend the night.

The "HoJo" story wasn't just a matter of traveling customers turning in off the highway, however. Locals liked the restaurants, too. They featured fried clams and the Wednesday and Friday night fish fry, as well as ham quickies, corn toasties, "3-D" burgers, and 28 flavors of ice cream. By the 1970s, Howard Deering Johnson had built one of the first great restaurant chains, along with one of the first mid-priced hotel chains.

In the process (see Figure 1.1), he pioneered many of the most successful food service and hospitality innovations in the industry. Putting restaurants along busy freeways and turnpikes, offering themed restaurants and motor lodges, commissary-based food distribution, the franchise development concept, even super-premium ice cream, was significantly shaped by Howard Johnson, the man and the company.

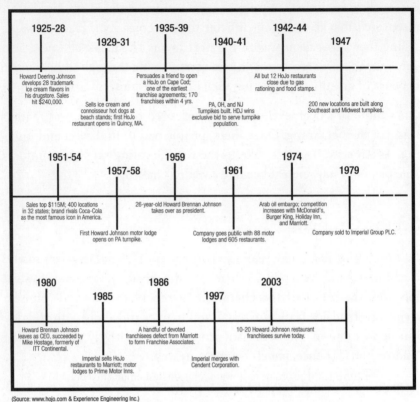

Figure 1.1 Howard Johnson Inc. timeline.

In those days, an orange roof served as a distinctive clue for comfort, cleanliness, and consistency, regardless of time zone or what state's name dominated the license plates in the parking lot (Figure 1.2). "To travel-weary Americans, with the kids bawling in the back seat and Pop bleary from driving, the sight of an orange roof was like the first palm of an oasis to a thirsty Arab and his camel," recalled *Forbes Magazine* in a 1985 report, [1]

> "This you knew: HoJo's would be a clean place with nice washrooms, the food would be predictable but wholesome, and the ice cream and popcorn would quiet the brats. In short, a homey, familiar place away from home. Some of the Motor Lodges even featured swimming pools and color television, which was a big deal at a time when most families had black and white televisions at home. The alternative to HoJo's? A greasy hamburger joint? A fleabag motel?"

Figure 1.2 The profile of Howard Johnson Restaurants that dotted
the U.S. landscape with its distinctive orange roof.

How many experiential "signals"—some rational, some more emotional in nature—can you unearth in that short description? Weary, bawling, bleary, orange roof, oasis, clean, nice, predictable, wholesome, quiet, homey, familiar, greasy, fleabag—and those are just the directly stated ones. In that moment of customer time, when travel was something families did more than businesspeople and the travel experience was relatively basic, what customers valued was a sense that they were stopping at a comfortable, safe, clean place. Howard Johnson helped pioneer that emotion-laden travel experience.

Making Clues Systematic

Providing reliable, consistent, experiential reassurance gave rise, among other things, to the hospitality franchise movement. Businesses that had the same names were built to the same or similar floor plans, offered the same products, recipes, and amenities, the same uniforms and décor, and catered to the same clientele. This took a lot of the worry out of exploring strange new places far from home for travelers. The names could be the same. The clues could be the same.

Even in those early days, experience-oriented thinking was in evidence. Charles Kemmon Wilson, the contemporary of Howard Johnson who founded the Holiday Inn chain in 1951, originally considered putting fly swatters in each room and trampolines in each hotel. The former he rejected for sending the "wrong message," the latter for being too dangerous [2]—both judgments that applied directly to clues embedded in the total experience being provided to customers.

Perhaps nothing better illustrates the power of experience-based customer loyalty in building business success than the rise of national and ultimately international brands over the last 50 years.

The growth and success of Howard Johnson in those days reflected the power of that far-reaching dynamic of customer experience management. Beyond the business efficiencies—providing consistent customer experiences, regardless of the locale—franchising systematically transformed entire industries. When satisfying experiences were richly imprinted, they left customers with a penchant to repeat those experiences. Perhaps nothing better illustrates the power of experience-based customer loyalty in building businesses than the rise of national and ultimately international brands over the last 50 years, often at the expense of individualistic Mom-and-Pop operations.

Relatively speaking, franchising is a very recent business model. According to McGrow Consulting of Hingham, Massachusetts, which is one of the specialized firms serving the franchising field, only about 3% of all franchise organizations around today can trace their histories back prior to 1950. [3] In other words, most of the familiar roadside signs (a common clue) you're accustomed to seeing today are less than half a century old.

Which raises a provocative question: If Howard Johnson was an early giant among them, why aren't orange roofs a powerful icon of the modern food and hospitality business? Why isn't Johnson an icon ranked with Kroc, Marriott, Nordstrom, and Sanders? After all, in 1965, Howard Johnson sales were greater than the combined totals of McDonald's, Burger King, and Kentucky Fried Chicken, and *Forbes Magazine* quoted Bill Marriott, Jr. as once telling his father, "I hope one day we can be as big as Howard Johnson." [1]

Had things played out differently, this book might today be celebrating HoJo's as the pioneer of experience management systems. How did such an apparently clued-in company become so clueless?

In the late 1970s, I had a ringside seat for the later stages of this proud company's decline, and the early, painful stumbles were still fresh enough to be recalled by many of the Howard Johnson people with whom I worked at that time.

At the New York City office of Campbell Ewald Co., an advertising agency, I was the management representative and liaison on accounts that were "participants" with The Walt Disney Company. Howard Johnson was one of the "official" lodging companies of Disneyland and Walt Disney World, just as National Car Rental was the official car rental company and Eastern Airlines was the official airline of Walt Disney World.

As an outsider inside the walls of Howard Johnson, I witnessed the erosion of a once-robust company rich in experiential value. Beleaguered by earlier trends ranging from the rise of competing choices to the OPEC oil crisis of the 1970s, the Howard Johnson organization that I saw was clearly struggling.

It showed in so many little ways. I remember going to HoJo's suburban Boston headquarters for meetings in which weary executives would shake their heads and talk about new ways to cut costs: How much money could be saved by taking a fraction of an inch off the straws, or going from a four-ply paper napkin to a two-ply napkin, or reducing the number of ice-cream flavors from 28 to 24 to 16.

What they were doing appeared to make sense financially, but it just didn't add up experientially for customers. Under the short-lived leadership of the founder's son, Howard Brennon Johnson, HoJo was following the management wisdom of the time, striving to become the low-cost producer at any cost, including customers. It was an approach born from a manufacturing perspective that had little or no sensitivity for a service business, let alone the customer experience.

The company whose founder operated under a simple axiom—"quality sells"—had bought into the current business thinking of the time, aided and abetted by consulting firms pushing the company to gain a supposed competitive advantage as the low-cost producer.

To do so, the restaurant organization in particular was nibbling away at itself, cutting any corner, no matter how customer-valued, to reduce costs with the promise of driving more revenue to the bottom line for investors. Cleanliness and maintenance became huge issues. Commissaries were closed and food specifications were compromised. The company name was even removed from tractor-trailer trucks delivering supplies to the restaurants because it cost too much to keep them clean. In fact, numerous closed restaurant locations were simply boarded up, leaving the distinctive orange roof as a monument to the once-proud brand's decline—a megaclue that reinforced the organization's disenfranchisement from its customers (see Figure 1.3).

Howard Johnson had become better at managing the clues of extinction than the clues of distinction.

In my observations there was seldom a mention of what was happening to the organization's most valuable asset as a result of this whittling-away process. The *trust* Howard Johnson had built up in the minds of its loyal customers over so many years was still significant, even bankable. But as financial difficulties mounted and the organization turned defensive, it didn't figure into management discussions in any meaningful way.

Figure 1.3 The peeling orange roof, a testament to the extinction of the restaurants, is depicted in this photo taken in the summer of 2002 in Dallas, Texas.

Broken Connections

Few seemed concerned that the manic urge to cut ever closer to the bone was whacking away at hard-earned experiential trust—a different but highly significant form of equity—inflicting wounds that made the organization itself steadily weaker as it further encouraged its customers to seek alternative suppliers where their experiences would be better.

The world in which Howard Johnson had to compete had indeed changed immensely. Unfortunately for customers, employees, and shareholders alike, the company didn't seem to notice. Nor did it react effectively. It seemed to be operating without a customer-based vision. Its experiential Clue Sensitivity had gone from 20/20 to virtual blindness. In essence, Howard Johnson lost sight of the value of the customer experience it had pioneered. Once that trend got underway, it became impossible for the management team to reserve.

By contrast, aggressive new pacesetters such as Marriott and McDonald's had painstakingly ensured that their operations would continuously and consistently sync up with customer needs and expectations. Sales, earnings, and operating income comparisons between

Marriott and Howard Johnson for the 1970s and 1980s are shown in Figure 1.4, Figure 1.5, and Figure 1.6.

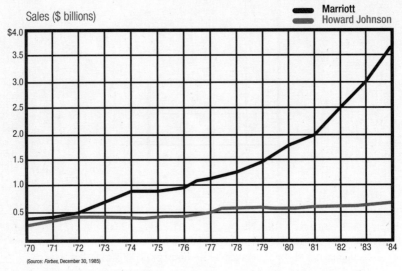

(Source: *Forbes*, December 30, 1985)

Figure 1.4 By the mid-1980s, Marriott sales had greatly surpassed those of Howard Johnson.

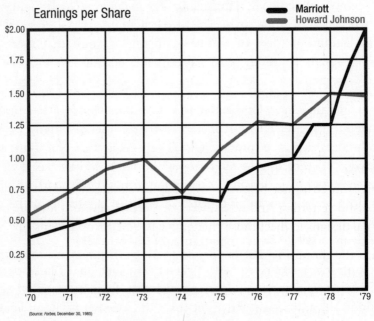

(Source: *Forbes*, December 30, 1985)

Figure 1.5 Earnings per share.

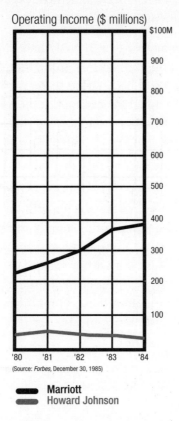

Operating Income ($ millions)

(Source: *Forbes*, December 30, 1985)

Marriott
Howard Johnson

Figure 1.6 Operating income.

With the benefit of hindsight, it's easy to conclude that the creation and constant evolution of effectively managed experiences require a long-term commitment to a sustained system. Take your eye off *the customer's concept* of experience-based value and you can lose—big time. You must constantly monitor the essential clues involved in what you're doing for changes in customer behavior that may invalidate strategies that were successful yesterday. And when necessary, create new and inviting experiential designs to meet those changing customer expectations.

That's the moral in what happened to Howard Johnson in the 1970s and early 1980s. The family travel market was still there, of course. And it was growing. But because the Howard Johnson organization had little understanding of the experiential equity it had built, it had no context for how to react to competitors or how to sharpen its appeal to customers as their tastes changed and their experiential expectations became more discriminating.

As customer tastes changed, new models had emerged. Instead of a mass migration looking for simple, something-for-everyone coffee shops, families on the road had started to segment into more specialized preferences. Some opted for fast food; others drove by a variety of sit-down alternatives until they found a place whose clues promised the steak or fish they were craving at that moment. Customers evolved. HoJo didn't adapt.

At the same time, business travel exploded. Arthur Miller's "traveling salesman" was replaced by road warriors with an evolving set of very different priorities and needs from the family market. "Business travelers didn't want a frank and a soda," *Forbes* recalled, "and they didn't want to sit next to a noisy kid with a sticky face. The business types wanted a drink and a steak, and maybe a little action in the bar. The HoJo restaurant offered them little. . . Frankfurters and ice cream just didn't mix with martinis and rock music." [1]

The problem remained lack of customer focus: Howard Johnson got progressively better at doing the wrong things.

Through it all, I watched the management of the original Howard Johnson and the foreign investment group that bought and later sold parts of it act as though they mostly didn't have a clue about what was really happening. Even though the company placed a high priority on research into customer satisfaction, and major initiatives were put in place as a result, the pressure on earnings was now insurmountable, and the problem remained lack of customer focus. Howard Johnson got progressively better at doing the wrong things.

Sadly, preventing customer defections and not improving customer value was too often the focus of the meetings I attended. I'd hear managers talking about creating a revitalized process to document that workers were indeed cleaning the restrooms, as though a pronouncement from the head office would make it so. But I knew I could stop by any HoJo at nine in the morning and find cleanliness surveys already checkmarked positively for the entire day. Although cleanliness is certainly important, as is keeping employees on task to accomplish it, a major insight was missed: People don't turn into a restaurant's parking lot because they're attracted solely by the prospect of sparkling bathroom fixtures. That's a commodity, not a differentiator. Customers rightfully expect that any organization in the roadside hospitality business will have clean restrooms. It's the careful orchestration of *all* clues in combination that creates the distinctive value of the total experience for the customer.

I also suspected that one of the brand's most powerful clues was actively working against it. Here and there, dotted across the landscape, were locations that had failed and had been closed. The buildings were dark. The signs were gone. But those closed-up casualties of changing customer desires still wore their distinctive orange roofs. They were huge, negative clues associated with the total Howard Johnson experience.

A World Apart

The experience of working with Howard Johnson had so much impact for me because after meetings with those Howard Johnson's executives, many times I would hop a flight to central Florida as the agency's Disney liaison. At that time, that organization's best and brightest were busily building EPCOT Center every bit as carefully planned as its Magic Kingdom counterpart.

The differences between Howard Johnson and Disney were profound. At HoJo, they were constantly looking for yet another way to cut a corner. Howard Johnson no longer was providing a unified, meaningful, holistic experience.

At Walt Disney World, meanwhile, the buzz was about "imagineers"—Disney's distinctive word for people who try to creatively engineer every piece of an experience a guest (aka customer) can even imagine. (Disney, as many business people know, divides the world into just two kinds of people: "guests" and the "cast members" whose job it is to perform for them.)

With the full support of management, the imagineers were thinking about anything and everything that might impact the experience they were committed to providing. It didn't take long to see that what they were up to went way beyond any definition of customer service.

At Walt Disney World, corners were not being cut. To the contrary, even the corners were seen as integral to the experiential system being created. Disney's designers were sweating out how corners should be designed and integrated into the surrounding environment so that they, too, would be a seamless part of the customer experience. (Take a close look at a Disney trash can, and odds are you'll find that its location is incorporated into the paint scheme of the sidewalk or curb to help ensure that it will be put back in just the right place every time it's emptied.)

Disney's attention to this kind of detail is legendary—and deservedly so. Once, when Mickey, Donald, and Goofy accompanied Walt Disney to a baseball game where Walt was to throw out the first pitch, the young man in the Goofy costume—Carl Andrews, who years later would "grow up" to become the head of Walt Disney Travel Company—found himself nose to nose with the founder. After the pitch, the ball was to be tossed among the Disney characters, and Goofy was to be the last in line. Walt wanted to make sure his young cast member understood the role of being Goofy in even this brief experiential vignette.

"What are you going to do?" Disney inquired with trademark intensity.

"I'm going to catch the ball," Andrews replied with some confusion.

"You're going to do what!" Disney barked. "Who are you?"

The question flummoxed the young man for a moment. Why did "the" Disney want to know his name? Was he in trouble for some unconscious mistake? Was he about to get fired?

"Who are you?" Walt insisted, intensity rising. Happily, Andrews caught on.

"I'm Goofy," he said, finally beginning to see the experiential light.

"So what are you going to do?"

"I'm going to drop the ball." And he did.

Experience by Design

That's a simple illustration of multilayered experience management and deep understanding of the roles performed by employees. Done right, nothing is left to chance. For example, when Mickey and Minnie Mouse were booked for receptions at National Car Rental, they came with an extensive list of conditions designed to make sure the characters indeed could stay in character. Among the conditions: no alcohol in the room with them. Imagine corporate cocktail receptions transformed into ice cream socials. That's exactly what National had to do if it wanted to involve the trademark representatives of its sought-after partner. So it did.

During the time I was bouncing between Boston and Orlando, EPCOT Center was under construction. Unbelievable effort was being committed to manage everything that visitors to this international showcase would see, hear, feel, touch, smell, even sense and imagine. After meetings with HoJo, where managers were obsessed with seeking to save an incremental slice here or there, I'd find myself with Disney executives such as Dick Nuness, Chip Eichman, Jack Lindquist, Pete Clark, Mike McPhillips, Phil Lengyel, Tom Elrod, and many others—people who were talking to me about things like temperature and velocity of the wind within Spaceship Earth. What would guests see? What would they feel? What would they walk away from the experience thinking about? What would they remember?

In some organizations, that level of conversation would be mere posturing—just some momentary hot air about the air. At Disney, it was as serious a design consideration as the structural supports for the attraction.

When businesses accept the idea that the quality of the total experience has powerful effects on long-term loyalty and advocacy, the plane on which the organization can compete broadens remarkably.

You can encounter similar levels of attention to customer-centric detail in organizations as outwardly dissimilar as Harley-Davidson and Mayo Clinic. When businesses accept the idea that the total experience has powerful effects on long-term loyalty and advocacy, the plane on which the organization can compete broadens remarkably.

For Disney, such attention to detail clearly emanated from the founder. Walt Disney wasn't building standardized amusement parks. He was creating complex, finely detailed experiences, including clues that tell you where to stand to take the kind of pictures that will best help you recollect those experiences. Those signs prompting guests to stop, point, and capture carefully composed Kodak moments are a lot more than casual evidence of a marketing partnership. They're part of managing the total experience, and are carefully located to make sure you remember your Disney day in the most idyllic way.

Everyone I rubbed shoulders with at Disney in those days had a ton of "Walt stories" to tell, just as the old-timers at Howard Johnson did of that company's founder—and I'm sure just as contemporaries of Ray Kroc, Dave Thomas, Harlan Sanders, Bill Marriott, Sr., Stanley Marcus, the Nordstroms, and a host of other clued-in leaders can recall about their own formative influences.

To me, it's always an intriguing clue when the stories people tell about the founders or later generation leaders in pacesetting organizations involve customer connectivity rather than bottom-line achievements. By the same token, one of the most chilling experiences I've ever had at Disney came just a couple of years ago, when a marketing manager proudly told me how they had "finally" started benchmarking their practices against others. From my perspective, this was like Tiger Woods revealing that he had just agreed to be coached by someone with a 12 handicap. If you're in the business of providing excellence, why are you looking for ways to copy what could be mediocrity? And if the mediocrity you're benchmarking truly is better than what you're doing, what happened to you?

Experiential Vision

Some readers may be thinking, "Well, of course they would obsess about all that stuff at Disney. That's their business: It's all entertainment to them. It's all make-believe. That kind of stuff just doesn't translate to the real world."

That's what I thought until one day I was being told about the *temperature* of the ice cream they were going to sell in the park. Not just the flavor. Not just the serving size. Not just the cost efficiencies they wanted to negotiate with suppliers. The temperature.

In central Florida, this was important. Wherever the concessions were going to be placed, the temperature was going to have to be cold enough to make sure the ice cream didn't immediately start to melt and drip on people's hands or on the sidewalks. Dripping on the hands could have messy consequences for the type of experience Disney wanted its guests to be having.

Of course, dripping on the sidewalk also could have messy consequences for cleanup, affecting staffing costs, maintenance costs, and pest-management costs. But the total customer experience was the primary preoccupation. Have you ever had an ice cream bar drip all over you or—worse—one of your children? How did it make you feel? What did it do to your wardrobe, your day? How much attention were you able to pay to the other aspects of the experience? And what did you remember most vividly? That range of perspective is what sets imagineers and Disney apart.

Enduring Lessons

In particular, those formative years convinced me that it is maximizing the *total* customer experience that truly creates value and builds preference. While individual experts at Howard Johnson deconstructed their tiny piece of the whole, I began to notice how Disney's people worked together to meticulously orchestrate everything that customers might encounter. They recognized that gaining efficiency in one small place but degrading the overall experience as a result actually reduces the value being delivered—to customers and to the bottom line.

It's a philosophy that anchors Disney regardless of the times. Reacting to a downturn in business in 2003 due to disruption in travel and tourism and the uncertainty caused by the war in Iraq, Jay Rasulo, the senior executive in charge of Walt Disney's parks and resorts, stated, "We want to manage in a scientific way to run our business but not ever allowing cost management to affect the guest experience." [4]

Does Disney stumble? Certainly. Are there glitches and failures and even (in its vocabulary) "visual violations" that challenge its ability to satisfy all guests? Of course. But from Disney you can learn that not only is the experience central to creating and sustaining value, but the system indeed can also be the solution. An entire complex, multidimensional operation built to function on an incredible scale can be designed and run on the premise of leaving nothing to chance.

To this day, I remain convinced of the extraordinary opportunity for any business with the patience and dedication to emulate Disney's experience-based systems approach to everything it tries to do. Just as I became an avid student of what I saw happening there, I've remained a dedicated advocate for applying those principles to businesses as diverse as auto dealerships, banks, colleges, grocery stores, hospitals, insurance agencies, and rental car companies.

At Disney, they weren't concerned just with measuring how much popcorn they sold (an item that turned up periodically in a Howard Johnson sales report). They were every bit as concerned with creating a complete experience around selling that popcorn; they understood the two were intimately linked.

They didn't consider just what a specific building façade should look like (which Howard Johnson approached in terms of architectural design, maintenance, and capital expenditure). They calculated how the size, color, and texture would mix with other sights around it, how that mix would affect sight lines to distant attractions, and even how the mysterious (to most guests) business names on the second-floor false fronts along Main Street could be clues that keep alive the memories of legendary Disney cast members.

To Disney, lines aren't just a place to store customers until they can be shunted onto the next ride. Every year, countless businesses (as well as U.S. government agencies) come to Disney to learn how lines can be made an integral part of the experience being delivered to customers. The experiential science involved has even generated a buzzword— "metawaiting"—for the discipline of elevating simply standing in line to an experiential component of the business.

For example, the experience of *waiting* to board a ride such as Space Mountain—hearing the background chatter of mission-control announcements, reading the warning signs, working your way down through the blue-lit corridors, wondering while you wait what the ride itself will feel like—is an essential part of *riding* Space Mountain. The Disney imagineers want you to wait and wonder. Otherwise, all you're experiencing is two minutes on a small roller coaster in a dark building.

Even though the result of this obsessive attention to detail isn't always obvious to the customer, it can provide powerful subliminal clues. In Florida's Magic Kingdom, when you look down Main Street toward Cinderella's Castle (Snow White's Castle in California), the subtle angling and relative height of the various floors of the buildings along the street make the castle look farther away than it really is. In the trade, it's called a "Hollywood perspective," and it helps build your anticipation as you're walking up from the main gates and looking forward to a long, enjoyable day.

When you stand in front of the castle and look back toward the main gates from the other end of Main Street, on the other hand, the building angles seem to minimize the distance between you and the parking lot—a welcome sight at the end of the day when legs are leaden, the kids are dragging, and you're looking forward to winding down.

A Constant Learning Process

This is meant to be neither an unqualified paean to Disney nor an unrelenting critique of Howard Johnson. As noted, the HoJo brand survives and continues to evolve. And as times changed—and customers revamped their expectations—Disney has had to struggle with many of the same operational issues as other organizations.

Clearly, Disney's experience is not perfect. Some excitement-jazzed classes of customers now consider its theme parks a little stodgy. The sheer scale of Disney World daunts some families. The price daunts others. But Disney has a history of being willing to work on them in the context of an experience, not just a balance sheet.

For example, the travails of Euro Disney (39% of which is owned by The Walt Disney Company) have been widely reported—and, to be honest, occasionally gloated over—since Disneyland Paris opened in 1992. With the benefit of hindsight, it's now apparent that simply replicating a distinctively American experience in a European time zone was something less than a true experiential value proposition. Disney's fabled imagineers overlooked or underestimated a lot of the realities of a new base of customers:

- In America, alcohol too often leads to rowdiness, so Disney minimizes its availability. In Europe, alcohol is simply a beverage, and its absence is on a par with going into Denny's and not being able to order a cup of coffee. Euro Disney's food service venues have been changed to reflect that.

- Though visitors from outside the United States are significant subsets at Disneyland and Walt Disney World, the bulk of the people coming through the gates are Americans. By contrast, only 40% of guests to Disneyland Paris are French, which dictates multilingual (French and English) live presentations and headphones that offer culturally specific translations in six other languages.

- Americans display relatively predictable eating patterns, which makes food service largely an exercise in queue management. Europeans don't tend to eat at the same time; often eat later, slower, and less at any given meal; and are prone to see a meal as an entertainment experience in its own right. The fact that Disneyland Paris is now France's largest tourist attraction suggests that a better experiential connection has been created. [5]

Experience Evolution

The opportunity to be deeply involved with two organizations working with two very different approaches to the customer experience was a turning point for me. It crystallized some of my early thoughts about experience management. It turned me into a soulmate of organizations interested in putting the experience at the center of how to create value for customers.

Their subsequent evolutions, in turn, have had a profound impact on my role as a coach, supporter, and pathfinder for companies committed to leveraging experience as a value proposition. It's no accident that I named my business *Experience Engineering*. It's exactly what I set out to help companies achieve. What is now being labeled the *experience economy* was in its formative stages in those days. It has taken another couple of decades to create the conditions in which the management of the customer's total experience can now come to the fore of the business value proposition.

Before we venture deeper into the world of experience management, it will be instructive to see how we arrived at this opportune moment and how we can maximize the value derived from it.

References

1. John Merwin. "The Sad Case of the Dwindling Orange Roofs," *Forbes*, page 78 (December 30, 1985).

2. "Charles Kemmon Wilson," *The Economist* (February 27, 2003).

3. *History*. McGrow Consulting (August 2003). http://www.mcgrow.com/history.htm.

4. Tim Burt. "Disney Aims to Ride High Again," *Financial Times* (October 8, 2003).

5. John Tagliabue. "Disney's New Paris Park Has a European Accent," *The New York Times* (June 9, 2002).

2

EXPERIENCE AS A VALUE PROPOSITION

Starbucks didn't start out as a purveyor of experience. From its initial roots as a product retailer over time, the organization shifted its value proposition to customer experience. When Starbucks' first location opened on the Seattle waterfront in 1971, it was a bean shop in the literal sense: It sold whole or ground, gourmet roasted coffee beans right off the boat (hence the siren-of-the-sea logo that 30 years later still puzzles some customers).

Back in those early days, the only brewing involved at Starbucks was for product tastings, or, as they're appropriately referred to in the business, "cuppings." The original theme tried to evoke the feelings of the seafaring tradition of coffee traders returning from exotic parts of the world with their precious cargoes. The actual brewing, consuming, and creation of a "place" that is now at the heart of the Starbucks coffee experience was intended to happen off site, mostly in people's homes.

In essence, Starbucks was a state-of-the-art business for the 1970s. It had a commodity-derived product. It provided just a little service (also basically a commodity). And, even though its customers had constant individual experiences with it for more than 10 years, it clearly did not provide a broader totally managed experience as its value proposition. Without that important change of emphasis—from experience as simply a transactional by-product to experience as the focal point and essence of the value proposition—it's unlikely that many people would know the Starbucks name today. What happened?

In *Pour Your Heart Into It* [1], his 1997 recounting of the company's phenomenal rise to cultural icon, chairman and CEO Howard Schultz credits the Starbucks we know today to a trip to a housewares show in Milan, Italy, in 1983 (Figure 2.1). He'd been with the company for a little over a year at that point, and he hadn't crossed an ocean looking for an epiphany. But that trip turned out to be an important milestone in the developing world of experience as the value proposition.

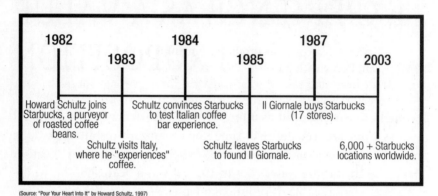

(Source: "Pour Your Heart Into It" by Howard Schultz, 1997)

Figure 2.1 A Starbucks timeline depicts some critical dates in the evolution of experience as a value proposition.

While at the show, Schultz recalls, he wandered into an espresso bar. He'd already begun to register, piecemeal, some sensory data from the way food was handled in Italy, compared with the Pacific Northwest— the way products as simple as figs were wrapped, packaged, and handed off to customers. In the espresso bar, he encountered a multisensory environment literally worlds different than the shop he'd left behind on the Seattle wharf.

You could say he woke up and smelled the coffee. And he saw the coffee. And he registered the sights and sounds and flavors and smells of fresh ground coffee being artfully woven into an *experience* with the coffee at the espresso bar. The *barista* gracefully moving around behind the counter; the grinding of beans and the pouring of shots; the intermittent sounds of people greeting one another; and the conversation of the staff with the customers waiting expectantly nearby. Newspapers were rustling; the grinder was grinding and clanking as new grounds were dispensed for brewing. Even the thumping sound of the used grounds being tamped down into a bucket, the sound of steaming milk, and the sound of Italian opera playing as a backdrop to all this action was embedded in the experience.

Schultz realized that Italians had turned coffee drinking into a symphony for the senses—an experiential rapture. As a direct result of his experiences in Milan, he returned to the United States with a passion to unlock the experiential romance and history of coffee and to explore the deep connection that could be developed between a business and its customers using the experience as the value proposition. In his book, he describes what that was going to mean for the way Starbucks did business:

> "We treated coffee as produce, something to be bagged and sent home with groceries. We stayed one big step away from the heart and soul of what coffee has meant throughout the centuries. If we could recreate in America the authentic Italian coffee bar culture, it might resonate with Americans the way it did with me. Starbucks could be a great experience, not just another great retail store." [1]

Smelling the Coffee

The rest really is history. Starbucks has grown to over 6,000 stores and was recognized by *Business Week* as the fastest growing global brand. [2]

But it's more than that because it's also current events. What Starbucks does—and what Disney's Attractions Group, Mayo Clinic, Harley-Davidson, and countless other businesses are beginning to do—is something that most businesses will need to learn how to do in the years to come.

The one-dimensional, accounting-driven approach to managing value creation is a matter of "counting the wrong beans."

As more and more companies realize that they cannot rely on standard, unimaginative pricing moves, continuous cost reduction, promotions, and "white sales that never end." Unleashing the power of creating experiential value is becoming more widely recognized. Companies are realizing that experience-based value strategies can provide a significant payback. Even the product life cycle of entire companies can be extended experientially.

In a sense, the one-dimensional, accounting-driven approach to value creation is a matter of "counting the wrong beans." By contrast, creating value around multidimensional, well-integrated, and consciously managed experiences will challenge you to connect to the unconscious emotional passions of your customers and in the process, you'll discover how to differentiate yourself from competitors in ways that can be almost impossible to copy and commoditize.

That's a very significant aspect of the Starbucks story. The design point for the customer value being created is on a deeper emotional level and not just on the level of a commodity, a product, or a service. It's a complete value proposition, emotional and rational, created and managed throughout the total customer experience. The smell of roasted coffee is a sensory clue. It engages sensory memories below the level of conscious thought. The experience surrounding brewing coffee at Starbucks releases a form of emotional economic value that's well beyond the strictly tangible attributes of the product alone.

Simply roasting coffee, brewing it, or pouring it into a cup for someone is merely the performance of a simple service. In the absence of wider experiential understanding, all you're doing is putting a hot liquid into a mug. On the other hand, when you're clued in to what customers actively desire and when the clues you're providing are validating and enriching that value proposition, you've taken a step up the value progression ladder. And you will reap significant economic efficiencies (Figure 2.2).

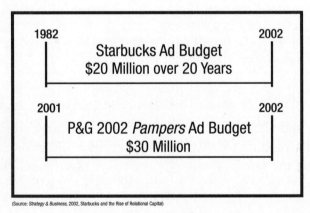

(Source: *Strategy & Business*, 2002, Starbucks and the Rise of Relational Capital)

Figure 2.2 Starbucks advertising expense.

That's why Starbucks and others of its genre have people lined up every morning. There were more than 6,000 locations worldwide in 2002, not to mention competitors with their own variations on the experiential theme. The restaurant on the corner may be *called* a coffee shop, but coffee isn't central to the total experience you have when you're there. You don't see coffee, hear coffee, smell coffee, feel coffee.

"Starbucks is a place that allows the customer experience to happen. Things in the store are just props to the experience."

On the other hand, Starbucks makes the complete "coffee" experience its focus. It consciously provides, then manages wide-ranging clues embedded throughout the experience that enhance and influence how you feel about the experience, the brand, and yourself as you recall the experience. At Starbucks, the nation's premier coffee experience management system, they consider their locations to be "a place that allows the customer experience to personally happen, with things in the store just props in staging the experience." [1]

Beyond the Starbucks success story, coffee the commodity also provides a useful way to illustrate the larger evolution that has been at work in the economies of the developed world over the last 50 years. In essence, value creation and value creation management are moving along a continuum that began with a raw commodity, then progressed to a focus on product, then to service, and now to the total customer experience.

A Valuable Cup of "Joe"

The value and willingness to pay increase as you move from a commodity to a product to a service to an experience. Let me illustrate. Joseph Pine and James Gilmore [3] use coffee as a general example to demonstrate the progression of economic value. A coffee cherry, the commodity, looks surprisingly just like its name. It's small. It's round. It's red. It grows on small trees and bushes that yield about 3,500 cherry seeds (or beans) a year. Even though coffee crops are still harvested mostly by hand and the yield of an average bush is only about a pound

---

of coffee, coffee beans are relatively inexpensive. A sack of beans on the world market often can be had for as little as 25 cents a pound. That's a commodity in its rawest, truest sense.

On the shelf in the supermarket, the commodity—embellished by processing, roasting, packaging, promoting, and moving it to market—results in a value-added product with a price between $2.50 and $6.99 a pound. This is the tangible product world with which we're so familiar, where "things" are packaged, stacked, and counted as inventory.

If you're a consumer rather than a connoisseur, you can brew about 50 pots from a large $5 can of vacuum-packed coffee, which typically contains a little over 2 pounds of ground, roasted beans. At four mugs per pot, your utilitarian cup of Joe (no pun intended) is costing you less than 3 cents. Even if you're buying beans and grinding them yourself, you'll have to work pretty hard to push the per-cup price much over a dime.

When you add the restaurant-style service of brewing the coffee and bringing it to your table, you raise the willingness to pay to somewhere between a dollar and a buck and a half. The cost now includes the commodity, the product, and delivering the service.

So why do millions willingly pay prices of $2 or more a cup for the same basic coffee when it's served up at a Starbucks or other similar establishments? And—equally germane to this narrative—why do they just as willingly continue to accept that price, yet complain when the franchised chain restaurant down the street charges them appreciably less for an endlessly refilled cup of a something-less-than-gourmet brew?

In a word: experience.

In two words (to be more precise): total experience.

The total experience is how a 3-cent cup of commodity coffee becomes a $2 form of emotionally vested consumer involvement. The total experience is what transforms the combination of product and service, making it more valuable than the basic components alone. By the same token, no matter how the coffee shop java tastes compared with the more expensive brew being dispensed at the gourmet place around the corner, it's the presence of a managed, complete, integrated, and focused experience that makes the difference that causes customers to feel committed about indulging in a $4 latte on a daily basis.

Experience Decisions

As it turns out, not only is the marketplace indicating that the total experience is central to customer value, but scientific data and marketing research are also validating it—and beginning to offer explanations for why this has always been the case.

"The tangible attributes of a product or service have far less influence on consumer preference than the subconscious sensory and emotional elements derived from the total experience."

Provocative findings in the pure sciences as well as market research are proving that the *unconscious* plays a far more central role in decision making than traditionally thought. In fact, much like the tip of a very large iceberg, as much as 95% of what influences consumers' conscious choices resides below awareness [4].

As these insights have begun to seep into the business world, they are setting the stage for major changes in fields as diverse as market research, customer relationship management, advertising, organizational development, and experience design.

Perhaps most prominent in this area of understanding is the distinguished Dr. Gerald Zaltman, the Joseph B. Wilson chair of the Marketing Department at the Harvard Business School. Founder of the "Mind of the Market Laboratory" at Harvard and author of the 2003 book, *How Customers Think: Essential Insights into the Mind of the Market,* I've had the great pleasure of knowing and working with Jerry for almost a decade. On the basis of his extensive research and his patented tools for surfacing unconscious emotional drivers, he states the case for managing the total experience in its most basic form: "The tangible attributes of a product or service have far less influence on consumer preference than the subconscious sensory and emotional elements *derived from the total experience*" (author's emphasis). [5] This assessment underscores the central value of the total experience. It also points to the potential impact that systematically managing the sensory and emotional elements—the "clues" being emitted throughout an experience—can have on customer value creation and competitive advantage. It also helps us see that even when product attributes or service quality formed the core of value propositions, an entire experience was always still taking place, made up of important sensory and emotion-based information that form a composite impression.

Dollars and Donuts

Over the last several years, perhaps no company demonstrates the results of the managed-experience phenomenon better than Krispy Kreme. [6] And the numbers are impressive. Consider:

- As of June 2003, there were 285 Krispy Kreme stores in the United States and Canada. By comparison, Dunkin' Donuts—the largest coffee and baked goods chain in the world—had some 5,300 locations, about 70% of them in the States, the rest spread from Aruba and Brazil to Thailand and the United Arab Emirates.
- A Krispy Kreme location is, however, designed as a manufacturing facility as well as a doughnut store and in an average year will post sales of $3.4 million, compared with $744,000 for a Dunkin' Donuts counterpart (Figure 2.3).

Krispy Kreme		Dunkin' Donuts
219	Number of Stores	5,300
$3.4 Million	Avg. Yearly Sales per Unit	$744,000
$2 Billion	Doughnuts Produced per Yr.	$2.3 Billion
12.8%	Sales Growth 2000-2001	7.4%

Figure 2.3 Krispy Kreme and Dunkin Donuts.

- As a result, Krispy Kreme systemwide—with about a twentieth as many physical locations—produces about the same number of doughnuts as its larger rival: on the order of 2.5 *billion*.
- More to the point, it produces an exponentially greater level of word-

of-mouth advocacy. Dunkin' Donuts, as part of a corporate family that includes Baskin-Robbins ice cream and Togo's sandwiches, talks about "trombos" (locations featuring all three brands), "dayparts" (numerical abstracts of consumer buying patterns), and "share-of-stomach." Krispy Kreme talks about experiences.

As CEO Scott Livengood told David and Tom Gardner on their *The Motley Fool Radio Show* in May 2003 [7], "I am in the fortunate position of knowing probably better than anybody what I consider to be the power of the Krispy Kreme brand: the connection that we have with customers. To have been a part of the experience here with the company, I have seen the business model evolve. We repositioned the business from a wholesale business, which created some retail opportunities, to this management team—the one that repositioned our brand around the retail store experience."

Yes, both Krispy Kreme and Dunkin' Donuts are in the business of selling tasty fried dough. That's the common product—the stuff that keeps accountants and operations management software busy counting things. But what makes one a retail store and the other a storied experience is how the customer feels in one place, compared with the other.

To extend that advantage, in recent years Krispy Kreme has been rolling out as a "super signature experience clue" its own proprietary Hot Doughnut Machine: a more portable conveyor oven and glazing system based on its traditional store equipment that allows it to "bring the Krispy Kreme experience" to customers in locations such as regional malls, airports, downtown office buildings, and more.

Even when customers find boxes of Krispy Kreme doughnuts in grocery stores, department stores, convenience stores, or church fundraisers, there's little danger that the experience itself is being diluted. To the contrary, it's being reinforced. Customers know that what they're buying in these peripheral locations is a good product but nowhere near as emotionally satisfying as the experience they will have wherever they find one of those Pavlovian "Hot Doughnuts Now" signs lit. One form of consuming behavior simply reinforces the other.

Even the rollout of locations has been part of the very controlled experience. Krispy Kreme has opened a limited number of stores annually, maintaining a sense of scarcity. In fact, I used to take dozens of Krispy

Kreme doughnuts home to my family from Atlanta, Tampa, and other markets before they opened in Minneapolis. I remember a particular incident where an airline gate agent in Atlanta jokingly tried to confiscate my smuggled doughnuts, saying "Krispy Kremes aren't allowed to be taken out of state." Grand openings have caused traffic jams several miles long. People camp out for days to be first in line for an opening. Cars were lined up for three and four hours even a week after Krispy Kreme made its debut in Minnesota. That's consumer behavior that's very difficult to attribute to rational thought.

The Krispy Kreme phenomenon is powerful and so are the experience clues at its locations, including the open-view production of the doughnuts, the "waterfall" of thick glaze that cascades over the doughnuts, the smell of the doughnuts frying, even the people waiting in line to scoop up their dozen "hot" off the production line.

Close your eyes for a moment and recollect your last visit to Dunkin' Donuts. Perhaps you envision as I do, a few doughnuts sitting on pink liner paper with hardened glaze and grease stains displayed in a doughnut case that constantly seems to be shrinking to make room for line extensions such as bagels, soup, and even ice cream now. It must be very frustrating for the Dunkin' Donuts management and operators to watch the incredible success that Starbucks and Krispy Kreme have realized with coffee and doughnuts in what was once their domain.

Customers, Coffee, and Doughnuts

In the examples above, the commodity is raw coffee beans or flour. The product is produced by roasting those beans or making the batter. The service involves brewing those processed beans and frying the batter into doughnuts. In the main, these are elements that exhibit a high degree of rationality. Businesses can and do quantitatively measure those rational aspects: cost, volume, purity, temperature, speed, product turns, and return on investment.

However, what's significant is that Starbucks and Krispy Kreme understand the impact that changing their focus to experience as the value proposition has for them. They know that it's not the rational elements that engender a customer commitment but the emotional bonding to the experience that transforms those commodity, product, and service components into something uniquely memorable—something that indelibly connects with customers. Realizing that purely rational explanations are not adequate, accurate, or effective in today's competitive marketplace, both organizations have demonstrated the courage and conviction to leverage the total experience as their value proposition.

The creation of value has been documented and written about for years by others, such as Morris Holbrook, the W. T. Dillard Professor of Marketing at the Columbia Business School, who has said, "Customer value resides in the consumption *experience*."[8]

Although I won't take the time to mention every noteworthy explorer in this area,[1] the implications are becoming more visible and clear. As experience becomes the new focus of the value proposition, not only will businesses need to change the way they operate, but the customer's role will also be transformed and enlarged in important ways. Writing in the magazine *strategy + business*, for example, authors C. K. Prahalad and Venkatram Ramaswamy envision customers becoming outright co-creators of value, increasingly working toward common objectives in partnership with the businesses trying to serve their needs.

"For more than 100 years," they theorize, "a company-centric, efficiency-driven view of value creation has shaped our industrial infrastructure and the entire business system. Although this perspective often conflicts with what consumers value—the *quality of their experiences* with goods and services—companies see value creation as a process of cost-effectively producing goods and services."

The authors further point out that such a cost-centered obsession sometimes works at cross purposes with the interests of the organization's customers, who "appreciate and expect efficiency when it improves their experience with a product or service" but are less inclined to tolerate

---

1. Commentators on the value of experience—notably Joe Pine and Jim Gilmore in their 1999 book, *The Experience Economy*—also have sensed the growing power of the experiential value proposition. In particular, they also deserve thanks for giving the world a useful name for what's at work as well as their references to theater as a metaphor for experience. Also noteworthy is Bernd Schmitt's most recent work in the area of "experience marketing." In *There's No Business That's Not Show Business*, he raises the curtain higher—literally—by showing how organizations can understand experiences in the context of show business as a metaphor. His work demonstrates the intimate relationship between experience and traditional approaches to branding and marketing.

managers "so preoccupied with operating efficiently that they don't even think about value in terms of the consumer's experience." [9]

An Alan Wrench for Your Thinking

Memorable experiences can come in any form and can involve services as well as products. In the mid-1990s, when enhanced service was still being listed under the heading of silver bullets, an interesting book appeared, shortly to be accompanied by a companion videotape. In *The Real Heroes of Business . . . and Not a CEO Among Them*, [12] author Bill Fromm and contributor Len Schlesinger advanced the idea that "uncommon individuals" were challenging their employers to take customer service to new heights as a way to win the battle for customer loyalty.

Curiously, the heroes they profiled were in many cases extremely common—a hotel doorman, an airline flight attendant, a health care billing troubleshooter—men and women whose real contribution was guiding the experiences their customers had with them, sometimes despite the mixed signals they were receiving from the folks who signed their paychecks.

One such individual was Alan Wilk, a Roto-Rooter route driver in New York. Alan Wilk knew his way around a drain snake, but that wasn't what made him a hero in the eyes of Fromm and Schlesinger or his customers. It was the way he tinkered with virtually everything provided by his employer—even though often that was against official company policy. Then, from the moment he got out of his truck, he worked to make sure that everything his customers saw, heard, smelled, or wondered about added up to a complete (and therefore preference-generating) experience.

Because he understood the emotional value of his response time, Wilk wasn't content to flip through street guides. In the absence of GPS technology, he'd wrapped a pull-down map around a window-shade roller and attached it to the visor on the passenger side of his truck. Whenever he found himself stopped in traffic, he could simply pull down the map and reorient himself. Though the truck itself was neither large nor lavish, Wilk had rigged a toilet and even a modest shower in the back so he wouldn't arrive sweaty and smelly from previous jobs; a simple sink handled smaller cleanup needs.

Once out of the truck, Wilk did more than haul a pile of gear into someone's home. He took pains to relax and reassure the nervous homeowners or tenants who were waiting for him to unclog whatever was currently clogging up not just their drains but also their lives. Freshened up with cologne, he rescued lost socks, dispensed treats for watching pets, and made sure his work area was cleaner and smelled better (he carried his own can of air freshener) when he left than it had been before the problem ever occurred.

It is on the basis of those unconscious feelings that the customer will decide not only who to call the next time but also who to recommend to friends and neighbors if they face a similar need.

None of that, speaking strictly from a financial accounting perspective, is a part of the actual, rational service that Roto-Rooter is charging for. But all of it is part of the total experience the customer will remember long after the service has been delivered. And it is on the basis of those unconscious feelings that the customer will decide not only who to call the next time, but also who to recommend to friends and neighbors if they face a similar need.

Over the years, Fromm and Schlesinger reported, Roto-Rooter had learned to *tolerate* Wilk's eccentricities. It even adopted some of his equipment modifications. But it didn't seem to give much thought to what the possible net effect would be on its business, had the Alan Wilks among its workforce become the norm and not exceptions to the rule. To this day, the company still remains steadfastly focused on selling a franchise built around a piece of drain-cleaning equipment, rather than a systematically managed customer experience in which that signature piece of equipment plays a part.

(After his brief moment in the limelight, Wilk was still happily on the job in 2003, mostly fixing people's everyday problems but occasionally popping in on a training session to serve as something of a behavioral visual aid, however out of the ordinary.)

Do you have a feeling that there may have been a missed opportunity here?

- For Roto-Rooter, much of the business concentration is on the *product*—the flexible Roto-Rooter "snake" that cleans out drain pipes. It's a known commodity. It works very well. The clues surrounding it are fairly rational and tangible: It can be seen, touched, measured, inventoried on a truck, and watched in operation.
- The unclogging process itself is the *service* being provided, and it also regularly achieves good reviews. Here, too, customers can observe some tangible attributes: a worker, a truck, tubing, cords, water flowing. They also record other, more sensory forms of data, as well: the sounds and smells of the work being done, the appearance of the worker and the equipment, the look of the mess before arrival and the job site afterward.
- Beyond these purely product and service clues, however, the *total experience* the customer has—and on which the customer will make an emotional and a rational decision of who to call or recommend the next time a plumbing problem is encountered—involves much more.

Whether the arriving tech is named Alan Wilk or Wilhelmina Allen, Roto-Rooter's collective future will be determined by how its customers feel about everything that happens from the time they discover a problem until the driver departs, the drain running unobstructed again. This involves things such as how long it takes for someone to come, compared with how long the homeowner expected to wait; what that someone looks and sounds (and smells) like; whether he or she leaves behind a cleaned-up drain area or gooey footprints, offers helpful troubleshooting tips or a view of low-riding pants, makes the customer feel confident in the value received, or leaves the customer making a mental note to look for some other alternative the next time they have a problem.

For the entire experience to succeed, all the clues have to be managed toward the desired experiential end frame, which raises a salient question: However admirable it may be to celebrate the Alan Wilks individually, how much more powerful might it be if *every* Roto-Rooter customer had the experience that Wilk's customers do, no matter whose name is stitched on the service provider's coveralls?

Perhaps someday Roto-Rooter will take that next step along the value-proposition continuum. There's nothing wrong with what it has done to this point in building a respected brand name. It just hasn't fully leveraged the business proposition to move it to a higher level.

Taking the Next Step

As noted earlier, experiences aren't new. Businesses have been creating them since the dawn of business time. They've just been doing it piecemeal and generally without a deep understanding of how central it is to the customer value they are creating. More and more companies today are attempting to understand and leverage the value created by customer experience.

In fact, a review of the studies conducted for members by the Marketing Science Institute (MSI) in recent years shows a growing number of investigations designed to better understand the nature of the customer experience. Director of Research Ross Rizley reports that although there is no firm consensus within the organization on the meaning of "the customer experience," it is continuously popping up under various terms and titles and in a number of prominent studies. He predicts it will become an increasingly common element in the organization's future studies. [11]

For his part, William Ghormley, a former president of MSI, sums up the interest this way: "Not everyone sees experience in its holistic sense, and some can't get beyond customer service as the experience. But by and large, almost everyone seems to sense there's a great deal more to be learned." [12]

Most significantly, there's an ever-increasing need and desire for new models, disciplines, competencies, and tools to enable business to fully leverage and manage experiences. Len Berry, whose work has guided so many to a deeper understanding of customer value for so many years, is a guiding light in this area. Harvard's John Deighton has contributed seminal work in areas such as customer service as a performance, laying a firm foundation for the more recent experience-oriented investigations.

Fortunately, these insights, along with the leadership of inspiring early adopters and market leaders, are now being spotlighted in today's business world. And they are setting a new bar for how organizations will present and brand themselves to customers in the future. Those that develop a system to manage the sensory and emotional signals—the "clues"—being emitted throughout a customer's experience will gain powerful competitive advantages. Through experience management, businesses will be better equipped to tap into the underlying "iceberg" to forge stronger bonds with their customers that lead to long-term preference and loyalty.

As you begin to build a successful value proposition around the customers total experiences, you're going to find that the future becomes a lot more manageable and your competitive advantage a lot more distinctive—and considerably more sustainable.

References

1. Howard Schultz with Dori Jones Yang. *Pour Your Heart Into It* (New York: Hyperion,1997).

2. Gerry Khermouch with Stanley Holmes and Moon Ihlwan, "The Best Global Brands," *Business Week* (August 6, 2003).

3. B. Joseph Pine, II and James H. Gilmore. *The Experience Economy, Work Is Theatre & Every Business a Stage,* page 2 (Boston: Harvard Business School Press, 1999).

4. Gerald Zaltman. *How Customers Think: Essential Insights into the Mind of the Market,* page 58 (Boston: Harvard Business School Press, 2003).

5. Gerald Zaltman. "Lighting Up the Shadows," a presentation at Procter & Gamble's Future Forces Conference, Cincinnati, Ohio (1997).

6. Carlye Adler, "Would You Pay $2 Million for This Franchise?" Fortune Small Business (May 1, 2002); Dan Ackman, Forbes.com, "Investors Peruse Hole in Doughnut Sales." Posted on Fortune.com (9/16/03).

7. Scott Livengood interviewed on The Motley Fool Radio Show (May 2003). David Gardner and Tom Gardner. "Krispy Kreme's Competition." Posted on www.thefool.com (June 12, 2003).

8. Morris B. Holbrook. *Consumer Research: Introspective Essays on the Study of Consumption,* page 51 (Thousand Oaks, CA: Sage, 1995).

9. C. K. Prahalad and Venkatram Ramaswamy. "The Co-Creation Connection," *strategy + business,* page 1, (2nd Quarter 2002).

10. Bill Fromm with Len Schlesinger. *The Real Heroes of Business ... and not a CEO Among Them* (New York: Doubleday, 1994).

11. Ross Rizley, Director of Research, Marketing Science Institute. Personal communication (May and June 2003).

12. William A. Ghormley, Chief Catalyst, Snap Out of It! Personal communication (May 2003)

3

THE BRAND CANYON

By one informal count, more than 275 books have been written on the subject of brand and brand management in American business, not to mention numerous articles. So perhaps it's a surprise to find that there's a chapter related to brand management in a book about experience management. The simple reason is that the two are directly related yet distinctly different. Managing a brand is not the same as managing experiences to create value, and managing experiences is not brand management per se.

Clearly, brand has a prodigious head start where "the literature" is concerned. With so many voices arguing for so many different interpretations of brand, especially as business conditions change and traditional assumptions are being challenged, the term has become commonplace, venerated, and as sprawling as the Grand Canyon. In the process, a vast chasm has opened up between brand as rooted in the old "make-and-sell" [1] world and where it needs to be in a "sense-and-respond world," in which Experience Value Management is critical.

Because this is among the first books to lay out a practical, systematic approach to creating and managing the total customer experience as a value proposition, it's essential to establish a more concise understanding of the relationship between the two. Brand management and experience management are different: The former is more focused on how customers feel about the company and the latter on how customers and/or employees feel about themselves.

In the past, many have framed experience management predominantly in terms of brand management. Perhaps this is because a robust approach to managing experiences had not yet been articulated or described in terms of principles, disciplines, competencies, and tools. Nor had the differences between brand and experience been sharply articulated. In truth, more time and energy have been expended trying to make brand and experience one and the same. Using brand as the context for experience management can create more difficulties that it solves because it lacks the clarity and priority for managing what customers feel about *themselves* in their dealings with an organization.

What customers value is the experience. And that's what they associate with the brand (brand association).

The longer this state of affairs persists, the deeper and wider the "Brand Canyon" will become, and the greater will be the organizational engineering task for bridging the chasm between creating value for the customer and creating value for the company.

What customers value is the experience. And that's what they associate with the brand (brand association).

Brand and Experience

Consider Starbucks again, but this time, first think about Starbucks as a brand, then think about it as an experience. If you are considering how you feel *about* Starbucks, you are thinking about the Starbucks brand. If you think about how *you yourself feel* as a result of a visit to Starbucks, you are relating to the experience. Often, comments that reflect value for the experience will be framed by statements such as, "When I'm at Starbucks I feel like . . . " or "Starbucks makes me feel . . . " Experience comments (and indications of experience value) are framed by both the emotional and rational value being created on the surface and, even more importantly, on a deeper emotional level. Figure 3.1 summarizes these value relationships.

Brand Value	How I feel about the company
Customer Value	How I feel in the experience

Figure 3.1 Value relationships.

Experience and brand are not one and the same and therefore shouldn't be used interchangeably if you want to optimize the value of both. For example, consider the Marriott master brand and the company's numerous sub-brands of Marriott Courtyard, Marriott Hotels, Residence Inn, Ritz-Carlton, Renaissance, Summerfield Suites, Fairfield Inn, and so forth. When you're at Marriott Courtyard, the experience is different from at a Marriott Hotel or at the Ritz–Carlton. The value perceived by customers is based on how they personally feel about their individual experiences, not how they recall the Ritz-Carlton brand when they stay at a Marriott Courtyard. Each sub-brand has distinctive experiences associated with it, which reflects the company's understanding of the distinctive experiential value of each.

However, take the co-branded locations where Taco Bell, KFC, and Pizza Hut are all served under one roof (in order to leverage real estate opportunities by the parent company). Or where National Car Rental and Alamo Rent A Car (owned by the same company) share the same shuttle buses, facilities, and even the same fleet. When you rent a car at National, the experience is almost a mirror image of the experience you get at Alamo. The point is there's a tremendous blurring of the experiences each brand delivers, and as such, an unwitting erosion of the company's ability to optimize both experiential and brand value.

In fact, National/Alamo's parent company claimed Chapter 11 reorganization on November 13, 2001, and was purchased by Vanguard Car Rental USA Inc. in October of 2003. The new CEO, William Lobek, stated the new leadership's intent to experientially emphasize each brands' distinction (National as a leader with high-frequency business customers; Alamo as a value, vacation rental brand). "Our most important focus is to restore National and Alamo to their former prominence," he said. [2] "What I would like (customers) to see when they get to an airport is an Alamo counter and a National counter. They may be side by side and separated by a very thin wall, but they will be separate. If you're an Alamo customer you will not stand in a National line and vice versa." [3]

It's a delicate balance to optimize both brand and experience. When they are perceived as being interchangeable, it can lead to a quagmire of confusion for an organization and thus, widen the chasm of the Brand Canyon.

Figure 3.2 depicts a framework to think about the relationship of brand and experience in value creation:

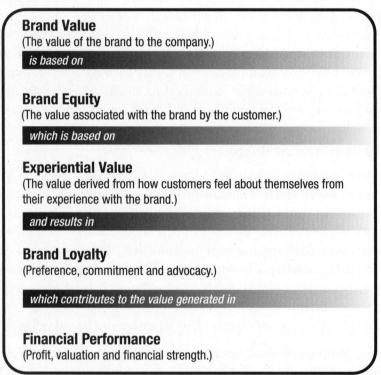

Figure 3.2 Brand experience relationships.

Ultimately, how your customers feel as a result of doing business with you reflects what they value on an unconscious level.

That experience-derived value perception is what customers become bonded to—not the brand attributes. It's on the basis of that deeper bond that customers become totally committed to a brand.

This subtle clarification is crucial at a time when brand perspectives are being stretched from simply achieving top-of-mind awareness and positive associations to forging more lasting and deeper emotional bonds with customers.

Because the customer is the ultimate arbiter of value, "smoke and mirrors" won't induce people to be loyal to a brand. Customers value the "reality" they perceive and feel. They will reward or punish you by voting with their feet (or fingers on the phone or in cyberspace), returning to organizations that create experiences that connect with their deeper needs and desires, and walking away from those that don't.

The management of authentic experiences requires a robust system that simultaneously upholds the integrity and perceived value of what customers themselves feel.

Experience Authenticity

The deep emotional bond customers establish through experience can be transformational. The authenticity of the experience is a factor in the creation and strength of that commitment. So it follows that the management of authentic experiences requires a robust system that simultaneously upholds the integrity and perceived value of what customers themselves feel.

It's an important if not vital consideration in the creation of value for customers in an authentic and genuine manner to consider what different customer subsets have in common and what makes them different. For example, authenticity for various generations is summed up in a study conducted by Yankelovich, Inc. It describes generational "cohorts" as Echoes (age 16–23), Xers (24–37), Boomers (38–56), and Matures (57+). The study goes on to highlight characteristics that contribute to authentic connections for each: Authenticity for Boomers is based on "telling the truth"; with Xers it means showing savvy; and with Echoes it means facilitating involvement. [4]

As you'll see in the second section of this book, the disciplines, competencies, and tools utilized in managing experiences provide the capability to understand such commonalities and differences and to customize and manage clues to each group's unique characteristics.

You can put bug-ridden software in a pretty box, put shabby clothes on a big-name model, or spend millions of dollars hyping a movie before it debuts at the multiplex. But as soon as customers have their experiences, their word-of-mouth reviews will define your future and fortunes. Significantly, those reviews are more credible than any brand-polishing efforts you can commission precisely because they reflect how customers felt during real experiences. Experience truly is the best teacher.

Strangely, that's a phenomenon that can have some curious side effects. For example, loyal customers of Krispy Kreme routinely complain to the company's management when they see the company doing anything that resembles advertising. They are such firm, committed patrons of the authenticity of the experience that they actually become upset when they perceive that their role as experience advocates is being diminished by the company's marketing efforts.

Stretching Brand

Embracing experience as the focal point of a company's value proposition transforms the management imperative. Without minimizing the importance of brand, it places a new priority on managing what customers feel about *themselves* in their dealings with an organization and its offerings. As Len Berry notes in *The Soul of Customer Service*, "The marketed brand contributes to brand meaning·, but not as strongly as the customer's actual experience with the company." [5]

The growing recognition of the importance of experience led some to attempt to bridge the brand/experience gap by slapping a convenient label on the effort—"branded experience" or "experiencing the brand" being the most obvious. But those labels may miss the essence of the challenge as well as the real opportunity. These well-intentioned discussions about whether the experience is the brand or whether an experience can be branded further illustrate the need for deeper understanding and clarity concerning what the two have in common and where they part company.

Exploring Experience Motifs

Often, brand management will deal with "emotion" as ascribed to the brand rather than emotion felt by the customer. Further, it's based on the emotions a customer feels *about the company*, not what *customers themselves feel* when interacting with it.

Many will point to the "brand persona" as the emotional connecting point for customers, but again, the problem is that the persona is defined by emotional attributes ascribed to the brand and not what customers feel about themselves.

In the practice of managing experiences, I recommend that organizations develop a three-word Experience Motif that focuses on the feelings customers desire as the goal of the experiences they're committed to delivering to their customers. (You'll see specific applications of this technique in Chapter 9, which deals with the discipline of designing.) Whether you do it formally or informally, however, the exercise of developing an Experience Motif is worthwhile because it helps you concisely express the emotional values of the customer experience that often is only vaguely defined in traditional strategic discussions.

A pragmatic way to orient yourself to the concept of motif is to think in terms of the perspective of direction. Brand very often is an expression from an *organization* out: The business wants to deliver a message that it controls and leave an impression that it believes will favorably position it in the customer's mind. An Experience Motif literally is "customer-back": It starts by identifying emotions *customers* want to feel as a result of an experience (which recognizes that the customer is in control), then works back to what the organization has to do to get to that emotional end frame.

Brand is by nature self-aggrandizing. It's about projecting rather than providing. To build up the company's image and stature . . . control vests in the originator of the message, not the receiver. An Experience Motif is essentially selfless. . . . The organization acknowledges that its stature and future prospects hinge on the value its customers distill from their experiences.

These are subtle but very real and important differences. For a company, brand is by nature self-aggrandizing. It's about projecting rather than providing. Ultimate control and determinations of value vest in the originator of the message, not the receiver. It seeks to build up the company's image and stature. Figure 3.3 shows how perspective changes with the experience managed as a value proposition.

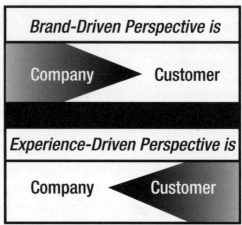

Figure 3.3 Brand vs. Experience perspective.

An Experience Motif is essentially selfless. Rather than seek to control an image that originates with the company, by creating a motif, the organization acknowledges that its stature and future prospects hinge on the value its customers distill from their experiences. In Experience Value Management, a motif becomes the overarching filter for all the clues customers encounter (see Figure 3.4).

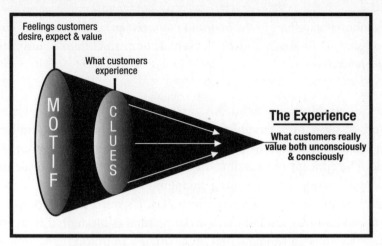

Figure 3.4   Experience Value and Clue Management.

Defining Brand

Evidence of the confusion around brand can even be found in the various definitions for the word itself.

Merriam Webster Dictionary offers the definition [6]: "A word, name, symbol, etc., especially one legally registered as a trademark, used by a manufacturer or merchant to identify its products distinctively from others of the same type and usually prominently displayed on its goods, in advertising, etc." . . . "A product, line of products, or service bearing a widely known brand name," even "A person notable or famous, esp. in a particular field: The reception was replete with brand names from politics and the arts (1925)."

The *New Oxford American Dictionary* [7] defines brand as:

- "A trademark or distinctive name identifying a product or a manufacturer."
- "A product line so identified: *a popular brand of soap.*"
- "A distinctive category; a particular kind: *a brand of comedy that I do not care for.*"
- "A mark indicating identity or ownership, burned on the hide of an animal with a hot iron."

A fundamental point of view in brand management is the emphasis on an organization's interests, sometimes override or distract from a customer's value perception.

You can readily understand how marketers would connect putting a brand on something tangible, such as a cow, with product branding. In that sense, brand is a way to demonstrate ownership of something tangible. The concept of branding an experience is an attempt to demonstrate ownership of something intangible. But you can begin to see where the Brand Canyon comes into play. It's much more complex to try to put a similar kind of mark on something as intangible as an experience. As noted, a fundamental point of view in brand management is the subtle emphasis on an organization's interests, which often can override or distract from creating real customer value perception.

If you're deeply involved in customer experience management, you can definitely become frustrated if you fail to recognize the differences and similarities between brand and experience. Not only can the "fogginess" hamper your efforts to fully leverage the experiential value management opportunity, but it can also unwittingly lead you right over the edge of the Brand Canyon, leaving even the best-intentioned brand or experience management efforts smashed on the all-too-familiar rocks of failed programs.

Virtually every author who has engaged the subject of brand in recent years has taken a stab at redefining or stretching the term, recognizing the need for deeper understanding. Scott Bedbury, who held senior marketing positions at firms that represent two acclaimed brand development stories of recent times—Nike (1987–1994) and Starbucks (1995–1998)—told *Fast Company* [8], way back in 1997:

> "They recognize that consumers live in an emotional world. Emotions drive most, if not all, of our decisions. Not many people sit around and discuss the benefits of encapsulated gas in the mid-sole of a basketball shoe or the advantages of the dynamic-fit system. They will talk about Michael Jordan's winning shot against Utah the other night—and they'll experience the dreams and the aspirations and the awe that go with that last-second, game-winning shot."

In his book *A New Brand World* [9], Bedbury goes on to say that he did what he could "to shape these products into more valuable, more relevant, more exciting, and more rewarding experiences."

Management of the experience, in other words, is where the real customer value was distinctively created. When you know what to look for, you can see that some of the brightest megabrand development stories have a powerful experience component woven through them.

Brand Reviving Experiences

It's the effective combination of brand management and Experience Value Management that can breathe new life into customer loyalty and the revitalization of a brand.

Effectively managing both the customer's total experience and the brand has the power to resurrect even all-but-extinct brands. It's not a matter of one or the other—it's the effective combination of brand management and Experience Value Management that can breathe new life into customer preference and loyalty and revitalize a brand.

Business lore offers no shortage of brands that, like Howard Johnson Restaurants, reached extinction or near extinction from not managing experiential value. Some eventually revived. Many did not. Remember Burger Chef? Eastern Air Lines? Burroughs?

Retailing, in fact, is littered with the stories of once-great brands gone into eclipse—or gone entirely—among them Garfinkle's, Sterns, Wanamaker, Gimble's, and more recently, Montgomery Ward.

Do you remember the "old" Abercrombie & Fitch? At one time, A&F was renowned as the clothier that outfitted the likes of Ernest Hemingway and Teddy Roosevelt. But over the years, the name lost its luster and was eventually snuffed out. I remember going into the A&F store in Bal Harbor, Florida, in November of 1977 like it was yesterday. There are two reasons the memory is so sharp: My wife and I were on our honeymoon, and it was the store's going-out-of-business sale. I bought a pair of boat shoes and recall telling my wife what a sad sight it was to see such a storied company seemingly on the verge of extinction.

In the early 1980s, much to my surprise, we encountered a miracu-lously resurrected A&F at the Stamford Town Mall in Stamford, Con-necticut, where we were living at the time. It boasted plaid carpeting reminiscent of a men's club but delivered an experience more rooted in its brand heritage.

Eventually, the Griffin Company, the real estate developer that had led the attempt to revitalize the brand, sold Abercrombie & Fitch to The Limited (now Limited Brands), whose companies include The Limited, Express and Express Men's, Victoria's Secret, and Bath & Body Works. There, Les Wexler, retail and merchandising wizard (and president), led efforts that reignited the brand before it was spun off as a once-again independent company in 1996.

Today, the A&F experience that The Limited created resonates with an entirely new generation of consumers, especially those of college age who may have no idea of the brand's deep heritage. No matter: The new experience clearly connects. Back in November of 1977, I never dreamed my children would be sporting the A&F logo as a fashion statement in the 1990s. That they and millions of their contemporaries did is a working testament to the ability of a revitalized experience to breath life into a nearly extinct brand.

What The Limited, in particular, understood is the connection between the power of brand and the need to manage the creation of a form of experiential value that is in sync with customers' needs and desires. Granted, some of the tactics employed have contributed to periodic controversy around the Abercrombie image. Nonetheless, A&F's rise—like a phoenix from the brand ashes—is an outstanding example of the ability of a well-managed total experience to help reconstitute a brand.

Brand Junction

As experience increasingly becomes woven into the way organizations conceive of and manage customer value, your organization will find itself at a critical junction point along the Brand Canyon. When the heritage of brand management is viewed as the foundation for effective experience management, the road will be obscured and eventually lead you right over the edge. But where brand strengths are effectively integrated with the practice of experience management, you'll find a way to bridge the chasm.

If we truly expect to leverage experience as a value proposition and reap significant benefits as a result, the time has never been better to understand the relationship between these two powerful concepts. Sorting out the relationship of experience to brand is a critical key to unlocking the full potential of any experience management system you hope to create. To optimize the opportunity, understand that just as they cannot be substituted for each other, they also are not mutually exclusive or opposing forces. Rather, the trick is to manage brand and experience in a distinctive yet complimentary manner.

In fact, a complete relational separation of brand and experience is impossible: The natural attraction that pulls them together is much like the positive and negative poles in an electromagnetic field. If anything, the synergistic nature of the relationship underscores the need for a system where the interaction of the parts results in a greater whole and greater value creation for the customer. That is completely evident and natural when you fully understand the relationship between experience and brand.

A Tipping Point?

Keeping a clear and consistent perspective on the relationship of brand to experience—and avoiding the dangers created by the Brand Canyon—is a huge challenge. Product-based "make-and-sell" roots run deep in business history and brand tradition, resisting any simple changeover.

Moving from a make-and-sell world to a new perspective based on sense-and-respond won't be easy. But it is definitely possible—and an extraordinary opportunity. Already, some firms are beginning to bridge the gap and reap benefits, even without fully fleshing out a sustainable experience management system.

Below the Radar

Consider most airline experiences. On a functional and operational level, they're all pretty much in parity. The industry has used loyalty programs to keep frequent customers from feeling worse about the deteriorating experiences they are having, thus extending the concept of "mileage as a reward" to make up for what has become a commodity experience.

From the passenger standpoint, flying has probably never been worse. Pricing that can change from one minute to the next is not only incomprehensible, it's reprehensible. Hub-and-spoke systems make the prospect of getting from point A to point B a multiple-flight ordeal that often requires going by way of point C and sometimes point D. Security is intrusive, intimidating, and sometimes nonsensical.

Interestingly, since the federal government's Transportation Safety Administration (TSA) has taken over the security experience, studies have shown some visible change in the way passengers feel. Compared with what once seemed random and haphazard, TSA's personnel impress passengers as being both more knowledgeable about what they're doing and more conscientious in the way they do it. It's no accident: TSA enlisted Disney's experience specialists to help train people and design systems involved in the process. Although a better experience than was initially delivered after 9/11, it remains far from perfect, and still contributes significantly to travel stress.

Once on-board, the passenger's experience hardly improves. Seats are uncomfortable, restrooms Spartan, and even fresh air in the cabin is being rationed these days to improve on-flight mileage efficiency. Creature comforts from basic beverage service to meals have been reduced, eliminated, or on a pay-as-you-go basis.

It's noteworthy that even though all carriers operate on a theoretically level landing field, a couple—in particular, Southwest and JetBlue—have managed to differentiate themselves. Not coincidentally, both focus on how passengers feel about themselves, which has encouraged their passengers to have a strong preference for the companies involved. Now, United with Ted and Delta with Song are attempting to crack the low-cost airline experience code and blunt inroads made by JetBlue and Southwest.

JetBlue Airways made news in June 2003 when it placed a $3 billion order for 100 new planes. [10] While most familiar airline names have been flirting with bankruptcy headlines, reducing flight schedules, and having to play hardball with unions over continuing cutbacks, Jet-Blue—profitable since 2001—was building on its experience in smaller markets and shorter routes to plot an ambitious growth course.

For its part, since its founding in 1971, Southwest Airlines has risen from an upstart to the nation's fourth largest carrier and has done so while being almost continually profitable. The "secret" is posted on its Web site for the whole world to share [11]:

> More than 30 years ago, Rollin King and Herb Kelleher got together and decided to start a different kind of airline. They began with one simple notion: If you get your passengers to their destinations when they want to get there, on time, at the lowest possible fares, and make darn sure they have a good time doing it, people will fly your airline. And you know what? They were right.

It's not precisely about having a good time—it's about feeling good about the time you're having.

Neither carrier pampers its passengers. Both, in fact, are justifiably labeled as "no frills." But both understand that it isn't frills that bring passengers back. It's what happens at the ticket counter, in the gate areas, on the planes, down in baggage claim, on the phone, on the Web site, in the countless moments when customers experience the various facets of the business.

People feel good about themselves when they fly those airlines. It's not precisely about having a good time—it's about feeling good about the time you are having. It's about an experience that provides you with a specific set of feelings you yourself have and then associate with how you feel about the airline. What Herb Kelleher understood and built a thriving business on is that a good time can create feelings of freedom and trust.

High amenity or no frills, every airline dutifully works to polish its brand image, and each boasts of various measures of customer satisfaction and loyalty. They each have very well-developed and managed brands, but if a magic wand was waved tonight, and tomorrow passengers were able to choose among four different carriers, each with flights going to their chosen destinations at similar times and for similar fares, who would benefit? If a customer's experiential preference rather than "fortress hub" reality (where one carrier often controls 60–80% of the seats available at any given airport) were the primary arbiter of winners and losers in the airline marketplace, who would soar and who would be left at the gate?

This is not to say that brand is unimportant—either as a conceptual framework or as an operational concern. But if an organization doesn't keep focused on the emotional component of the interaction and how customers want to feel, it isn't going to enjoy the kind of long-term loyalty that can be generated from a total experience that connects on all levels.

Consider how often customers leave brands and companies, even those that have met their functional needs, because of the way they feel—frustrated, tense, weakened, victimized, ignored, devalued. Obviously, these are not emotions about the brand. They are clearly people's emotions. And they influence customer loyalty and have a profound impact on the bottom line.

It's important to add a caveat here: Defection, disappointment, and even disenfranchisement are not simply a result of experiences that customers don't think of as "fun." Fun may indeed be a part of the experience. But the emotional forces working in the customer's mind involve far more than just having fun. It's putting a priority on how customers feel about themselves that speaks to their unconscious perceptions of emotional needs that they derive from the experience and in turn yields greater loyal and committed customers.

There's an incredible richness latent in experiences. If you can tap it, you can turn blasé customers into passionate advocates for the experiences you provide and for the brands that are woven into that fabric. In particular, you will need to develop a more complete and deeper understanding of the clues that customers process and interpret and the fundamental role they play in creating experience value. This is where becoming *clued in* really begins.

References

1. "Make-and-Sell" and "Sense-and-Respond" are terms coined by Stephan H. Haeckel in his book, *Adaptive Enterprise: Creating and Leading Sense-and-Respond Organizations* (Harvard Business Press, 2000).

2. "Alamo and National Car Rental Purchase Completed," Travel Industry Highlights (October 10, 2001).

3. Patrick Danner. "For 2 Car Renters, a New Map," The Miami Herald.com (October 16, 2003).

4. *The Multicultural Marketplace of Tomorrow*. Presentation by J. Walker Smith, President, Yakelovich Partners, at the SRI Institute 10th Annual Ethnic Marketing Conference, Chicago, Illinois (September 30, 2003).

5. Leonard Berry. *Discovering the Soul of Service,* page 201 (New York: The Free Press, 1999).

6. *Merriam Webster Dictionary,* page 62 (Springfield, MA, *G&C* Merriam Company, 1999).

7. *The New Oxford American Dictionary,* page 208 (Boston, New York, Houghton, Mifflin, 2001).

8. Alan Webber. "What Great Brands Do," *Fast Company,* page 96 (August/ September 1996).

9. Scott Bedbury and Stephen Fenichell (contributor). *A New Brand World: Eight Principles for Achieving Brand Leadership in the 21st Century* (New York: Viking Press, 2002).

10. "JetBlue Orders 100 Jetliners from Brazilian Manufacturer in $3 Billion Contract," *Minneapolis Star-Tribune* (June 11, 2003).

11. "We Weren't Just Airborne Yesterday," www.iflyswa.com/about_swa/airborne.html.

4

EXPERIENCE VALUE MANAGEMENT

Are there experiences that you feel provide greater personal value than others? Is there a grocery store where you prefer shopping over any other? Do you pass by other grocery stores to get there? Do you feel different when you shop there? Are there grocery stores you outwardly reject and would never consider going to? Are there others that you consider just okay, not better or worse than any other?

How about restaurants you prefer, a particular barbershop or hair salon you've frequented for years? How about the physician you use? Experiences and the clues embedded in them are valued or devalued by our feelings as we encounter them. That becomes the reality of how we build our loyalties.

Clearly, people prefer some experiences more than others. That preference is based on both functional (or rational) value and emotional value personally derived from the experience. When we prefer an experience, we become committed to it and seek it out over and over again. The result is that we become loyal customers.

Regardless of the business you're in or the nature of your customers, you can manage experiences that are more distinctive and powerful and result in bringing committed customers back again and again.

To leverage experience as a value proposition, it's critical to understand the dynamics of experience and how perceptions of experience value become reality.

The Preference Model™

For starters, consider a simple Experience Preference Model (see Figure 4.1). Some people I've worked with call it "the Band-Aid® chart" [1] because that's what it looks like.) It can be used to visualize where both customer experiences and specific experience clues fall along a spectrum that goes from negative through neutral to the positive value assessments that determine preference and loyalty.

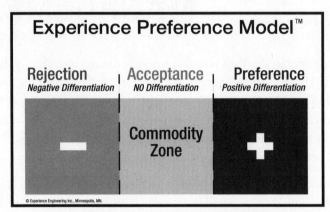

Figure 4.1 Experience Preference Model.

Reactions or impressions of experiences fall into one of the three "zones" of the model as a result of how customers feel about their total experience:

- *Negative or Rejection Distinction (Experiences that Create Burners).* These are experiences that are perceived as negative and are rejected. Customers who categorize their experiences in this space are also apt to be a source of negative word-of-mouth commentary.
- *Neutral or No Distinction (Experiences that Create Churners).* These are experiences that don't create strong impressions in either a positive or a negative sense. In essence, they perceive this as what I call "the commodity zone," where experiences are no better or worse—or distinctive—than any others.
- *Positive or Preferential Distinction (Experiences that Create Committed Advocates).* These are experiences that clearly move out of the commodity zone and foster a commitment for repeating it and talking about it to others. Experiences categorized by customers in this zone will engender the kind of long-term loyalty that is both remarkably resilient and financially desirable.

Satisfaction and even loyalty are not necessarily accurate measurements or correlations to commitment and advocacy.

Significantly, customers often may pronounce themselves "satisfied" or even "very satisfied" when surveyed for traditional customer service feedback, which can lead to a highly misleading reading of their real preference and long-term loyalty. In fact, in *The Loyalty Effect* [1], Frederick Reichheld points out that most defectors are customers who label themselves as "satisfied." Satisfaction is not necessarily an accurate measurement or correlation to commitment and advocacy.

Truly understanding customer preferences can provide deeper insight into what builds loyalty versus mere satisfaction. This is vital because satisfaction in and of itself is not enough to fuel and sustain loyal customer behavior.

Just as the Preference Model can be used to plot customers' reactions to experiences, it can also be used to plot customer reaction to specific experience clues:

- *Rejection (negative) clues* detract from perceived customer value and act to burn away any sense of loyalty.
- *Acceptance (neutral) clues* do not detract from the experience but don't create strong feelings; they are almost expected.
- *Preference (positive) clues* strongly contribute to experiential value and either reinforce the Experience Motif or are extremely distinctive. They foster emotional fulfillment and desire to return again and again, and they also encourage storytelling. These clues can contribute to word-of-mouth power and they are the Holy Grail of experiential or "buzz" marketing.

Tying a Ribbon Around Experience

Experiences do not have a beginning or an end: They are a continuum. Take for example the experience of the Mall of America in Bloomington, Minnesota. If you've never been there, or even if you've never heard of it before, you still have some perception of the experience. If you've never heard of it, you still have perceptions of malls, Minnesota, and so forth, and in your mind's eye you have some impression of what the Mall of America should be like. If you have the opportunity to visit, you'll have another dimension of the experience, and you'll have memories and recollections of the mall. In any case, you continue to add data and information from clues to your Mall of America experience, whether it's the experience in your "mind's eye" or 20 visits to the mall.

The Experience Ribbon (Figure 4.2) is a three-dimensional way to think about a customer's total experience. It is especially useful in illustrating an experience's breadth and depth. It usually has three stages, and it uses a simple form of chronology:

Experience Ribbon™

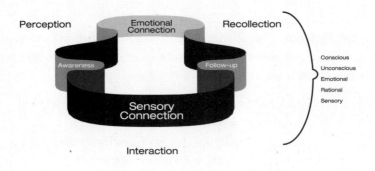

Figure 4.2 The Experience Ribbon.

1. *Perception* starts with customers' preconceived ideas and feelings whether conscious or latent, good or bad, accurate or inaccurate, relevant or irrelevant. Customers bring these thoughts and feelings with them to the encounter. They may be created by advertising, word of mouth, and their own previous experiences. Customer perceptions reflect the feelings and experiences they have developed through life experiences, not only within your specific competitive set, but also across a very broad spectrum. For example, businesses such as Federal Express and Domino's Pizza have impacted the way customers perceive speed and reliability in sectors far removed from overnight or pizza delivery services.

2. *Interaction* involves customers' contact with the people, physical environment and systems of the experience. As part of this stage in particular, they have "moments of truth" (to use the phrase made popular by Scandinavian Air Service's Jan Carlzon these past 20 years). [3] However, experiences and clues occur throughout an experience and are not neatly arranged in a linear process traditionally associated with considerations of "moments of truth" or "points of contact." During experiences, expectations are modified and further shaped—for better or for worse—as customers process the multitude of impressions, thoughts, and feelings they absorb. In the encounter, the connection is primarily sensory in nature. Customers sense what's going on and respond accordingly: They encounter numerous clues through which they process the experience in their conscious and unconscious mind.

3. *Recollection* involves the way customers remember the experience. It combines all their thoughts and feelings, whether rational or emotional, about their recently completed encounter. This, in turn, sets their expectations for future interactions. Recollection is the critical crossroads for the conscious and unconscious functions of the mind. Experience clues are first collected, stored, and "felt" unconsciously, then "rationalized" later as customers become conscious of value perceptions and brand associations.

In the aftermath of a transaction, the way people remember and value an experience emotionally will have everything to do with their ultimate commitment to an organization or brand—far more than what actually did or did not happen in the purely rational sense.

This is where the use of traditional marketing research can easily lead companies astray. Customers can (and will) intellectualize an experience, literally creating an intellectual alibi or rationalization that even incorporates specific experience clues into a rational explanations. In fact, how customers "feel" about what happened to them is much more important than their rational explanation.

In the aftermath of an interaction, the way people remember and value an experience emotionally will have everything to do with their ultimate commitment to the organization or brand—far more than what actually did or did not happen in a purely rational sense. That, in turn (as the Experience Preference Model illustrates), influences their loyalty, their degree of commitment and advocacy, and whether they will want to repeat or avoid a similar experience in the future.

If the feelings they have about the experience are strongly positive and emotionally bonding, they will be motivated to come full circle around the Experience Ribbon, repeating the experience and advocating it to others.

If the feelings they retain are negative or often simply neutral, the odds are high that they will choose to abandon the experience, taking with them the residue of their less-than-preferential experiences as a challenge for the new provider to meet. How many customers come to you with expectations preconditioned by negative or lackluster experiences with your competitors? They are also influenced by all of their experiences in various secondary, unrelated catagories. And how loyal do they become when you demonstrate that you can indeed provide them with what they feel they need and want?

Notice that the path customers travel around the Experience Ribbon involves more than the time they spend in the actual interaction with your company. It also encompasses parts of the experience that occur well before and after they interact with your people and systems.

No matter: The objective is to constantly manage a continuous experience cycle. Experiences are not point-to-point timelines with distinct beginnings and ends. Instead, they start at a point you may never specifically be aware of and continue well beyond a customer's momentary interaction with your particular business.

The path customers follow around the Experience Ribbon involves more than the time they spend in the actual interaction with you. It also encompasses parts of the experience that occur before and after they interact with your people and systems.

Clue Math

Another element that affects the perception of value is the interaction of clues in an experience. When an experience is unmanaged, it's not uncommon for prevalent negative or commodity clues to cancel out even the most high-impact positive clues. Consider, for example, the hospital emergency department that invests in a state-of-the-art registration system but fails to give any thought or attention to the dreary, impersonal, and frustratingly long waiting room experience. Subtle clue interactions also have impact. For example, a clue that evokes joy interacting with a clue that evokes surprise will result in a general feeling of delight. Recognizing the dynamics of clue interaction spotlights the critical importance of a management system that ensures maximum experience value is being created and leveraged.

Distinguished Professor of Marketing at Texas A&M University, and my good friend, Dr. Len Berry, has developed what I consider a form of experiential math. [4] Though originally designed to focus on the specifics of service delivery, it ably demonstrates the intricacy and complexity of clue-laden experience management. It has some marked similarities to the Experience Ribbon in its use of simple chronology. And, like the Preference Model, it considers three potential outcomes.

Berry maintains that to compute overall value accurately, three distinct variables must be mastered and managed:

1. Customers' *expectations* of what is about to happen.

2. The *outcome* that actually does happen.

3. Customers' *observations* of everything that goes on in between.

What is especially important about this formula is the way you do the math. The three separate variables don't *add up* to a cumulative total. They are *multiplied*. That difference is crucial. When you add 6 + 4 + 0, you get 10, no matter which way you rearrange the order of the numbers. On the other hand, when you multiply 6 × 4 × 0, you get zero, again regardless of the numerical sequence.

When you're adding, the presence of a zero doesn't change the total. But clue interaction is like multiplication, not addition. When one of the numbers you are multiplying is zero (or a negative clue), it wipes out everything else, regardless of the other numbers involved. All three variables have to be positives for anything significant to be produced.

It follows that if the value of the total experience is going to be managed, each significant clue on which the customer relies in processing the experience must be properly recognized and managed so that it contributes to generating preference and building loyalty. If just one significant clue leaves the customer stuck back on zero, it can jeopardize the value of the entire experience.

Imagine going into a grocery store for a gallon of milk and a dozen eggs. The store has what you want. The cooler's not hard to find. The price is right. But, the aisles are slippery with broken eggs, the whole store smells of sour milk, and the stock clerks look like they haven't mastered the use of soap and water. How likely are you to return to that store compared with any other handy source of milk and eggs?

Even though the products you bought may have been perfectly fresh and fine (in other words, you achieved the rational outcome you intended), the store didn't look or feel the way you expected it to look and feel. And both consciously and unconsciously, the experience of shopping there probably did a pretty fair job of ruining your appetite. If the place had been spotless and the help positively glowing with cleanliness and courtesy but the cooler was empty, the experience would have failed for different reasons, but it would have failed nonetheless.

The converse can be equally powerful. How do you feel when the drop-ship order you thought would take ten days to arrive shows up in three days instead? How do you feel when, instead of snapping at you and making you feel inept, the person at the counter or on the phone quickly and graciously figures out a simpler solution to your problem than you could ever imagine? Surprised? Delighted? Impressed? All of the above?

That makes becoming clue-conscious a powerful management mindset. By creating and orchestrating consistent, compatible clues tied to customer impressions that substantiate value, your business can engineer the way customers "do the math."

The compounding of positive feelings, expectations, outcomes, and observations generates a powerful reason to return—a natural impulse to be loyal. That's why a business needs to actively and systematically manage clues toward a planned positive emotional end frame. Every customer that a business encounters—every customer who has an experience with a business—does Len Berry's math. Each can be located along the spectrum of the Preference Model. Each builds a uniquely personal Experience Ribbon.

That makes becoming clue-conscious a powerful management mind-set. By creating and orchestrating consistent, compatible clues tied to specific customer impressions that substantiate value, your business can engineer the way customers "do the math," moving the needle on their preference and loyalty.

Experience value management also requires understanding clues, clue creation, and clue management in depth. The next chapter is dedicated to that deeper understanding of clues.

Principles of Experience Value Management

Managing experiences to be distinctive and powerful creators of value derives from the following premises:

1. *Experience* is *a value proposition*. The elements that make up a complete and coherent total experience can be identified, expressed in an Experience Motif, and managed to create distinctive value for customers.

2. *Clues are drivers of experiences.* Experiences are composed of identifiable indicators, signals, and stimuli—some of them rational, some of them emotional—that are registered consciously and unconsciously by the senses. In combination, they evoke the aggregate feeling experienced by a customer. In a designed and managed experience, that aggregate feeling should be the Experience Motif selected to reflect the firm's customer value proposition. Customers value what they are receiving on the basis of the way those clues are woven into an overall experience. It's that combination or fabric of clues that drives long-term loyalty and advocacy.

3. *Systems to manage experiences are built by means of clues.* The key to cost-effectively connecting to what customers want and value is first to get clued in to how your customers experience your business. Then, to design and manage experience clues systematically.

In addition to these foundational premises, three general principles have evolved as organizations have made strides toward managing experiences as a value proposition. These principles reflect more than 20 years of studying and working with experience-driven businesses that have succeeded in creating extraordinary and lasting loyalty. The validity of these principles continues to be proven every day in organizations of all sizes and descriptions.

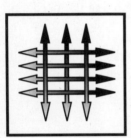

Principle 1:
Manage Experiential Breadth and Depth

An experiential value proposition can transform a commodity product business into a highly differentiated one. Remember Starbucks' heritage as strictly a purveyor of a commodity (coffee beans)? Effective experience management systems have breadth and depth. Extending the system in either direction will create the desired impression more consistently and anchor the impression in the customer's mind for a longer period of time.

Consider the way you think about the value of the following:

- Commodity medicine is practiced coast to coast, but medical care is a distinctively different experience at Mayo Clinic, Cleveland Clinic, and other leading medical centers.
- Bakeries and doughnut shops are a dime a dozen from big cities to small towns, but the Krispy Kreme experience serves up a lot more than fried dough.
- It's hard to imagine a colleague rolling up his or her sleeve to reveal a tattoo that reads *Maxwell House* or *Sears* or *Pizza Hut* or *General Electric*, but Harley-Davidson inspires a form of distinctive lifestyle loyalty that often literally gets under the skin of its riders.

In each case, commodity forms of products and services have been built into broad, deep, and full-featured experiences. They have been designed and are being actively managed to connect with customers on multiple levels. The result clearly is a noteworthy form of competitive advantage.

Experiential breadth refers to the boundaries of the managed experience. Are the clues in every phase of the Experience Ribbon managed throughout or only in certain areas? Is the full continuum of the experience being leveraged? For example, a hotel guest begins to "experience" a hotel long before walking into the lobby, by surfing the facility's Web site or flipping through its brochure, by making the reservation (sometimes through a third party not employed by the hotel), arranging ground transportation, or finding the right shuttle van from the airport. Once the stay has occurred, there's the myriad of recollections the guest departs with. Anticipation, interaction and recollection are all part of the breadth of the experience and present an opportunity to deepen positive impressions.

Progressive Auto Insurance expanded the breadth of their customer experience when they instituted Instant Response Vehicles (IRVs). This made it possible to move claims processing to the scene of an accident to be a managed part of the customer's experience that hadn't previously been focused on by auto insurers.

It's impossible to overemphasize the extent of linking the breadth and depth of an experience. As customers proceed along their identifiable cycles on their experiential journeys, the number, diversity, and intensity of the clues encountered will also contribute a sense of distinctiveness and differentiation (see Figure 4.3). As clues that reinforce the targeted customer feeling grow in number, uniqueness, sensory diversity and imprinting ability, greater experience depth is achieved.

The key word here is *sense*, as in the senses through which customers observe and respond to the world around them.

When someone tells you that his or her room at the Excelsior Hotel in Florence glowed like honey from the reflection of the sunrise on the surrounding buildings, you don't have to be holding a brochure to get the picture he or she is trying to convey.

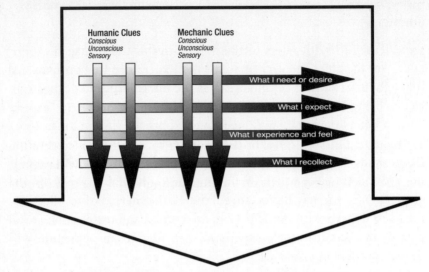

Humanic Clues
Conscious
Unconscious
Sensory

Mechanic Clues
Conscious
Unconscious
Sensory

What I need or desire

What I expect

What I experience and feel

What I recollect

Figure 4.3 Illustration of experiential breadth and depth.

All of the senses should be involved in the management of a memorable experience because they are the input channels for impressions. It's the way the human brain processes information. At a hypothetical hotel, for example:

- The eyes see the elegance or shabbiness of the décor, the way the staff is dressed and behaves, the way the physical facility is maintained, the newspaper carefully laid outside the door for the morning, and the battered housekeeping cart that blocks two-thirds of the hallway most of the afternoon—all are visual clues to the quality of the experience being created.

- The ears pick up the soft bubbling of a lobby fountain, the courtesy and professionalism of a desk clerk's voice, enticing music from a lobby lounge, loud laughter from the room next door at 2:00 A.M., an unusually loud ice machine down the hall.

- The nose registers odors as mesmerizing as hot chocolate-chip cookies and as off-putting as an overchlorinated pool, as reassuring as the lingering hint of cleaners and polishes and as worrisome as a phantom whiff of smoke in a corridor or a moldy, musty scent in the room.

- Taste assesses aromas coming from the restaurant, the sound and velocity of water coming out of the tap in the bathroom, and the smell of the mint left on the pillow.

- Touch registers the softness of the carpeting and the firmness of the bed, the thread count of the sheets, and the plushness of a bath towel.

Not only are the specific stages and sensory aspects of the individual clues important, but they must also fit together effectively into a coherent whole. If the lobby is expansive but the room cramped, or the room lavish but the lobby down-at-the-heels, the clues don't mesh appropriately. The customer senses that something is not quite right.

Finding a couple of bottles of spring water thoughtfully placed in the room can be a pleasant surprise. But, discovering when you check out that the hotel charges a princely—and unannounced—five bucks a bottle can leave a bad taste.

Managing experiential clues can indeed be challenging. In fact, it's likely to take as much focus and energy as anything you've previously undertaken. But don't forget that the clues are already there in the experiences you are currently providing. Why not manage them for a greater return?

The rewards are more than substantial. When all of the clues fit together and the customer's perception of value is validated, their bond to the experience is clarified and reinforced—and that will determine where they return again and again, and with what level of passion.

The tactile and sensory experience surrounding Westin Hotel's "Heavenly Bed" have very effectively imprinted the Westin experience.

Principle 2: Design and Manage Humanic and Mechanic Clues Simultaneously

In experience management, there are elements of the experience that are *humanic* (those feelings from clues and interactions produced by people) and those that are *mechanic* (feelings produced by reactions to the environment, the process, or the more physical aspects of the experience).

The fusion of designing and managing mechanic and humanic elements simultaneously is critical to creating cohesive experiences that fully realize their value potential. But organizations seldom design the environment and people skills synchronously because of organizational silos and far-flung company programs. Companies spend enormous amounts of time planning and building new facilities, store locations, call centers, and so forth, yet almost always think about educating and training people separately from planning the physical aspects. Fusing mechanic and humanic clues can have a significant impact on the feel of the total experience and its alignment, as well as customer feelings and thoughts.

For example, when designing some of the early McDonald's restaurants, founder Ray Kroc insisted that the french fry, beverage, and hamburger stations be positioned in full view of customers to show off the restaurant's cleanliness. He was also known to choreograph employee movement behind the counter to suggest speed, agility, and efficiency, all adding up to "fast" food.

The Doylestown Health and Wellness Center in Warrentown, Pennsylvania, was highly aware of designing humanics and mechanics to strengthen and reinforce each other. Processes that once involved four or five separate appointments, usually days or even weeks apart, now are completed in one or, at the most, two visits conducted with the same medical team. In an initial visit to the cardiac risk program, for example, patients are introduced to a Health Design nurse who is their main contact. They then complete a profile, blood is drawn, and "speed passes" are issued to expedite movement through the center for other related tests. Within no more than two days, as soon as lab results are back, patients return for a calcium scoring CT scan and an immediate review of their profiles with the same doctor/nurse teams and the radiologists, who review scans with the patients. Together, the doctor, health design nurse, and patient then design heart-healthy approaches on the spot, with the option for follow-up visits to a Health Design Center that links them to a personal medical team in order to monitor eating and exercise habits, as well as stress management and more.

Principle 3: Experiences Must *Connect* Emotionally

It's a given that in managing any experience, the functional aspects of a transaction or encounter must meet basic expectations (Does the razor cut? Does the watch tell time? Did the reservation agent secure the flight?). But organizations with effective experience value propositions understand that they must also positively connect to the emotional needs and desires of their customers. In fact, this emotional connection—because it involves so much more understanding and management of the clues involved—is critical in the customer's total experience.

Adding an imaginary doughnut to your virtual cup of coffee from the Starbucks discussion in Chapter 2 may help drive home the point. Consider how the complete, sensory-loaded experience of buying and consuming Krispy Kreme doughnuts illustrates the power of creating positive emotional connections with customers.

Bakeries and doughnut shops are certainly nothing new or uncommon. Yet the rapid growth of Krispy Kreme has been nothing short of a phenomenon. It's not by accident. Krispy Kreme isn't selling doughnuts. It's creating an experience in much the same way that Starbucks "dispenses" coffee.

Everything the customer sees, smells, tastes, functionally encounters, or emotionally senses, is orchestrated into an experience that goes far beyond the simple "transaction" of buying doughnuts. The experience includes the almost Pavlovian neon sign advertising "Hot Doughnuts Now"; the fully visible conveyor along which pressed dough becomes a fresh, tasty treat; the smiling folks behind the counter, busily picking, bagging, boxing—and reacting gracefully when the customer points and says, "No, no, I want *that* one."

Does it work? In Denver, 3,000 people lined up along three city blocks for the chain's opening day a couple of years back. That's a phenomenon that simply cannot be explained in strictly rational terms. Somehow, the act of eating an "unhealthy" food has been transformed into a form of celebration. If you're going to eat something that supposedly is not that good for you physically, it had better be good for you emotionally.

An emotional connection indeed has been made. Preference expressed on such a scale, and not just in Denver, has made Krispy Kreme a rising star when other sales at doughnut chains today are flat.

Value-Added Education

Okay, so Krispy Kreme can do a number on the senses and have emotional impact. But what about more commonplace forms of experiences? Can experience truly make a difference in the value propositions of businesses such as hospitals, for example? Or technical schools?

Absolutely. Experience value management has the potential to generate powerful returns on investment from even basic adjustments to the way you've "always" done something, no matter how regulated, regimented, or routine the experience you provide. Once you break out of the traditional make-and-sell pattern and see beyond your processes to the rich ground provided by your customer experiences, the potential impact of even a modest redeployment of resources has the potential to become phenomenal.

At Northcentral Technical College (NTC), a regional adult-education system with a central campus in Wausau, Wisconsin, and satellite locations in five other towns in the east-central portion of the state, Bob Ernst and Tom Mercier—respectively the school's CEO/President and Vice President of Administration—opted to utilize the context of experience management when the college was preparing to build a new Health and Sciences Center.

Traditionally, additions to campus infrastructure adhere to a time-honored pattern. The board conceives a plan and a budget. An architectural firm comes in and does research on the physical aspects of the building. An interior decorator or design firm spends time and money to evaluate the inside layouts. Facilities management, grounds-keeping personnel, and outside landscapers perform similarly isolated evaluations. Dr. Ernst, who envisioned the opportunity said no one ever considers the total experience that the users of the building (students, faculty, and staff, all of whom are customers) will have.

Well, as NTC is demonstrating, this is no longer entirely true. From their years of experience in continuous improvement efforts under the general heading of quality, Ernst knew they had been doing a great job of eliminating defects in their educational setting. But once they latched onto the idea of experience as a value proposition, they recognized that they had done very little to understand customer preference and experience value management, let alone begin to factor that preference into the design and operational decisions they were making.

To their credit and the benefit of their institution, they opted to explore a different course for the Health and Sciences Center. They took funds that would traditionally have been put into architectural fees and invested it, in an "experience assessment" (more about that in Chapter 7) to create an experiential framework instead. That understanding has become the basis of all subsequent planning at NTC and provides an experiential perspective that has been used to fuel every other piece of the puzzle that resulted.

There's no shortage of potential customers: Career-oriented students and busy adults, many of whom have been away from classrooms for years, are bringing much more exacting expectations to the way they choose schools and programs. To connect with them experientially, everything from physical facilities to everyday processes such as registration must be designed to promote a unified and positive experiential end frame.[1]

NTC is creating an experiential design that already involves distinct experience clues, some specific to health sciences and others affecting all students. That foundation is being integrated into the physical facility that is taking form first as the new Health Sciences Center.

From the physical or mechanic side, a four-story atrium will greet students with a sense of expanding horizons. Classrooms will be configured to accommodate hands-on teaching techniques and the technology so deeply woven into modern health care today. Informal

---

1. "Adult learners are not just 'in school,' they're in life," Mercier told us. "NTC is a place of hope for a lot of people, and we wanted the experiences they have in the new facility to reflect that."

gathering spaces will encourage interaction outside of the classroom while providing simple comforts often excluded from colorless, utilitarian educational facilities. Signage and way-finding systematically anticipate as well as answer questions.

On the process side of the institution overall, improvements in both physical and computer infrastructure already are bringing significant experiential upgrades to such tasks as registering for classes. The lessons learned in and around the new Health and Sciences Center not only have changed the way student preferences are considered at NTC, but have also been extended to the entire system, including satellite facilities.

Importantly, the critical roles of staff and faculty as they relate to the learning experience have been characterized in a way that clearly supports making a meaningful connection with learners and stakeholders. It started simply by taking advantage of what the organization already knew, then redirecting resources it already had into more experiential channels.

Focusing on Clues

Up to now, we have stuffed a lot of different observations and assertions under the general umbrella of clues. As you begin to investigate the specific disciplines involved in creating and running effective experience management systems and the profound impact clue consciousness and clue management can have, you'll gain a better idea of how much ground this simple, little four-letter word can take in.

We'll go there next.

References

1. "Band-Aid" is a registered trademark of Johnson & Johnson.
2. Frederick F. Reichheld. *The Loyalty Effect: The Hidden Force Behind Growth, Profits, and Lasting Value* (Boston: Harvard Business School Press, 1996.)
3. Jan Carlzon. *Moments of Truth* (Cambridge, MA: Ballinger Publishing, 1987).
4. Leonard L. Berry, Valerie A. Zeithaml, and A. Parasuraman. "Quality Counts in Services, Too." *Business Horizons*, pp. 44-52, May-June 1985.

5

GETTING CLUED IN

Once you're *clued in*, the thrill of hunting for clues and the meaning and importance of clues in managing experiences can be exhilarating. Perhaps, putting the puzzle of experience clues together will remind some of you, as it does me, of the same thrill I remember when playing the board game Clue as a child—the excitement of adding up the clues and developing the hypothesis that the "perpetrator" of the crime was Colonel Mustard, using the rope in the dining room.

If you could see the atomic structure of an experience, you would find it comprised of a complex array of interlinked sensory clues. Sights. Sounds. Smells. Tastes. Tactile sensations. Conscious and unconscious thoughts and feelings and "real" data absorbed through the senses and the stimuli you feel, or imagine, or simply expect (often from previous experiences).

Each sensation is a clue. Each contributes to the cumulative sense of the total experience. But not all clues are created equal. Clues will be sensed and valued in different ways by different customers. What's more, subject to the way each person puts the pieces together, a specific clue may rank somewhere between largely insignificant and very significant in an individual's perception of the total experience. As the customer's mind combines all these stimuli, the experience happens, and preferences are created or amended.

Customer loyalty is more a result of how customers feel about the overall experience they receive from you than what they rationally think about your individual products and services.

Jerry Zaltman's concise assessment of what the total experience represents is a worthwhile preface for this more detailed examination of clues. Studies he conducted maintain that the unconscious sensory and emotional feelings have more power and influence on customer preference than do the tangible attributes of a product or service. [1] In other words, customer loyalty is more a result of how customers *feel* about the overall experience they receive from you than what they rationally think about your individual products and services.

Though many businesses believe that product attributes or service quality form the core of their value proposition, how customers feel is what builds preferences, and ultimately, growth. In a recent study that explored the top measurements businesses should focus on to predict growth, loyalty expert Frederick F. Reichhled found it came down to one simple metric: the enthusiasm your customers feel for the experiences they receive from you, and their willingness to recommend them to friends. Reichheld states, "In fact, such a recommendation is one of the best indicators of loyalty because of the customer's sacrifice, if you will, in making the recommendation. When customers act as references, they do more than indicate that they've received good economic value from a company; they put their own reputations on the line. And they will risk their reputations only if they feel intense loyalty." [2]

As experience takes on more relative importance in the way customers assess value and determine their loyalties, identifying and understanding how they arrive at those feelings must move front and center in business thinking.

More About Clues

Typically, clues in a criminal case refer to snippets of information or isolated bits of physical evidence that only the most painstakingly thorough or brilliantly intuitive detective can uncover, let alone interpret.

By contrast, the clues that make up a customer experience are literally everywhere and can be thought of as illustrated in Figure 5.1. They are more easily discerned, and their interpretation, though subject to some logical limitations, seldom requires the gifts of a Holmes, Poirot, Marple, or Columbo. Even better, you can hone your clue-sensing skills to an expert level by mastering a discrete set of experience management competencies.

Clue Bombardment

Figure 5.1 Experience Clue bombardment comes from everything a customer senses.

Anything that can be perceived or sensed by its presence or its absence is an Experience Clue. Once you know what to look for, they can provide a wealth of eyewitness detail. Simple classifications of clues will help you better understand how clues work within experiences. Experiences are formed through the combination of three different but inter-related types. [3]

- The first, *Functional Clues*, are perhaps the easiest to identify and understand. These are clues emitted by the functionality of the specific good or service. Does the razor cut? Does the car start? Does the refrigerator keep things cold? Does the brewer provide a piping hot cup of coffee?
  Functional Clues generally register most with the customer's rational thought processes. Their meaning and value are interpreted by the logical circuitry of the customer's brain as it assesses the functionality of the specific good or service being provided.

Beyond the functional, however, are two additional types of clues that are often overlooked or undervalued. [3] Nonetheless, these clues are extremely critical to any attempt to manage the customer's total experience.

- *Humanic Clues* involve stimuli produced by people: the way the customer perceives things such as choice of words, tone of voice, cadence of voice, voice level, enthusiasm, gestures, actions, body language, and so forth. Think of it as the human side of the business.
- *Mechanic Clues* come from the physical "things" that are intimately woven into the experience: the sights, sounds, smells, textures, and physical elements that contribute to the overall experience.

In contrast to purely Functional Clues, Humanic and Mechanic Clues tend to be registered and assessed unconsciously by the brain, with their meaning and value interpreted more emotionally (Figure 5.2).

Each clue—functional, humanic, or mechanic, carries a message, suggesting something negative, neutral, or positive to the customer, either consciously or unconsciously.

Type of Clue	Emitted by	Interpretation
Functional	Product or Service	Rational / Conscious
Mechanic	Environment	Emotional / Unconscious
Humanic	People	Emotional / Unconscious

Figure 5.2 Classifying clues.

Clues relating to the actual functioning of the good or service will be familiar to anyone who has been exposed to quality enhancement efforts over the past 20 years. Clues with emotional impact may be less familiar. The feel of leather upholstery, the sound and smell of a steak on the grill, the tone of voice of the person answering the customer-service line, the presence or lack of eye contact and sincerity in interpersonal transactions—all are signals that go well beyond basic functionality. Using Len Berry's formula [4], the composite of all the clues are tallied into the customer's total experience.

Because of the way clues (emotional and rational) surround or envelop the functional core of an experience (and do so in such a wide array of sensations), systematically managing them is the key to leveraging the total experience (Figure 5.3), which we now know powerfully affects future behavior and loyalty.

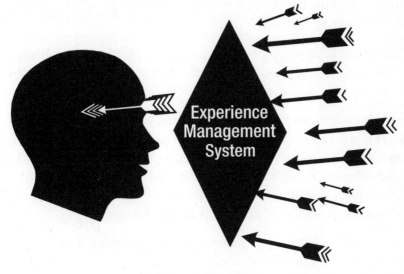

Figure 5.3 Managing clues.

Works Right, Feels Right

Just as customer value cannot be reduced to a matter of functionality versus price, neither can it be seen as a choice between aspects that make the customer feel good and those that assure that the basic product or service functions well. Instead, the value proposition is composed of both the functional and the emotional benefits customers derive, minus the financial and the nonfinancial burdens they bear. [4]

Clearly, Functional Clues are essential. If a product is perceived as shoddy or doesn't perform as expected, people won't buy it, period. Providing a car that starts when the key is turned, fixing the faucet so that it always shuts off, creating software that functions reliably and consistently—these are table stakes that companies must have to enter the game today, but they don't drive preference.

What is becoming clearer is that the emotional clues, the mechanics and humanics, are vitally important to the customer's experience and perception of value. When functional attributes are perceived as being equal—which is increasingly the case in industry after industry—it's the emotional clues and their impact that will gain or lose competitive advantage. When the humanics and mechanics are managed in combination with Functional Clues to create an integrated whole, the power of experience is unleashed.

The senses are the receptors for humanic and Mechanic Clues that help shape customer feelings. For example, we know that colors have been determined to have an emotional effect on people.

In business contexts, color can have meaning as a clue in the context of positioning. For example, in the rental car industry, red equals Avis, green equals National, and yellow equals Hertz. Among soft drinks, Coke comes in a red can, Pepsi in blue, and 7-Up in green. From "the purple pill" (Nexium) and "the power of brown" (UPS) to Little Golden Books and Big Blue, color is a powerful clue.

So, too, is sound. On a generic level, a rhythmic beeping sound out on the street warns people—functionally—that a vehicle is backing up. More emotionally, specific musical themes clue customers into specific brands from airlines to restaurants, and voices like the melodious tones of actor James Earl Jones lend a sense of character to offerings as prosaic as telephone service.

Sensory elements that are or become distinctive to a particular experience—such as Jones's voice, the castles at Disney's Magic Kingdoms, or the voice on the PA system aboard the Disney moonstation—are *Signature Clues*. However, not all are or can be "branded." On the telephone, a beep is a clue for you to leave a message, no matter who made the equipment. On the Web, an underlined or blue word indicates a hyperlink that will take you somewhere else, regardless of the site. The point is, these clues elicit specific responses and associations.

Some clues are tied to a specific moment in time; others linger. In the family car, smells tell you the car is new or remind you of the pizza you brought home last night. When you picked up this book, your senses unconsciously registered its shape, weight, the gloss of the cover, the texture of the pages; months from now, merely glancing down the shelf and unconsciously registering the look of the spine will call up residual images of content and value.

The science of clues and clue management is in its infancy, and the application of increasing knowledge and technology to this area will transform it forever.

Clued In

Getting clued in is about awareness; it's such an elemental process that most people never think twice about it. But if you're going to harness the power of experience as a new value proposition, you need to make the systematic identification and orchestration of clues—and the experiences they help to form—a critical business competency. By doing so, you'll learn to better manage and meet customer needs, as well as to build their preference for future experiences with your company, all the while providing tangible benefits to your organization's bottom line.

Clue Clusters

Clues can be devised and utilized as individual or in combination to achieve a specific goal. Think of these combinations as "clue clusters." For example, think about the act of waiting in line. Sometimes ropes or fabric belts are strung between poles that draw you into a minimaze and line you and others up in orderly fashion towards the next available teller, airline counter clerk, or amusement park ride. At Disney and other amusement parks, "waiting" clues are clustered in the form of rope guides combined with signs, music, and sometimes even a person to tell you how long you still have to wait at specific points along the way.

Even if you haven't given clues a moment of thought, you respond to them on both a conscious and an unconscious level. When you reach the head of the line and hear someone say, "Next," you don't have to think very hard or ask yourself (or the person behind you), "Next what?"

Think about the countless personal encounters in which men and women reach out and grasp each other's right hands for a moment. In a wide variety of cultures, the common handshake is a ceremonial contact that provides tactile and observational clues about the other person—some functional, some emotional—from which wide-ranging judgments will be made.

- You come close enough to see, hear, and even smell the other person, rapidly processing a barrage of vivid clues that wouldn't be obvious from several feet away.
- You form an impression about things such as character and sincerity on the basis of the firmness of other people's grips, the movement of their eyes, the temperature and dryness of their hands, and the aura of friendliness (or menace) they project in body language as well as words.
- You decide how to respond based on how your conscious (and especially your unconscious) mind interprets these myriad obvious and subtle clues.

As a clue-laden experience, the handshake dates back centuries to the days when men extended their sword hands—empty—to portray their peaceful intent as they approached anyone from a known friend to a stranger.

Clues in Action

Organizations that have succeeded in creating effective experiences have been able to string clusters of clues together to create an overall impression or feeling. The question is how purposeful they are in putting that system of clues together.

In the 1970s, Amerada Hess Corporation, a leading independent petroleum company with Hess service station retail outlets from Boston to Florida, had a set of clues embedded in their customer experience that clustered together to shape and form what we experience at the gas pumps throughout the country even today. The Hess gas stations in the 1970s were extremely well lit, bright, and clean while the rest of the industry by and large conjured up an image of dirt and grease. Hess used white as its predominant color, and accent colors were yellow and green. Curbs were painted white, the attendants wore white coveralls, and the gas pump islands were painted white. The white curbs were maintained so meticulously that it seemed as though they were freshly painted weekly. The clues embedded in the Hess experience, by contrast to other service stations, created a feeling that distinguished it from its competitors.

In a grocery store, the first clue clusters you encounter often set the tone for the total experience. That's why generally the first displays are likely to emphasize fresh, savory, and smell-laden clues. The sight and smell of fresh fruit, veggies, deli items, and baked goods (plus the occasional sample to taste) offer multiple clues to an experience where freshness and quality are going to be found. Compare that with being greeted by a pyramid of soup cans or motor-oil boxes. No matter how architecturally creative, that cluster of clues evokes feelings of a different kind of shopping experience to come.

Think about being online, searching for some new treasure in lieu of another trip to the mall. Before you share sensitive financial data, such as your credit card number, you may see a small padlock icon in the lower corner of the screen or a security notice dialog box. It's a visual clue that the personal information you're sharing is being encrypted and will be zealously safeguarded to keep it from falling into unwanted hands. How often do you click on the encryption notice? Or is the appearance of the "icon" clue sufficient to create the feeling of security?

Organizations are often familiar enough with Functional Clues that they don't require an extended discussion. But with the unconscious mind processing as much as 95% of the data throughout an experience, gaining a better understanding of how clues are being registered will create a sturdier foundation for the development of experiential disciplines that follow.

Here are two extended examples—one uniquely personal (but for which you may well have a counterpart) and one more universal—to illustrate how both humanic and mechanic emotional clues play a central role in the way customers have experiences. Also, it will be easier to see the weave of clues and their connection to customers on a deeper level.

The Mechanic Side

Consider the tale of the toilet-paper triangle . . . and the towel swan.

This may come as a revelation for younger generations of travelers, but many years ago, to provide a clue that the housekeeping staff really had cleaned the bathroom, hotels and motels would have the maid slip a loop of paper over the toilet seat. Typically, the paper said "Sanitized for Your Protection" or something similar.

Then as now, determining whether proper time and attention had been given to providing a clean, healthy place to spend the night was a legitimate concern for people checking in at inns, known or unknown, far from home. At home, they knew what standards of cleanliness and quality could be expected. On the road, how could they be sure? Finding that simple, silent wrapper on the toilet was a consistent and reliable indicator that their expectation was actually going to be met.

As a Mechanic Clue, that paper loop connected both functionally and emotionally. It actively contributed to a satisfying experience by indicating to customers that they weren't going to encounter something nasty left behind by the last occupant of the room. And, the wrapper could convey that message clearly without direct human involvement when the customer encountered it.

Over the years, the combination of rising environmental consciousness and increasing cost consciousness conspired to render the old paper wrappers outdated. (Somewhere, there's probably a collector's society whose members jealously hoard the remaining rare examples of this once-common roadside icon.) What to do instead?

No one has made a definitive claim of inventing the current practice, but somewhere along the line, housekeeping professionals recognized that they could provide an equally useful clue to cleanliness simply by having the person who cleans the bathroom fold the outer end of the toilet paper roll to form a triangle (Figure 5.4).

Figure 5.4 The toilet paper triangle.

It's a little thing, but because it conveys something meaningful to customers, it's also a big thing. In fact, this simple clue to cleanliness has become so effective that people see the *absence* of the toilet-paper triangle as significant. Also, embedding the clue into the experience insures the staff checks the roll of toilet paper to be certain there's an adequate supply.

Too Much of a Good Thing?

In a simpler, less competitive world, the story of this minor symbolic achievement in Mechanic Clues could end here. But in the modern business world, one-upping the competition, taking things to the proverbial next level—even though sometimes the customer would be perfectly content if things were left exactly where they are—is the name of the game. If a toilet-paper triangle can acquire power in the customer's eyes, how about embossing the end of the toilet-paper roll? Or sealing it with a little piece of gold foil? Or laying an orchid petal over the end?

All of these techniques and more (Figures 5.5 and 5.6) are in use in major hotel chains these days—all ostensibly driven by the supposed need to impress discerning customers who apparently expect to find ever more imaginative Mechanic Clues suggesting that their rooms are clean.

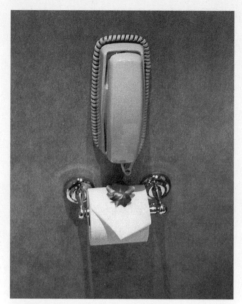

Figure 5.5 Creative toilet paper techniques.

Figure 5.6 Creative toilet paper techniques.

Unfortunately, it doesn't end there.

I recently encountered towel swans, or bathroom origami aspiring to absurd levels by folding towels into the shape of birds (Figure 5.7). No research I'm aware of remotely suggests that discriminating travelers consciously (or even unconsciously) plan their overnight stays, derive deep emotional value, or base their away-from-home lodging preferences on the presence or absence of absorbent linens that have been prefolded into the shapes of exotic birds and animals.

Figure 5.7   Towel swan.

Yet someone—probably someone relatively well-schooled in marketing or operations,—(a) thought this up, (b) had enough internal clout to decree that the organization would actually provide it on a continuing basis, and (c) found a way to budget not only for the training required to teach staff members how to do a credible job of it but also the supervisory time necessary to make sure it was being done.

An outlandish example? Perhaps. But it points out an important distinction. In successfully managing experiences for your customers, more isn't necessarily better. Better is better. And your customers' emotional needs decide what constitutes better.

The Humanic Side

Just as simple physical things can mean a lot in the context of customer experiences, individuals also can have a profound impact by what they do and how they do it. In big Italian families like mine, there's often someone who serves as the "patriarch" and mentors the next generation as it enters the world of working. His example provides essential insight into the management of Humanic Clues, as well as a template for how people should behave in the workplace.

In my family, it was my Uncle Pio. For more than 35 years, he worked as a store manager for the Great Atlantic and Pacific Tea Company (known to many simply as the "A&P"). His career dated back to the days when they used to fill orders and deliver them to people's houses in person. It ended in the mid 1970s as another once-dominant market leader slipped into decline.

As an experience manager as well as an intuitive merchant, Uncle Pio was an absolutely phenomenal "natural." He had a knack for developing new ways to display merchandise and was forever winning vendor-sponsored contests for effective display designs and promotions. But more significantly, he had an abiding sense for the ways his customers wanted to experience—and would experience—his particular store.

Under his guidance, many of my cousins and I received a lasting form of basic training in experience management that emphasized paying attention to detail and developing an unyielding sensitivity to what customers were sensing and feeling in the store.

The economic logic he employed was quite simple. Happy customers come back. More importantly, happy customers come back again and again, each time spending more and more of their money. Which means that stores with happy customers make money. Which makes the managers, executives, and stockholders of the company that owns those stores very happy. Uncle Pio's stores made lots of people happy and made lots of money for the company.

Most Saturdays as a young boy, I'd look forward to visiting his store. After all, I could count on a Pavlovian kind of reward: Uncle Pio's store gave out food samples to thank people for coming in. I'd walk in and there he'd be, up front with his manager's jacket and his plaid tie and the pin that told how many years he had been at A&P. He had risen through the company's ranks to become the youngest A&P manager in the northeast region and was given the most modern store at the time to run because of his record for producing results (Figure 5.8).

Figure 5.8 Uncle Pio at the A&P.

Not that there weren't occasional clues to discord. I remember a particular Saturday like it was yesterday. He had all of this Vermont cheddar cheese cut up and placed on top of an enormous cheddar cheese wheel on a table.

"Look at this," I remember him saying. "They just want us to put the cheese on the table. Just plain cut, plastic-wrapped cheese. It looks so much better sitting on top of a wheel of cheese. Why not let people know it's fresh and where it comes from?"

His boss had come through a little earlier and made some kind of off-hand remark: "That looks pretty good, Pete." My uncle was still growling about that encounter. "Well, of course it does!" To him, doing a little bit more, doing things to enhance the experience for "his" customers, was second nature.

Like so many characters of business legend, he genuinely loved mixing it up with his customers. That whole store was his kingdom, his stage. I'd be a couple of aisles over and I'd hear this loud voice, bigger than life: "Mrs. Andreozzi, how are you? What are you making for supper today? You're making veal and peas? Oh, my God. Your husband's a very lucky man. I wish I could be at your house for dinner tonight. We have some exceptional veal today. Come over here. Let me show you a meal fit for a king."

One of his favorite aisles was the coffee aisle, not just because customers could grind their own beans at the A&P, but also because the smell of coffee would carry over several aisles. "This aisle is worth its weight in gold," he'd say, "and the company doesn't realize it! This is what we're all about." He'd brew coffee in the store for the employees and customers just to make sure people could smell something other than whatever was in the mop buckets when we cleaned up the floors.

We'd go to church, and everybody would stop by to say hi to Uncle Pio. He was a legend in the neighborhood. But he was more than just a colorful local character. He had an innate sense of how people wanted to feel in their grocery shopping experience. His customers obviously connected to that—and not simply inside the store, but anywhere in the community they happened to encounter Uncle Pio. In essence, he helped their Experience Ribbons tie together the store, the neighborhood, the church, and more—and all of it worked to the financial benefit of A&P. Uncle Pio must have thought constantly about how he could make a mark on the business of his neighborhood that could not be erased.

You can't stop taking care of people as well as the physical elements of the business. You can never take the customer for granted.

Connecting with Customers

Over the years, I learned an important lesson from Uncle Pio. You can't stop taking care of people as well as the physical elements of the business. You can never take the customer for granted. The greatest pain in his life, I think, came from the way the company he loved and devoted his career to lost its edge over time—and lost so many of its customers in the process.

Often, the evidence of decline and stagnation is so simple. There was the time, as competing store chains started to encroach on A&P's turf, that a competitor called Almac's opened nearby. It drove Uncle Pio nuts because corporately they were so much more experientially advanced than A&P. Among other things, they played music in the store at Almac's.

There's another of those purely sensory inputs that on the surface seems to have nothing to do in a functional sense with the food on the shelves but a lot to do with the shopping experience in the emotional sense. It may not seem like much, but back in the late 1950s, it put Almac's a definitive step ahead of A&P in managing the customer's experience.

Uncle Pio loved music. He was in the University Glee Club in Providence and a huge opera fan. Predictably, he was distraught over the fact that a competitor was being permitted to gain a musical advantage. He told his bosses, "People need music. They need something in the background." Even though he couldn't have explained it in the words being used here, he instinctively knew that music could connect emotionally with his customers.

But the A&P management said, "Forget it."

Did that deter him? Nope. Uncle Pio went out and bought his own radio for the store, and out of the small office in the corner you would hear the opera on a Saturday afternoon and classical music at other times. It was his own private way of competing with the Almac's of the world . . . despite his own management's insensitivity to the customer experience.

To this day, I have a passion for the experience of grocery shopping. Once you've stocked shelves, there's something about pulling cans off instead of putting them on that makes winding your way through the aisles something akin to a religious experience. But I don't see very many Uncle Pios when I go shopping these days. I always look, but I seldom find them—not in the grocery stores, not in the malls, not in the auto dealerships, not in the theaters or pharmacies or restaurants.

Taking that personal, connection out of the business, whether in the name of greater efficiency or due to a simple lack of awareness, reduces the business to a sterile exercise in mathematics: how much, by how many, how fast, for how big a return. There's no real passion or pride in that way of doing business. There's no heart or soul. Ultimately, there's no lasting value for customers.

No wonder so many customers sound so irritable when they talk about the last airplane ride they took, the last fast-food drive-through they endured, or their last experience at the bank, drug store, post office, or supermarket. Functionally, all the indicators may be positive. The plane arrived on time. The fast-food restaurant put the right assortment of items in the bag. The bank statement balanced, the prescription was filled correctly, the mail was delivered, the milk was fresh. But customers are grumbling instead of glowing over the experiences they had.

It's no secret what's missing. There's no Uncle Pio showing people how to create and deliver an experience customers will enjoy so much they'll look forward to the next time they have a chance to repeat it. In far too many businesses, the humanics have been devalued and reduced to rote-learned, pat phrases delivered by indifferent people, indifferently managed.

The easy out is to claim that "You just can't get good help these days" or "People just don't want to work like they used to."

By the way, you can count me among those observers of business today who refuse to lay the blame for the state of service at the feet of "uncaring workers" or people who lack a work ethic. The easiest out in the world for bad Humanics is to claim that "You just can't get good help these days" or "People just don't want to work like they used to."

In my experience, most workers, regardless of their age, race, or gender, want to do a good job, provided that they know what a good job is. If they haven't been shown, if they aren't integrated into a well-run experience management system, if they aren't constantly surrounded by good role models—if there's no Uncle Pio to lead and inspire them— how will they ever learn what to do, why to do it and how to do it really, really well?

Uncle Pio knew his role, and he played it to the hilt. He led by example, but he also coached and managed—equally important hats to wear—

employing the everyday clues of a grocery store as though he were conducting the symphony orchestra for one of his beloved operas. If Puccini or Toscanini ever ran a grocery store, they'd have hired Uncle Pio in a heartbeat.

Making Clues Count

There's a certain sense of opening Pandora's box when you start down the road of exploring and actively trying to manage people's experiences. There's no silver bullet for experience management. It's not a one-time quick fix. It's not a way to turn thinking, feeling human beings into unconscious automatons who can be manipulated for profitable purposes simply by punching a few previously unidentified emotional buttons.

In fact, it can't be.

Experience management is a completely integrated set of disciplines that seeks to identify the clues—rational and emotional, humanic and mechanic—that customers consciously and unconsciously wish to find in their encounters with you. This set of disciplines helps you design and manage experiences around those clues in a way that consistently and deeply connects with your customers' emotions.

It starts with the customer. It ends with the customer. It's what happens in between, with your people and your systems, your humanics and mechanics, that will test your ability to build lasting customer loyalty.

The marketplace is here. Integrated, total experiences that are designed and delivered in keeping with experiential expectations are what it craves. A growing body of anecdotal evidence validates the rewards of a systematic approach to clue management. Research from marketing labs to neuroscience confirms that the underlying principles of experience management are valid and workable.

So how do you actually manage Experience Clues in a disciplined, focused way?

The solution is a system.

References

1. Gerald Zaltman. *How Customers Think: Essential Insights into the Mind of the Market*, page 58, (Harvard Business School Press, 2003).

2. Frederick F. Reichheld, "The One Number You Need to Grow," *Harvard Business Review* (December 2003).

3. Leonard L. Berry, Lewis P. Carbone, and Stephan H. Haeckel. "Managing the Total Customer Experience," *Sloan Management Review* (Spring 2002).

4. Leonard L. Berry, Valerie A. Zeithaml, and A. Parasuraman. "Quality Counts in Services, Too," pages 44-52 (*Business Horizons*, May-June 1985).

5. Lewis P. Carbone and Stephan H. Haeckel. "Engineering Customer Experiences," *Marketing Management 3*, pages 8–19 (Winter 1994).

6

APPROACH TO EXPERIENCE VALUE MANAGEMENT

Managing experience as the value proposition requires a shift from a make-and-sell mentality to that of sense-and-respond. Implicit in this is a commitment to a customer focus.

Most of us have grown up in a world that fostered an appreciation of the value and importance of process, from the efficiencies of assembly line production introduced by Henry Ford and later to the refinement and maximization of that model through quality control and continuous process improvement.

The notion of process improvement through quality management came very early in my own development. I grew up in the late 1950s and early 1960s, and I recall textbooks on statistical quality control stacked on bookshelves in my home because my father's work was quality. In fact, he had a fanatical obsession with it, particularly as it applied to the Nike Zeus, a Cold War antimissile program contracted to AT&T by the federal government. My father, Salvatore, who died a 35-year veteran of Western Electric and AT&T, was a field inspector for the Source and Supply Inspection Organization.

At the time, I didn't have an understanding of what was in those books, but as I personally experienced the "quality movement" in the late 1970s, I developed a much deeper appreciation for the approaches they represented and what my dad did for a living.

Philip Crosby fashioned and popularized the concept of "zero defects" based on the widespread premise that manufacturing to an "acceptable quality level" of less than perfect simply ensured that there would be defects.

That was the era that spawned thinking from people such as Philip Crosby, author of numerous books on quality, who at that time was working on defense programs at Martin Marietta. Out of his work there he fashioned the concept of "zero defects" based on the widespread premise that manufacturing to an "acceptable quality level" (i.e., less than perfect) simply ensured that there would be defects.

The collective work of Crosby, W. Edwards Deming, Joseph Juran, and others would ultimately coalesce into a full-fledged "quality movement" in the 1970s and 1980s. Its phenomenal contribution to business was based primarily on process improvement—taking highly methodical approaches to achieve elevated quality requirements through quality management process improvement.

One impressive business, owned by a friend, that has embraced quality process improvement is Gallery Furniture in Houston, Texas, under the visionary leadership of founder and owner Jim "Mattress Mack" McIgnvale. Gallery Furniture sells more furniture per square foot of retail space than any store in the world and is the world's largest single-unit furniture store.

In his book, *Always Think Big* [1], Mattress Mack credits his success to applying what he learned as a student of Deming to the way he developed processes for his business. One of his favorite illustrations is the "red bead" experiment that will be familiar to anyone who has attended a Deming seminar. In this exercise, participants use a trowel to scoop up beads from a box. The goal is to scoop up only white beads. But the box contains one red bead for every four white beads.

Using the trowel under Deming's demanding eye, McInvale recalls, red beads were scooped up again and again. No matter how people scooped, red beads appeared. No matter how Deming praised, barked instructions, or asked for new participants, success continued to elude his intrepid scoopers.

The lesson: The failure wasn't a result of the people. The "process" was at fault. [1] McIngvale has utilized the best of quality process management to affect his organization's ability for operationally delivering a distinctive customer experience. His firm delivers furniture to customers the same day they purchase it.

Managing Experience Value

The concept of quality management provides a basis for understanding the value of process management to operate a system effectively. But quality management in and of itself cannot provide the framework for designing and adaptively managing the total value created by experiences. As with our earlier discussion about making important distinctions between brand and experience, there's a similar need to sharpen understanding of the relationship between quality process initiatives and Experience Value Management.

There are firms that have tried to simply overlay quality process improvement to leverage customer experience through programs such as ISO 9000 or Six Sigma. And they stand to miss the opportunity to fully leverage the value that can be created by the experience because their purview is limited to process and not a holistic "customer-back"[1] systems approach to Experience Value Management.

I first realized the relevance of a systems approach to experience management when I was observing Disney and I've watched other organizations embrace the idea.

For example, while working with Progressive Auto Insurance in the mid-1980s, a group of executives attended several educational seminars at Disney. They returned somewhat confused by the relevance for their organization of what they'd been exposed to. They found Disney interesting and even saw some best-practice aspects, but the group essen-

---

1. *Customer back*, *sense-and-respond*, *make-and-sell*, and *managing by wire* are terms coined by Stephan H. Haeckel in his book *Adaptive Enterprise: Leading Sense-and-Respond Organizations* (Harvard Business Press, 2000).

tially dismissed everything from roles to staging as relevant only to "entertainment." Where could it ever apply in the insurance business?

The light bulb went on for them, however, as they realized that the customer-focused system and the processes to support the system that were in place at Disney were the very things that enabled the company to execute on the myriad details that they managed so efficiently. The Progressive executives' attention was piqued because of their familiarity with and appreciation for the management of quality.

For many on the team, that insight was the starting point for future inspired experiential thinking and initiatives at Progressive.

Process and Experience

When considering process improvement and its relationship to Experience Value Management, you must remember that:

1. Quality process improvement is by nature company-centric; it is derived from product manufacturing requirements that the company has set, not requirements that the customer has helped co-create.

2. The primary goal of quality process improvement is conformance to manufacturing requirements and product defect elimination, *not* customer preference generation.

3. Focusing on process improvement runs the risk of getting better at doing the wrong thing if it isn't fully aligned and supported by a system focused on customer-based value creation.

Additionally, quality management theories in the context of experiential value creation often are limited because unfortunately, they have been leveraged as a way to gain cost efficiency for a company without consideration of the customer's desires.

When an organization embraces experience as its focal point, it transforms the value imperative. If the way an organization defines and maintains quality fails to reflect the deep needs and desires that drive customer behavior, those efforts will work against the interests of the organization and ultimately undermine a customer-back system.

Experience management must be designed as an overarching system, then operationalized by processes that are aligned with the customer-focused goals of the system. The processes within the system must be designed to support the system and must not be an end unto themselves. The system is the representation of the sum of the parts to create a specific outcome—in this case, customer preference, commitment, and advocacy.

Think of it this way: Process design must follow systems design just as the design of a computer program follows the design of the computer architecture, which in fact is a systems design.

Establishing a Context

It's the system, not the individual components, that creates the leverage to truly turn customer experiences into a manageable value proposition for virtually any company in any industry.

Today, many organizations are thinking about experience but are not at all sure how to come to terms with it. This chapter and those that follow draw on more than two decades of work with a wide variety of businesses and academics dedicated to the subject. Starting with understanding how the human brain consciously and unconsciously processes information, it's possible to design and deploy systems composed of embedded clues that provide a practical way to manage customer experiences for greater value creation.

It's the system, not the individual components, that creates the leverage to truly turn customer experiences into a manageable value proposition for virtually any company in any industry.

A system succeeds when all the separate parts, all the discreet subsystems, mesh together to create a dynamic, cohesive whole. When subsystems of clues work together to create distinctive customer value, an experience management system is in place and operating successfully.

Deliberate Systems

The practice of managing experiences is all about being deliberate and purposefully organizing clues around a customer-back defined goal and thoroughly understanding the effect the designed clues and their interdependencies will have on the whole. Managing from this perspective requires a directional shift in thinking to a point of view that proceeds from the whole to its parts, rather than the traditional from the isolated parts to the whole. That's where a systems thinking focus comes to the fore.

Russell Ackoff, the Anheuser-Busch Professor Emeritus of Management Science at the Wharton School of Business, University of Pennsylvania, and noted founder of the discipline called General Systems Theory, defines a system as "any entity, conceptual or physical, which consists of independent parts" yet at the same time "is a whole that cannot be divided into independent parts." [2]

Take, for example, the ultimate system—the human body. Each of its parts—the heart, lungs, stomach, and so on—has an effect on the performance of the whole. However, no single element stands alone and no element has an independent effect on the whole,. How the heart functions and its effect on the entire body depend on the behavior of the brain, the lungs, the vascular system, and so on. If any one of those elements is removed from the body, the whole structure of interconnected systems cannot continue to operate as before. Indeed, often eliminating any one part is fatal to the whole.

From this perspective, you can see two of the primary characteristics of a system:

1. Every part of a system has properties that it loses when that part is separated from the whole.

2. Every system has some properties—its essential ones—that none of the other parts of the system possess. [2]

Ackoff and C. West Churchman, among others, have given us the term *systems thinking* to describe "seeing the 'structures' that underlie complex situations . . . seeing the whole . . . as a framework for interrelationships." [2]

That's one of the problems many organizations have faced in trying to adapt to the promise of digital transformation. Too often, companies have jumped into Information Technology (IT) and Customer Relationship Management initiatives, firmly convinced that building state-of-the-art systems will make or keep the business competitive but with little to no idea about the internal interdependencies or true customer value to be derived. Carol Moore, former technology consultant and now Director of the Design Lab at Parsons School of Design warns companies to "invest in what is valued, not in what is possible." [4] Small wonder money for IT and CRM has diminished considerably in the last few years.

The performance of the system depends more on how its parts interact than on how they act independently.

The tendency to invest in technology for technology's sake highlights the validity of a related systems principle that illustrates a form of reverse synergy: If each part of a system is looked at independently and is made to operate as efficiently as possible, the system as a whole will *not* operate as effectively as possible.

To illustrate this point, Ackoff suggests imagining a large number of different makes and models of automobiles assembled in a giant garage. With the help of auto mechanics, you can determine which car possesses the best carburetor, which has the best engine, which has the most superior brake system, and so forth. Then, extract those parts from their respective cars. With all the parts needed to make a functioning automobile laid out on the garage floor, imagine assembling them into a new automobile. Would you emerge with the best possible automobile?

Of course not. Though individually superior, the parts would not fit together and function properly. The way the parts fit together, relate to each other, and function in an effective rhythm is critical. Consequently, the performance of the system depends more on how its parts interact than on how they act independently.

Systems Perspective

Systems theory thinking in the context of the practice of experience management is a new perspective—and one that holds a unique challenge, due to the tendency of modern business to seek quick fixes. Businesses almost always think in terms of *linear, independent* processes as opposed to *integrated, system-scale* values and outcomes.

Steve Haeckel [5] offers a simple description of the principles of systems design applied to experience management principles (see Figure 6.1). Here's how they translate:

- Design from the top down (i.e., with the motif as the customer value proposition)
- Design the interactions between the parts (clues)
- Define the boundaries of the system in terms of constraints/restraints
- Depict the Experience Design as a system of roles and accountabilities; each role being defined by the clues (functional, humanic, mechanic) it must produce

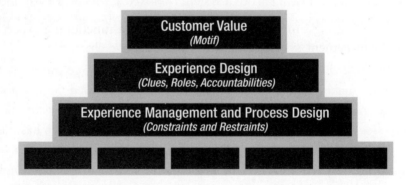

Figure 6.1 Experience Management and Systems design.

Start at the End First

End frame is the term for this crucial discussion. For cartoonists, the end frame is the last panel in a comic strip where the connection or resolution is found (see Figure 6.2). Knowing the end frame, the cartoonist creates a systematic story line that logically leads the reader (aka customer) to that outcome in the few short panels preceding it. In this context, the cartoonist's words and images become clues for the reader, telling a coherent story despite the limitations of time and space.

That end frame becomes the design focal point for the cartoonist, and all of the clues efficiently support that end frame. The same can be said about a good comedian who demonstrates system thinking by using the punch line as the design point for a joke.

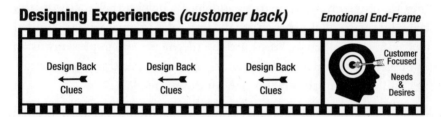

Figure 6.2 In designing experiences, clues are designed from the customers' emotional needs and desires back.

It's no coincidence that Walt Disney, who created one of the most evolved and sophisticated experience management systems to date, was a cartoonist. Creating an experience management system is, in a way, doing something similar. As you begin to build a functioning experience management system, you will learn to weave clues into concise story lines that move your customers along to the desired end frame.

Understanding, adeptly positioning, and continually monitoring meaningful (to the customer) clues are what provide the leverage to "manage the unmanageable." Don't think of experience management as linear and process-driven. Once underway and running, you'll find that it's a dynamically stable framework (one that thrives in ever-changing and inconsistent environments, facilitating high adaptivity) that a company can use to continuously align its actions with changing customer desires and values.

Systematic Stagecraft

Another important aspect of a system is that it's measured in terms of performance, whereas process is often measured more in terms of adherence. "Theater" has become a useful metaphor for understanding this distinction.

From a live theater audience's perspective, the actual performance on any given night appears to occur in a specific and predictable linear sequence: Act 1 leading to Act 2, and so forth. But on closer examination, we see experience management systems design throughout.

First, consider the playwrights and directors who start with the message they want to communicate to an audience. The play they then conceive can be thought of as a design for the way roles interact with each other and with the audience. Props are the mechanics, stage presence is an example of humanics, and actors are trained to perform their characters and roles consistently throughout the entire play.

Behind the scenes, the repertory company staging the performance has been engaged in a systematic regimen that may extend and repeat itself over years. A location is found, sets and costumes created, lighting configured, sound and sight-lines evaluated. A cast is selected with each member assigned to learn a specific role or multiple roles—and probably also understudying several others to provide for unexpected absences. A behind-the-scenes staff also is recruited to handle curtains, lights, set changes, and the countless logistical details involved in the performance.

Long before opening night, the director and producer assess how to stage the show within their budget and resources. Through constant practice, the company refines the myriad of interconnected elements of dialog and staging around that message and feeling that will resonate with the audience. On the basis of that "motif," the sets created may be simple or elaborate, the lighting stark or flattering, the costumes staid or revealing, the performances restrained or over the top.

Eventually, the production is advertised, creating expectations about the kind of entertainment experience that will be provided. On opening night, the first audience arrives, the curtain rises, the actors hit their marks, and the performance is delivered. All the hard advance work at last is laid before its intended audience, and everyone involved listens carefully for the timbre of the applause and the enthusiasm of a curtain call.

Then the cycle repeats. But before each new performance, the observations of the production staff are combined with feedback from previous audiences, critics, and even word-of-mouth reviews relayed by friends of the company to keep the show fresh and on target.

No matter how good or bad any single performance may be, everyone involved knows they will take the stage again—in front of a new audience who will judge their work solely on their experiencing of what happens on stage during that specific production. But although the audience's focus is entirely on a single performance, the company's craft must systematically extend on either side of those few important hours—the whole run, not any specific performance, will define the company's success.

Hit shows aren't accidents. Hits become hits because those involved, whether onstage or behind the scenes, are very systematic at doing the necessary things again and again, continually refreshing strong points while making changes and improvements where needed. Each time the curtain goes up, a new audience's Experience Ribbon stretches in front of them.

It's Really About Performance

"All the world's a stage" is as apt an observation at Walt Disney World as it is down at the local community playhouse or in any experience in any business. The entire entertainment industry, in fact, is less a service industry than an *experience* industry in which companies succeed or fail based on their ability to deliver the fun and beauty their customers value.

"All the world's a stage" is as apt an observation at Walt Disney World as it is down at the local community playhouse or in any experience in any business.

How does all this connect to experience management? Just as theater delivers its value proposition with carefully staged performances, so, too, do businesses focus on providing preference-building total experiences that rise and fall on their own performances.

John Deighton, the Harold M. Brierley Professor of Business Administration at the Harvard Business School, first wrote about theater and business management as a performance model in 1989. [6] Pine and Gilmore [7] and Bernd Schmidt [8] have since elaborated on that perspective.

To Deighton, a story is the natural way for humans to articulate an experience. Stories, along with performances, are how people learn from each other. Good stories encapsulate memorable experiences. Deighton holds that interacting with customers is an "intrinsically dramatistic discipline" because customers react to the way firms market to them by responding to or participating in performances. He states, "Marketers often refer to a market offering as a product, but a product is merely the frozen potential for performance." [9]

It follows from this point that there are strategic choices to be made regarding the type of performance your organization chooses to design and deliver. "What is fake in one context might be fun in another," says Deighton. And the customer decides which is which. Customers decide what's authentic, what they will bond with, and what they will value.

For this reason, good theatrical producers and directors spend as much time on the context in which a performance is delivered as they do on the content delivered by both the script and the actors. What they do, you can do—the same dynamic applies for those who set out to engineer the experiences of their customers.

Casting Calls

Extending the theater metaphor to one final point, there's a significant, systems-oriented difference between a job description that is focused on job function and a role focused on outcomes and accountabilities.

With the notable exception of Disney and a few others, most people in the corporate workplace have become accustomed to seeing themselves in the context of job descriptions, not roles. As have their organizations.

And therein lies another opportunity in the shift to effective experience management systems. It means an individual's behavior doesn't have to be scripted but can be coached. And their roles can be supported by "costumes" or dress, both providing important clues to customers.

A medical professional's bedside manner reflects a powerful set of Humanic Clues. Clues such as a lab coat or stethoscope help distinguish the role and support the performance. It's interesting that this set of clues is not as distinguishable in medicine today as it was decades ago.

Interestingly, roles often inspire more trust than the people playing them. Millions of people who may blanch if an otherwise well-groomed young person approaches their children don't think twice when the individual is wearing a Mickey Mouse costume. And as long as the role of Mickey is consistently portrayed, that trust is sustained.

In actuality, workers today are regularly asked to play multiple roles: manager, mentor, team member, presenter, creator, implementer. The experience management system you create will succeed to the extent that it encourages and enables your people to be improvisational—to tailor their vocabulary, humor, degree of candor, and tone of voice, among other things, to correspond with what is appropriate to a particular role, audience, or setting.

Realistic Expectations

Many organizations start out earnestly articulating a vision for their products, services, brands, and competitive positions, only to lose momentum as conflicting demands compete for limited time and attention. In remarkably short order, once-clear visions and simple, deliberate approaches can become disjointed, even counterproductive.

Much of this misalignment and conflict reflects the lack of a defined system and set of accountabilities that constantly bring all the activities into view whenever a decision is to be made. Employees tend to lose their sense of continuous commitment when efforts aren't integrated into a systematic approach that constantly renews its focus on delivering real value for the customer. They very often shift the priority from delivering value to customers back to managing limited resources and serving internal forces.

Admittedly, the term *experience management* is a bit of a misnomer. You don't (can't) manage experiences in the literal sense of being able to exert control over exactly what your customers sense and assign value to and the feelings they carry forward. But gaining a deeper understanding of how customers needs and desires affect their preferences will help you create the clues that matter. From that point, systematically managing those relevant clues toward an "end frame" that reflects the customer's desired value, will help to shape how your customers feel about your business and how inclined they are to come back and do business with you again—in even the most highly competitive of marketplaces.

Managing the Value Proposition

There is a pronounced tendency in business today to talk about change initiatives as programs rather than comprehensive value propositions. Steve Haeckel appropriately refers to this as the "bolt-on" theory.[5] Haeckel observes that businesses tend to bolt things onto existing practices rather than consider the best way to comprehensively configure and implement something new.

In recent memory, for example, it's clear that many organizations have viewed customer service and even quality management as bolt-ons— just another isolated thing to do. Even the best of intentions succumb to "continuous confusion," becoming the kind of program *du jour* that in time is easily scrapped. To succeed in leveraging experience as a value proposition, it will be critical to think in terms of system design rather than process or program design.

Whether you are committed to fully leveraging experience as a value proposition—and reconfiguring your entire organization as a result— or simply want to gain some useful insights into actions that can provide short-term, incremental improvements, you'll be making progress. Ultimately, however, you'll have to do more than fix some pieces in order to gain a substantial competitive advantage.

You're already creating experiences in the de facto sense—you cannot *not* create an experience. What you want, however, is to purposefully manage the value created by the experience rather than having it be a random happening.

A growing body of anecdotal evidence validates the rewards of taking a systematic approach to improving customer experience value as a way to move the needle at the bottom line. The challenge now is to avoid the temptation to rush into frenzied activity. How you proceed, however, shouldn't be defined in terms of time but rather pace. It's not about how much you do how quickly. It's about how much you do that truly creates value and results.

Consider the following as context for your efforts:

Observation #1

Perceived as an instinctive, almost intuitive art form as recently as a few years ago, systematic experience management is now ready to become a management science. As greater knowledge about how customers make decisions converges with developing concepts in the field of experience management, the opportunity to deliver more fully integrated customer experiences will continue to expand.

Conclusion: In the future, experience management will be a prerequisite to compete effectively.

Observation #2

The competitive advantage that can be realized from experience management is directly proportionate to an organization's ability to design and maintain effective, integrated, and meaningful experiences. The sum, indeed, is greater than the parts.

Conclusion: Your organization will benefit from experience management to the extent that it invests in it on a systemic scale.

Observation #3

Much like compound interest, the full potential of experience as a value proposition will be realized cumulatively over time, with rewards that grow exponentially once a successful system is in place.

Conclusion: Experience as a value proposition on a widespread basis is not a quick fix but an agent for long-term transformation, sustainable value and competitive advantage.

There isn't a universal, pure linear process for every organization to follow to create this focus. But methodically approaching experience management from a systems design and development perspective will get you there.

A Disciplined Approach

It's a disciplined approach to an experience management system that will help you continually configure and reconfigure your efforts for maximum customer impact, providing the kind of adaptive approach that continually focuses the organization on exactly what's right for your specific customers and marketplace at any point in time.

The design and development of an experience management system involves a wide variety of tools and competencies in support of distinct but interrelated disciplines. Configuring such a system relies on three fundamental principles:

1. Start by understanding the output of the system from a customer-back perspective: Relate customer needs and desires to the steps you take on their behalf.

2. Keep the big picture or end frame in mind; concentrate on the interactions between the parts, rather than actions within any particular segment.

3. Always measure progress in terms of the purpose of the system and its reason for being.

The ability to fully leverage experience as a value proposition for customers and employees is facilitated through the application of specific disciplines that unlock the power of experience that are performed with mastery of distinctive competencies aided by distinctive experience-based tools (Figure 6.3).

Practice of Experience Management

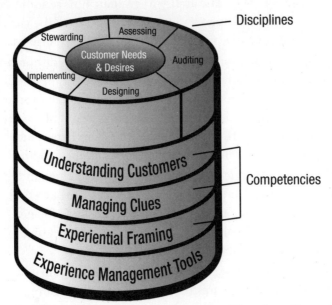

Figure 6.3 Disciplines and competencies in the practice of Experience Management.

No one competence, discipline, or tool will be a universal silver bullet or the experience management counterpart to Disney's coveted "pixie dust." It's the innovative blending of numerous perspectives and competencies that unlocks the full potential of experiential value creation.

The Disciplines of Experience Value Management

The disciplines you can depend on to create experience management systems and that will be individually explored in the chapters that follow include:

- *Assessing Experiences*: Defining and understanding your organization's creation of experiences for multiple audiences in the context of existing information and practices. It may be useful to think of this in terms of topography—learning the characteristics of the experiential terrain on which experiences are and can be created, optimized, and subsequently managed.

- *Auditing Experiences*: The ability to evaluate how random or haphazardly experiences happen and the identification of the gaps between what customers desire and what they currently experience.
- *Designing Experiences*: The deliberate articulation of humanic, mechanic, and Functional Clues created to be prompts that collectively deliver the experiential end frame and bond customers to the total experience. Designing clues and the removal of some existing clues to insure that they are consistent with an Experience Motif, brand, vision, and values are central to designing experiences.
- *Implementing Experiences*: Embedding selected clues and integrated experience designs into customer experiences, then testing, sourcing, building, and rolling them out economically and efficiently to accomplish specific objectives that loop back to creating value with customers and employees.
- *Stewarding Experiences*: Managing the system by continuously monitoring the effect and refreshing the clues for maximum impact on customer loyalty and advocacy.

Developing Competencies and Tools

In any trade or craft, competencies allow practitioners who understand the essential disciplines and principles involved to choose the tools that will help them produce workable results. The skills that electricians call on to install light switches or rewire outlets combine physical dexterity with an intellectual understanding of the principles of electricity. Based on their electrical competence, contractors can decide which actual tools and materials—wires, pliers, wire cutters, junction boxes, switches, and so forth—should be used for a given job.

As you embark on the creation of an experience management system, similar competencies will help you understand the principles and choose the tools appropriate for your situation. Some of these competencies are rooted in general design theory—architectural, interior, graphic, product, and retail. Others have been pioneered in fields such as engineering, psychology, organizational development, marketing research, communications, education, construction, set design, and event planning. Most are as useful to businesses with as few as half a dozen employees as they are to the Fortune 100, as applicable in government agencies and nonprofits as in modern corporations.

No one competence, discipline, or tool, for that matter, will be a universal silver bullet; rather it is the experience management counterpart to Disney's coveted "pixie dust." As Disney imagineers would be the first to point out, it's the innovative blending of numerous perspectives and competencies that unlocks the full potential of experience value creation. Unfortunately, there is a very human tendency to focus so intensely on a particular area of concern that you may lose a sense of perspective for other competencies and how they can contribute. Again, it's the combination rather than any one that will help you maximize the return on your investments in experience management.

No one competence, discipline, or tool will be a universal silver bullet; rather it is the experience management counterpart to Disney's coveted "pixie dust." It's the innovative blending of numerous perspectives and competencies that unlocks the full potential of experiential value creation.

The competencies include: understanding customers (via Experience Research and linguistics), managing clues (via Sensory Attentiveness and Clue Sensitivity), and experiential framing (via Experience Education, Experience Metrics and Experience Communication).

Thinking Systematically

The key to developing a successful experience management system is the masterful integration of positive clues, new and old, using experientially focused disciplines. The result is a synergy that is far more powerful and distinctive than simply the sum of the parts.

An organization ultimately must be able to configure its experience management system to integrate these disciplines. In the following chapters, you will see how organizations are learning to do just that.

References

1. Jim "Mattress Mack" MacIngvale. *Always Think Big*, pages 158–159 (Chicago: Dearborn Financial Publishing, 2002).

2. Russell L. Ackoff. *Ackoff's Best: His Classic Writings on Management*, page 16 (New York: John Wiley & Sons, 1999).

3. Vincent P. Barabba. *Meeting of the Minds: Creating the Market-Based Enterprise*, page 8 (Cambridge, MA: Harvard Business School Press, 1995).

4. Carol Moore. "The New Heart of Your Brand: Transforming Your Business through Customer Experience," page 1. *Design Management Journal* (2002).

5. Stephan H. Haeckel. "Leading on Demand Businesses—Executive as Architects," *IBM Systems Journal*, Vol. 42, No. 3 (2003).

6. John Deighton, Daniel Romer and Josh McQueen. "Using Drama to Persuade," *Journal of Consumer Research*, Vol. 16 (December 1989).

7. B. Joseph Pine II and James H. Gilmore. *The Experience Economy Work Is Theatre & Every Business a Stage* (Harvard Business School Press, 1999).

8. Bernd Schmitt, David Rogers and Karen Vrotsos. *There's No Business That's Not Show Business* (Financial Times Prentice Hall, 2003).

9. John A. Deighton. "The Consumption of Performance," *Journal of Consumer Research*, Vol. 19, page 368 (December 1992).

Part 2

THE PRACTICE OF EXPERIENCE MANAGEMENT

7

THE DISCIPLINE OF ASSESSING EXPERIENCE

A growing number of organizations—from Disney and Krispy Kreme to the likes of Harley-Davidson, Mayo Clinic, Target, and Kohl's Department Stores—have recognized how powerfully the customer's total experience can contribute to their competitive advantage. The discipline of *assessing*, the first of six distinct disciplines in the practice of experience management, focuses on identifying a link between your organization's internal resources and the experiential expectations of your customers.

Avis Rent A Car quickly learned about the reality of customer perceptions and their connection to customer loyalty. Ronald Masini, its former Vice President of Product Development, says it turned out that how customers felt about themselves during their rental experiences proved to be a far better indicator of customer retention than the traditional customer satisfaction measurements Avis had been using

He is emphatic that such insight "would never have surfaced had Avis not assessed the potential of customer experience as its value proposition rather than continuing to rely on quality improvement alone. Gaining deeper experiential insights moved us light years ahead of the pack. Just adopting the customer experience mindset itself became a competitive advantage." [1]

Why Assess?

The objective of assessing is twofold:

1. To determine how capable and willing an organization is to switch its emphasis to experience as the core of its value proposition

2. To identify the most logical places within an organization for experience-driven initiatives and how large or small those efforts should be

Assessing customer experience in your company and marketplace tells you where you are, which in turn helps you make decisions about what you can reasonably expect to do and over what period of time. Some companies can jump right in. Some can't. Some have the resources to launch broad initiatives. Some have to make their changes incrementally.

As with any quest for knowledge, a good place to start is by figuring out what you already know, identifying what you don't know but need to know, and being prepared to gain insight about what you don't know that you don't even know you don't know.

The more you learn about your customer and challenge the usual assumptions, the more accelerated your learning and ability to innovate will be.

Three questions are basic to the discipline of assessing:

1. What potential impact does managing customer experiences represent for the organization?

2. How is experiential value currently being created for customers?

3. What resources are available to improve and optimize the way your organization creates experience value?

As with any quest for knowledge, a good place to start is by figuring out what you already know, identifying what you don't know but need to know, and being prepared to gain insight about what you don't even know you don't know (Figure 7.1).

Insight Generation

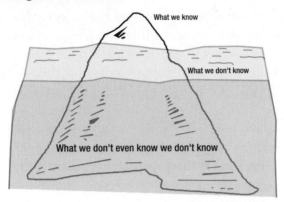

Figure 7.1 Generating knowledge insight and it is what is below
the tip of the iceberg that makes the difference.

Very often, exciting discoveries surface when you explore new territory and expect the unexpected. The discipline of assessing is not only about confirming assumptions but also about having the courage and patience to be open to using an array of tools and techniques that offer the most promising opportunity to gain distinctive insight and knowledge about your customers. Be prepared, however, because the learnings may challenge comfort zones and deeply entrenched thinking in an organization as well as an entire industry. Take it as a given that assessing your organization's experiential strengths and weaknesses will challenge you to think hard about how much you truly know about customers' needs and desires. Without that foundation, you can find yourself losing your edge, your market share, and the long-term loyalty of your customers.

As we will discuss later in this chapter, when Progressive Auto Insurance's Florida division decided to test settling claims on the spot at the scene of an accident, it was a major challenge to the accepted conventions in the industry at the time. In fact, the notion was unheard of. This unconventional move was completely driven by insights derived about customer needs. Under the leadership of Bob McMillan, their thinking was unencumbered by the way things had been traditionally done in the past.

Exploring Experience Topography

It's important to make the scope of your assessment as broad and unencumbered as possible. Steve Carlisle, a strategic planner at General Motors, an early adopter of experience as a value proposition, characterizes the challenge as moving from a desktop-sized whiteboard to a whiteboard the size of a drive-in movie screen. Customers are choosing to do business with you based on their total experience. That means throughout all stages of their Experience Ribbon, assessing uncovers far more opportunities to build preference than you probably have focused on before. As daunting as that prospect may sound, you should resolve to start with a clean slate and explore all the open white space available.

In some respects, assessing is a little like hiking in the woods. What you see is a function of where you are, how you got there, and where you want to go. As you move through the terrain, your vision changes. That changing perspective ultimately helps you to choose the best path to get where you want to go. For example, if there's a hill to your right, you can't be sure what's on the far side of it until you gain a better view that removes the obstruction.

Tempting as it may be, don't bring in the bulldozers and start rearranging the terrain right away. You can't know what to work on unless you've first developed good maps to guide your efforts. Start by identifying what the organization already knows about the delivery of the current customer experience and its value to customers. From that, you can begin to deduce what you need to know more about, and you may also get some indication of those uncharted areas that have yet to be discovered, which may unleash the ever more powerful opportunities.

Several years ago, as it pondered launching a customer experience effort, Office Depot was predisposed to rush right in and "move some dirt." It already had detailed information on selling patterns in its stores, competitive forces in its markets, the results of years of ongoing quality process initiatives, and barometric readings of general customer satisfaction.

Although Office Depot had for years asked customers basic *functional* questions about its products and services, it had not probed for insight into what value customers may have derived *emotionally* from shopping for office equipment and supplies. Accepting the idea that managing experiences was going to be something new and different, they concluded that they literally didn't know what they needed to know about what their customers were encountering in its stores. So they started looking. Assessing provided an eye-opening understanding of the experiential topography that led to a major refocus in how Office Depot might position itself with customers.

As part of its continuous improvement efforts, Office Depot had committed to building more than a dozen new prototype stores. To learn even more about what it didn't know, the company made a decision to use these prototypes progressively as real-world laboratories for research, Experience Design, and long-term tracking and learning.

Said Shawn McGhee, the president of Office Depot at the time: "It was an effort to reconfigure our thinking, to understand that 'experience' should be the value proposition and that everything in the experience represents clues and clusters of clues that 'shape' the way customers feel during their experience." [2]

Working on intuition alone, McGhee conceded, "the company might have lucked out and gotten it right. But it might just as easily have gotten lost, investing scarce resources and conscientious efforts only to get better at the wrong things instead of those that would have true impact on customer" preference and loyalty.

Assessing with Purpose

Today, what Office Depot did under McGhee's leadership can be referred to as *value proposition management*: in essence, integrating the customer's experiential perspective as a variable to be managed in decision-making, compared with just the more traditional focus on hot products and strong geographic presence.

Richard Nichter, who at that time was Office Depot's Vice President of Store Operations, recalled that in the past, the company had acted as though convenience and price—and very little else—drove customers to its door. Typically, management had thought of convenience mostly as a function of geographic location, with price as a factor influenced more by what competitors were doing than what customers were valuing.

And then? "The application of a set of systematic disciplines and a robust experiential approach made all the difference." "It gave us a valuable set of filters that changed the way we saw the world. It changed my personal perspective forever—taking something that had been intuitive and random and applying rigor." [3]

That change, according to Nichter, came about when Office Depot realized it had good insights into customers' rational needs and expectations but very little understanding of the emotional connections that created intense value for customers.

As with any form of situation analysis, the most obvious reason for assessing is to help develop a better understanding of your current situation. However, assessing isn't an end in itself. It helps sets the stage for the more action-oriented disciplines of auditing, designing, implementing, and stewarding experiences. Be prepared, however, for it to become a continuing process in its own right. With each new cycle of design and implementation, you will benefit from revisiting your assessments and updating them in light of the current environment. That additional knowledge, in turn, could lead you back into additional design change and new implementation as your experience management system evolves along with your customers.

Experience management systems never arrive fully conceived and smoothly functional across all the dimensions of a business. As thought leaders in the quality movement were prone to remind people a generation ago, improvement of any kind needs to be a long-term commitment, not a one-time happening. Experience management is no exception to that rule. For example, Avis learned that customers would actually spend more time at a rental facility if it helped reduce their stress. So the company installed work stations with Internet connections and fax capabilities in their locations. The stations have become more heavily utilized than management ever perceived, according to Ron Masini.

The customers never articulated the need for such work stations. In fact, customer data suggested that they wanted their car rental experience to be a "nonexperience," lasting no longer than a nanosecond. But deeper and continuous probing revealed customers' stress and anxiety in their travel experiences. Avis demonstrated that it understood those feelings, which led to a distinctive enhancement of the value of the Avis customer experience.

Although most assessment will be reality-based, idealized speculation is certainly in order. For example, suppose you had that rarest of rare opportunities in modern business: a "clean slate" to create a brand new experience (and the experience management system to make it sustainable). How would you reinvent the category you're in to create a totally new kind of value that customers would be relentlessly committed to and enthusiastically advocate to others?

If you literally could start over, how would that compare with what you're now doing? How would it gain momentum and provide even greater returns over time? In the end, the real measure of any strategy is its ability to generate the desired results along with a strong return on investment (ROI).

Now, how can you close the gap between how you manage experience value creation today and the optimized ideal?

Organizational Inclination

One predictable by-product of assessing is a sense of "experience management anxiety." As your organization begins to sense the full scope of the potential that experience management represents, it's natural to feel a little overwhelmed. Where do we start? How do we prioritize? Which initial successes will open the door to the greatest long-term opportunities and rewards?

Assessing will provide insights to set realistic priorities and make realistic decisions. In most organizations, internal limitations or external conditions—or probably a combination of both—will dictate that you find a scope and pace appropriate for your organization.

That is why management first needs to develop a meaningful sense of the long-term potential of experience management in your organization. In the short term, you may have to strike a balance between what has potential and what is digestible. Be patient: Shifting to experience as a value proposition can be an evolving pathway, not an event. Avis began its experience management efforts as a "toe in the water" test at a single location.

Although the need to move cautiously is understandable, the important thing is not to be reluctant to stretch. As the legendary advertising icon Leo Burnett once said, "When you reach for the stars, you may not quite get one, but you won't come up with a handful of mud either." [4] In the long run, an experiential focus can pyramid and extend your competitive advantage.

Audiences and Experiences

In assessing organizational readiness and inclination for experience initiatives, you'll need to address the different potential experience audiences that can be targeted.

Consider:

- The variety of experience audiences you must satisfy in your business; their similarities and differences;
- Their relative potential value to your company
- How systematic or haphazard current experiences appear, compared with what would be involved in bringing planned consistency to them
- The relative loyalty of each audience and their vulnerability to the efforts of competitors effects on your business

Once you've identified the priority of different experiences and target audiences as well as the internal organizational factors that can help or hinder switching your focus to experience management, move on to examining the information you have regarding the experiences you currently are creating. Even though you may not have addressed experience management issues before, you will be surprised to find that you have more information to work with than you might think. It's just a matter of starting from the vantage point of the customer and an experience management focus.

Start by reviewing all the available research and common organizational practices and asking the following questions:

- How well do you understand the unconscious emotional needs and desires of potential audiences?
- How does your current data reflect the customer's Experience Ribbon? Do you know anything about how customers anticipate your business? Or how they recollect it?
- Where do your organization's experiences fall in the context of the Experience Preference Model? Are your experiences rejected, accepted as a commodity or highly preferred?

Gaining a deeper understanding of what constitutes loyalty in your business and what your organization measures is another important area to explore. This knowledge will be invaluable in developing and later fine-tuning the metrics that will be needed to gauge the ROI realized from creating better managed experiences.

Assessing will help you identify gaps in your understanding of customer needs and desires, particularly when it involves the deeper unconscious emotions that traditional research rarely digs into. Don't be surprised if you find you have the equivalent of a Swiss-cheese perspective. Identifying the holes is the essence of assessing.

Experience Insight Wellsprings

In most organizations, there's a wealth of experiential information available, much of it provided by customers themselves:

- Some of this data may have come to you directly from your own customized research, including market reports and tracking studies.
- Some may have come indirectly from outside organizations (JD Power and Associates and others, for example) that seek to provide a snapshot of how various competitors are faring in head-to-head competition for perceptions of customer satisfaction and preference.
- "Anecdotal evidence"—correspondence, sales and call reports, complaint reports, and more—invariably is available in abundance.

- Call centers, Web sites, and field activities generate tons of information that can be mined for a sense of how well your current experiences are connecting with what you think customers desire.
- Company communication documents can yield unexpected information, as well. Check out employee manuals, orientation scripts, sales literature, annual reports, and other forms of stakeholder communications for clues to your experiential blind spots and opportunities.

A few years ago, Allstate discovered that its training modules all echoed the organization's familiar slogan by telling people that their jobs involved making customers feel that they were in "good hands," a metaphor for feeling secure and taken care of. But when Allstate looked at its materials from an experiential standpoint, it discovered that at no stage in its training did it ever define let alone provide useful techniques for producing what that "good hands" feeling consisted of—not in the customer's emotional frame of reference or from a rational standpoint, either.

Employee Experiences

Take full advantage of the body of material available from people within your organization. The front line of any organization is a tremendous in-depth resource for information and insight.

Listen to them as they share their personal experiences with customers. What from their "expert" vantage point consistently connects or disconnects with customers? What do they think are the consistent parts of a preference-building experience? What are the fail points?

Chances are, your people already know a great deal more than they've ever been asked to share about what your customers are experiencing. Assessing is the opportunity to begin to harvest such information. Just the simple act of asking your people about their experiences with customers and what it would take to manage them more optimally will create a bias for action. Such up-front involvement will help sensitize your organization to experience as the context for organizational value creation.

Also, you'll find out that having identified what you know, what you don't know, and what you previously didn't know you didn't know helps immensely in creating a plan for auditing activities that will be discussed in the next chapter.

The simple act of asking your people about their experiences with customers and what it would take to manage them more optimally creates a bias for action.

Leveraging the Moment

In assessing the experiential terrain on which your organization competes, examine whether you are leveraging the full breadth and depth of the experiences you are providing. Experiences don't simply start at your doorway, phone center, or Web site. Customers' experiences often begin long before they physically encounter the first tangible outposts of your organization. Make sure you are assessing this reality.

When Bob McMillan was the president of the Florida division of Progressive Auto Insurance in the early 1990s, he launched an initiative that used customer experience to develop a competitive advantage. Previously, Progressive had sold high-risk coverage through authorized agents. McMillan wanted to add broader direct sales. As he tried to diagram the policyholder's experience in his preliminary analysis, he found himself evolving from a conventional, linear process flow to a schematic that put the customer in the center of everything.

All of the company's capabilities and all of the experiences it created needed to be literally built *around* the customer and the customer's needs, he reasoned. However, not everything in his schematic reflected conditions Progressive could control or manage.

By assessing first, McMillan and his team recognized that the customer's experience relative to an automobile accident claim actually started well *before* a customer picked up a phone to call the Progressive agent or claims representative. In fact, the most vulnerable moment—for the customer and for Progressive as a business—turned out to be the moment of, well, impact. The scene of the accident was a moment of maximum emotional vulnerability for the customer. Yet neither Progressive nor any other insurance company had ever tried to manage the policyholder's experience in the immediate aftermath of an accident.

What could be a more distinctive and remarkable point to make a significant emotional connection, McMillan reasoned. How powerful would it be to actually have a Progressive presence *there*—if not at the actual moment of impact, then as soon afterward as possible? And not just a clerk—someone schooled in everything from basic trauma and grief counseling to arranging for towing to how to select a preferred provider for body work. Equally important, this would be someone equipped with a computer link to Progressive, so that the check for repairs could be written right there on the scene. What an incredible emotional connection could be forged by better managing the experiences at that moment of highest anxiety.

That was the genesis of Progressive's now-signature fleet of some 1,800 IRVs (Instant Response Vehicles). As it turned out, the customer experience wasn't the only thing IRVs improved. Not only has the program reaped customer loyalty benefits in recent years, it also has generated money-saving logistical efficiencies. It turned out to be incredibly more efficient to write checks on the scene than to push payment paperwork through layers of administrative sand over the following weeks and months of an accident—and perhaps on to litigation. It turned out that the more immediate the resolution, the less in administration it actually cost the company.

And lo and behold, including the customer experience at the scene of the accident led to more enthusiastic referral of new prospects to Progressive. In fact, Progressive found that a source of new business in the aftermath of the IRV experience was the person standing *opposite* its policyholder. For the other company's customer, watching a check being delivered on the spot is an equally powerful emotional moment. As a result of its strong customer-back perspective, Progressive became the fastest-growing auto insurer in the nation.

Most critically, McMillan's deep involvement in experience management development was a strong signal to the entire Progressive organization that reinforced the notion that customer-back perspective needed to be adopted.

Eye-Opening Discoveries

Be prepared for some surprises when assessing. Among other things, you may identify different potential customer targets than the ones you expected.

When Allstate began assessing experiential opportunities, for example, its going-in thinking was marketing-driven—in particular, ethnic marketing to improve preference and loyalty among Hispanics and Asians. But assessing surfaced the need for a very different primary target— Allstate's own sales and claims agents. Ray Celaya, Assistant Vice President of Emerging Markets, says that assessing the composition and nature of its ethnic experience delivery led to major learning that had implications for every customer. [5]

As a result of major restructuring to adjust to the deregulation of financial services (an industry-wide phenomenon), Allstate's agents had gone from employees of the company to independent contractors. In addition, the company's profile had broadened from a provider of insurance products alone to the larger arena of financial services. While assessing its own strengths and the key challenges to improving its customer experiences, Allstate began to recognize that its agents not only were wondering where they stood with the "new" company but were also struggling with the need for extensive training to acquire securities licenses so they could play a part in it. Regardless of their status or licensure aspects, agents were still the crucial experiential point of contact between the customer and the company. Building loyalty to Allstate still started as a link between customer and agent.

That drove home a simple reality: As the agent goes, so goes the customer. The experience of the customer was important, to be sure, but first the experience of Allstate's agents had to be addressed.

The need to manage the *agent's* experience better became a key contributing variable in managing the *customer's* experience. To be sure, in a crowded and highly competitive insurance marketplace, the customer's experience was still crucial to building long-term loyalty. But it turned out that the customer's loyalty reflected the agent's loyalty and actions. In recent years, Allstate has been redeploying resources and redefining programs accordingly.

Internal Experiences

Another major benefit of assessing is the way it sometimes reveals information that isn't always obvious. Audi of America had worked through some tough times before it began serious experiential explorations a few years ago. In particular, a major recall in the early 1990s had pushed the company's U.S. operations into a mostly defensive posture.

Over a period of years, however, Audi worked to correct its quality and logistical problems. Gradually, the improvements became obvious along the chain from factory to dealers to customers, allowing the auto maker to think ambitiously once again. As its resurgence as a viable brand in the United States gained momentum, the company at last was able to look forward to mounting a serious challenge to Mercedes and BMW.

To do so, Audi decided to focus on creating managed experiences in single-point dealerships—locations dedicated to selling only Audis. Previously, most Audi dealers had also offered Volkswagen or Porsche models, among other combinations. Audi felt that single-point dealerships would be the key to creating a distinctive brand experience for customers. But for its dealers, that meant a significant investment in new facilities.

John Peterson was Audi's Director of Dealer Development during this crucial time. He recognized that the company was now asking those who had stood by it through the lean times to make major investments in building new facilities. The last thing he wanted was for Audi dealers to feel as though they were being held hostage, even taken advantage of, just when the brand was beginning to prosper again.

He first assessed the full spectrum of existing experiences and the audiences to whom they were important, rather than simply jumping in with a laundry list of new, down-from-the-top initiatives. As a result, Peterson and Audi identified the *single-point dealer's* experience as a critical priority.

In response, he made sure that serious attention was paid to the emotional aspects of the single-point dealer experience, from the identification of the need for a new facility to construction design and all the way through the opening and operation of the new single-brand store and its operation. He applied his assessment-derived insights to focus on the emotional value the dealers needed to derive from their investing in single-point dealerships.

The resulting effort created extraordinary outcomes and significantly built loyalty among Audi dealers. Far from feeling taken advantage of, this key constituency instead felt that it had been recognized by Audi as a critical element in the future of the organization.

Creating a Sound Foundation

The goal of assessing is to understand better where your organization stands in its ability to manage meaningful customer experiences and how it will move forward on that front. The discipline of assessing should yield both a strategic understanding of how you'll leverage experience and a tactical work plan for how you will get there.

The trick in assessing is to deploy the right resources and launch efforts against the most meaningful audiences and activities. From that foundation, you will be able to set realistic priorities and maintain a sense of logic and order in all experience efforts that follow.

The discipline of assessing should yield both a strategic understanding of how you'll leverage experience and a tactical work plan for how you will get there.

The next consideration is to probe the full depth and breadth of the customer's actual and desired experience so that you understand what your potential experience audiences truly need and want from you, and how they perceive the clues that your business is currently providing, as well as the gap between the two. This discipline is called *auditing*.

References

1. Ronald Masini, personal communication (April 2003).
2. Shawn McGhee, personal communication (February 2003).
3. Richard Nichter, personal communication (March 2003).

4. Leo Burnett,Chairman, Leo Burnett Co. Inc, original citation, Readers Digest 1985, *Simpson's Contemporary Quotations,* quote number 2106, compiled by James B. Simpson, (Houghton Mifflin Company, 1988).

5. Ray Celaya, personal communication (October 2003).

8

THE DISCIPLINE OF AUDITING EXPERIENCES

Assessment of experiences is predominantly internal, but the discipline of *auditing* is driven from an external perspective—from the customer back to the business. Generally, you will find that there are things you don't know but need to know about the customer's experience. Auditing experiences is how you understand and fill in those gaps. Its objective is twofold:

1. To gain insights by evaluating the customer's experiences as they are now being delivered from the perspective of the hearts, minds, and senses of the customers

2. To identify the gap between what customers deeply desire and what they are experiencing

Throughout their everyday experiences, people continuously process signals—clues—both consciously and unconsciously. Auditing experiences helps to identify the clues they are experiencing and the feelings they create, then compare and contrast them with the feelings customers desire. Until you've confirmed what is working and what isn't and have identified the gaps between what customers value and what they are receiving, you can't begin to develop and design effective experiences.

Again, managing experiences is something of a misnomer in the sense that you can't really control what the customer thinks and feels about any given experience. Only the customer has that power. What you can control and manage toward a predetermined goal or end frame are the individual clues that customers process on both a conscious and an unconscious level so they create an experience that better meets their needs and desires. Auditing serves to deconstruct the Experience Clues so you can examine and evaluate the elements that comprise the experience.

Customers bond to a particular experience on the basis of the composite of all the clues they sense. Consequently, it's fundamental to an experience management system to be able to recognize, evaluate and then manage clues.

Up to now, however, organizations have not had a way to systematically evaluate and manage the clues that can lead to customer satisfaction, loyalty, and advocacy. Often, many clues have gone unnoticed or have been perceived as background noise, whereas others—simply by being obvious—have gained an importance not supported by true customer needs. Through auditing experiences, you will begin to see which clues have been discounted and under-leveraged, and which have been given more stature than they merit. By learning and better understanding customers' deep emotional needs and surfacing the thoughts and feelings being generated by existing experiences, you will begin to see what you could be doing to generate a greater emotional experiential impact.

Customers bond to a particular experience on the basis of the composite of all the clues they sense. Consequently, it's fundamental to an experience management system to be able to recognize and evaluate clues.

Multiple Perspectives

Characteristically, auditing benefits from using varied types of research to generate as many different perspectives of the experience as possible, rather than using just one or two forms of research to continuously sharpen a single view. Consider the imprecise, even misleading perception you would have of a table setting in a restaurant if you were limited to looking at it from only one perspective. From your vantage point, the salt shaker might be invisible because it's behind the napkin dispenser. It's there; you just can't see it because something else is blocking your view. Unless you can move either yourself or the napkin holder to gain a different perspective, you will be missing something significant and useful (Figure 8.1).

Figure 8.1 Seeing the same thing from different perspectives as in this tabletop illustration.

In some cases, experiential blind spots are obvious. In others, seemingly very minor details may make all the difference between an experience the customer registers as neutral and one that resides in the preference zone.

How important are the little things? In observational research done recently, customer service representatives (CSRs) were observed during the 10–15 minutes they typically spent with customers filling out credit applications. At completion, based on customer service best practices, the employees escorted the customers to the door and thanked them for their business. In a wide majority of the interactions observed, the

CSRs placed the completed applications on top of a stack of paperwork on their desks *before* escorting their customers to the door.

What's wrong with that? Think about the *unconscious* implications of that clue being processed by those customers. How significant do customers feel when they leave with the image of being just the latest addition to a huge stack of paperwork? Compare that with the clue involved when the CSRs were told to keep the application in their hands while escorting their customers to the door or to make a folder with the person's name on it to put the applications in while they were still in the office and keep it on the center of the desk. On an unconscious level, just that subtle change resulted in customers feeling that they were considered important.

The most effective experience auditing is something like studying a putt from different angles. Subtle aspects of the green's contour become visible as you develop multiple perspectives, such as the roll of the ground or differences in the grain of the grass—knowledge that increases your odds of sinking the putt. Multiple perspectives of your customers' experiences reduce the chances of being blindsided by an unknown in your examination of the customer experience.

In the past, many organizations have done very deep research studies, but generally only in a few specific areas. Gaining greater analytical depth certainly has its benefits, but it also can also build a false sense of confidence. No wonder so many narrowly but painstakingly researched new initiatives fail.

Gaining multiple perspectives reduces the risk of missing critical observations and consequently provides greater opportunity to manage the full breadth and depth of that experience in designing and implementing.

Jerry Zaltman is a strong proponent of drawing on research perspectives from an array of disciplines, believing that they are essential to a better understanding of "what happens in the complex system of mind, brain, body, and society when consumers evaluate products and the experiences they have with them." [1] He cites the example of a company that was seeking new ways to use consumer incentives. After meeting for two days with a neurobiologist, a psychiatrist, an Olympic coach, an adult learning specialist, and a public health sociologist, several new practical and innovative ideas were implemented—some within two weeks. Over the next seven months, the effectiveness of the company's consumer incentive program soared by almost 40%.

Gaining multiple perspectives reduces the risk of missing critical observations. Using multiple snapshots rather than a single one creates a more robust understanding, builds confidence in the insights gained, and consequently provides greater latitude and opportunity to manage the full breadth and depth of that experience in designing and implementing.

Auditing Components

Through the discipline of assessing you will also have emerged with an idea about your organization's readiness to adopt experience as a value proposition. In addition, you will hopefully have created a tactical plan for where it makes the most sense for you to start. Gathering knowledge in the following three areas will produce robust insights that guide subsequent actions in the practice of managing experiences.

1. Identify the Customer's Deepest Emotional Needs and Desires

Beyond the basic elements of product functionality (Does it do what it's supposed to do?) or service (How does the company perform?), you also need to develop a rich understanding of how customers want to— and do—feel about themselves during and after their experiences with your organization. Because people aren't consciously aware of these deeper feelings, using traditional focus groups and other methodologies will not access them. Most traditional research methodologies get primarily at people's "surface" thoughts, which is only about 5% of their total thought process, according to modern neuroscience. As much as 95% of what we process in an experience takes place in the unconscious mind. Uncovering, then probing people's more unconscious thoughts and feelings provides a more robust and accurate perspective for meaningful experiential learning and insight.

2. Deconstruct the Sensory Experience the Way the Customer Experiences It

You cannot address experience management in a meaningful and cost-effective manner until you are fully aware of the vast array and modulation of sensory clues that are present or absent. All Experience Clues can generate negative, neutral, or positive feelings. But some carry more weight than others. Individual clues that impact customers must be identified and evaluated until their individual significance is truly understood as well as their role in the cumulative clue experience mosaic.

3. Determine the Qualitative Gap Between Customers' Needs and Desires and How they Currently Feel in an Experience

By contrasting the effect of the clues, individually and cumulatively that are currently part of the experience, against the customer's deep-felt desires, you will gain insight into the gaps that may exist. And, you will be able to determine the relative value enhancement opportunities that are available to you. This will help you to recognize the opportunities that can be quickly and strategically leveraged and prioritize those clues that can be readily managed. Additionally, you will develop a more accurate understanding of how random and haphazard versus managed and purposeful experiences are in your organization. From this "gap analysis," you can make informed choices about designing, aligning, implementing, and managing experiences over the longer term (Figure 8.2).

Close The Experience Gap

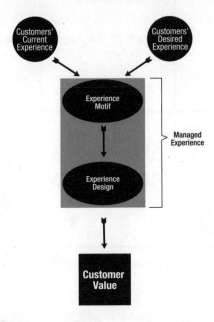

Figure 8.2 Close the experience gap with Experience Value Management.

Gathering information in these three critical areas requires a variety of tactical approaches. They include techniques such as Clue Scanning and experience mapping Psychological Pathways, observational research, interpersonal research, and communication research (Figure 8.3).

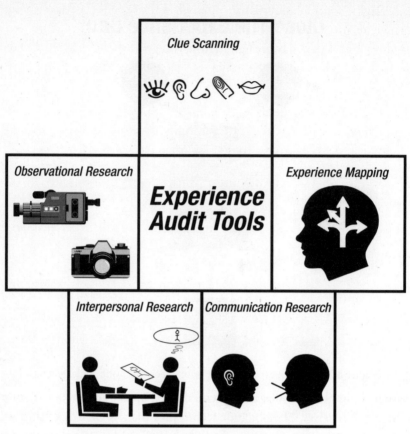

Figure 8.3 Experience Audit tools.

Scanning for Clues

Clue Scanning is one of the simplest yet most complex auditing tools. That's because it challenges you to get into the "customer's head"— more specifically, into the customer's eyes, ears, nose, mouth, and skin—looking for and examining clues.

A **Clue Scan** provides a sensory review of the physical environment, processes, and humanic behaviors of all of the various segments or layers of the experience. It can be as basic as cataloging every sensory input that can be registered in whatever order they are sensed, or as meticulous as making separate scans for each sense: sight, sound, smell, taste, and touch. The wealth of data a Clue Scan yields must then be sifted for the relative effect and importance of the clues. But if you're thorough in how you go about it, it will confront you with the full reality of experience management.

A Clue Scan is designed to enhance an organization's understanding of what its customers are feeling in reaction to the clues they are encountering with an eye toward gaining insights that will be used for more deliberate and strategic clue design and management.

Experience Mapping Psychological Pathways

In service literature over the last 20 years, the term *moments of truth* is often referred to. One difference between experience moments of truth and process mapping, is that the latter is often done in the absence of customers, while experience mapping is done through direct observation or interaction with customers. Thus, it is the difference of seeing the experience in the eyes and mind of the customer versus what we evaluate in processing the customer, which the organization defines and controls. This can make it difficult to break out of an internal mindset and begin to sense experiences the way customers experience them on the basis of sensory images and feelings.

The preconceived thoughts an organizations has about "processing" customers creates a clear tendency to see the customer's experience only from the company perspective. When I worked with Avis, for example, I found that the car rental industry traditionally disregarded where customers were coming from and where they were going, focusing its process mapping solely on what happened in the rental location itself. Yet from an experiential standpoint, a customer's state of anxiety or calm is influenced by the way they encounter the shuttle van, the ability to make a phone call or send a fax, find the restroom, get off the lot and into local traffic, and a host of other sensory stimuli they will recall from a specific rental location.

Mapping moments of truth or process looks like this: Customer comes to counter, rental paperwork is completed, car is assigned, customer locates car, customer leaves with car.

Experience mapping, on the other hand, looks like this: Customer gets off flight, stops in restroom, looks for baggage claim, waits for baggage, gets baggage, looks for car rental shuttle van stop, lugs baggage to stop, waits for van, lugs baggage onto van, rides van to various intermediate stops (perhaps retrieving messages from cell phone), rides van to rental location, lugs baggage from van to inside location, waits in line, keeps eye on baggage, hears parts of conversations in vicinity, can't quite hear what agent at counter is telling someone else, wonders if that means there's a wait, wonders why two clerks in the corner aren't working at the counter, sees the infant seats piled in a corner, smells the perspiration of the person waiting too close by, wonders where maps are, wonders whether the reservation is in computer, wishes that crying kid would shut up, moves up in line, comes to counter . . .

Obviously, these kinds of observations could be made about any industry, not just car rentals, if done from the perspective of what the customer's experience is, as opposed to what a company is doing to them.

When you're not thinking of the experience from inside the customer's head, you can easily miss not just minor nuances but also important pieces of the experience that the customer believes can and should be managed on his or her behalf.

It's quite understandable why businesses will often be closer to their processes than to their customer, but the emphasis has to be changed to customer-back thinking, which means paying closer attention to what customers are sensing and feeling—much of which will be at an unconscious level. When you're not thinking of the experience from inside the *customer's* head, you can easily miss not just minor nuances but also important whole pieces of the experience that customers believe can and should be managed on their behalf. That's a huge challenge for many firms making a transition from the make-and-sell model to sensing-and-responding.

Auditing can employ many forms of research, most of which are enhanced by new developments in neuroscience and communications theory. Observational research looks at what's happening on the surface and suggests what may be happening below the surface. Interpersonal research allows customers to describe what's happening on the surface with an opportunity to gain insight into what's going on below. Communication research looks for meaning beyond what is communicated by words and symbols and clues.

What You See

Observational research takes an anthropological approach to looking at customers in an experience. Observations of the experience can be made both "live" and through the use of video and audio recording and still photography. Capturing experiences for detailed deconstruction is like taking slices of the experience and mounting them on slides for examination under an experiential microscope. It includes the in-depth interpretation of everything from body language and facial expressions to tone of voice and traffic patterns. It can include the applications of the disciplines of ethnography—the study of human cultures and their influence on behavior. It allows you to see and take apart what customers are sensing and what effect it might be having on how they feel.

Digging Deeper

Interpersonal research mines customer thoughts and feelings for deeper insight into the way people perceive and interpret the value they're receiving. This auditing research technique is designed to unearth information in the customer's unconscious mind—the emotional elements that are difficult to surface from observational research alone. This can be accomplished through in-depth one-on-one interviews or customer-focused narratives, as well as forms of deep-probing qualitative research such as ZMET® (Harvard Business School Professor Gerald Zaltman's patented research technique).

What We Say and Hear

Communication research involves analyzing internal and external materials that the organization uses to communicate with customers. It also can include linguistic analysis of customer, employee, or common organizational language to determine the clarity of message and meaning from the company's perspective and critically the "take-away" and motivation on the customer's part. Such research represents increasingly sophisticated opportunities to study how information is exchanged in every communication between a customer and an organization.

The triangulations of these three research approaches—observational, interpersonal and communication—probe both the surface and what lies beneath. Understanding overt and hidden meanings in clues requires developing a more sensitive form of clue consciousness.

The use of observational research approaches and techniques such as ethnography, videography and understanding of cultural archetypes, as well as forms of deep probing qualitative interpersonal research, helps create considerably greater opportunities for distinction and differentiation in managing experiences toward emotional values, and in creating an experience management system.

Transforming Experiences by Observing

Anything perceived or sensed (or recognized by its absence) is an Experience Clue. Scanning for clues lets you walk the physical and Psychological Pathways of the customer's Experience Ribbon, not only noting how specific clues are making you feel but also gaining a sense of where the clues fall on the Preference Model—negative, neutral, or positive. In the process, you'll find that your general consciousness of the clues woven throughout an experience is constantly broadening and deepening.

Developing a hypersensitivity to what customers are seeing, hearing, smelling, tasting, and feeling in their experiences often is a transformative experience for employees.

To invoke that great American philosopher, Yogi Berra, "You can observe a lot just by watching." [2] Though it's not a direct objective, an extremely significant by-product of auditing is involving a cross-section of your employee team in the discipline. In addition to gathering valuable customer data, there's the potential for making everyone in the organization considerably more clue conscious.

Developing that hypersensitivity to what customers are seeing, hearing, smelling, tasting, and feeling often is a transformative experience for employees. A few years back, managers and store personnel of a Florida grocery store chain participated in Clue Scans of some of their stores, and suddenly they became aware of the impact of birds' nests growing out of their store's signage or milk racks quietly but visibly rusting away in the dairy case. To the extent that you can involve your people in meaningful auditing activities, they will become sensitized to the power of clues and develop a deeper appreciation for the impact of even the simplest things on the customer's experience.

The discipline of auditing experiences provides invaluable rigor. Far too many organizations lose sight of the customer's perspective in the routine of day-to-day operations. In this sense, familiarity breeds complacency. They can and often do unconsciously slip into the comfortable habit of focusing on elements of the routine or process itself, rather than the perspective of the customer for whom the products and services are intended and does good.

Be prepared, though: Auditing experiences can hold up an unflattering mirror. Often, the impact of significant clues that have been overlooked for years, and the size of the gap between what customers desire and what they are experiencing is so great that it has a shocking effect on an organization. Fortunately, that often fosters a greater sense of urgency and a bias for action. It also deepens an organization's sense of commitment and passion for what they do.

Emergency Sensitivities

Several years ago, when University Hospital (UH) in Augusta, Georgia, began auditing the experience that its emergency department delivered, the team performed Clue Scanning from various perspectives. A major "ah-ha" for Cindy Lundsford, Vice President of Community Services, and her staff was an enhanced appreciation of the patient's family in the hospital's emergency department experience.

The patient perspective, of course, was a natural focal point. However, as doctors, nurses, and support staff began observing the emergency department from the wider context of the clues family members encountered, they exposed many experiential elements at UH that had been routinely overlooked. One was the morgue.

The UH morgue consisted of a stretcher or gurney in the corner of a large but scuffed-up storage room. The effect was extraordinarily—if unintentionally—cold and somewhat foreboding, the more so because of the invariably flickering fluorescent lighting. There was also the periodic intrusion of staffers using the room for its other purpose as a storage area for surplus supplies such as mops and other utility items.

Unbelievably, families were being invited into this room as a gathering place to grieve and deal with the harsh reality of a loved one's death. But as the UH team, led by director George Ann Phillips, learned to look at experience in far more detail and from multiple perspectives, old familiar sights such as the morgue/storage room were seen in a whole new (and, in this case, far from flattering) light.

That eye opener created an immediate bias for action. The Clue Scanning team realized that family members at perhaps their most emotionally vulnerable point in the experience were being exposed to a highly unflattering memory of the hospital and its care providers. Even though it had never been articulated by patients or families, the team realized that negative clues were being digested, consciously and unconsciously, and would form the emotional basis for what they'd remember for years to come.

The team didn't need much time to figure out how to respond. There was very little they could do with the patient at that point, but team members were energized by what they could do simply and cost-effectively for the family. The very next weekend, doctors, nurses, and staff came in on their own time and created a whole new set of Humanic and Mechanic Clues for the morgue experience.

Among the humanics:

- They role-played, then literally choreographed the sequence involved in bringing family members into the morgue after the death of a loved one.
- They decided that someone needed to stay for the first few moments, then excuse themselves to leave the family with its grief, instead of just opening the door and letting people walk in unaccompanied.
- They worked through the dialog options that staff might say at such a vulnerable time.

In addition, still on their own time and initiative, staff members addressed the family experience on the mechanic side:

- They repainted the walls and purchased and put up a wallpaper border.
- To create softer, indirect lighting, they replaced the overhead fluorescents with lamps brought from their own homes or moved from other parts of the emergency department.
- They added a table with flowers and stocked it with spiritual reading material.
- They also provided two chairs—there had been none in the original morgue—and a curtain that could be pulled across the room to cover the storage area.

The simple act of scanning for clues helped transform the UH team's perspective and prompted immediate, effective responses.

"Experiencing what our patients experienced provided a distinctive perspective that altered how we came to view everything, from process to human interaction," according to Dr. Richard Eckert, M.D., the medical Director in the University Hospital Emergency Department.

Clue consciousness is not only an eye-opener but can also be a very strong motivator.

Widening the Vision

Other Experience Clues observed also inspired quick responses. Formerly, one of the first things that arriving emergency department patients and their families saw was a huge "Triage" sign over the check-in window. Triage is internal-speak, not customer-speak. The average person doesn't have the foggiest idea what it means. What does the replacement sign say? Simply, "Emergency Care Check-in."

Additionally, right in the emergency room entryway, arriving patients were confronted by a bright, yellow and black biochemical decontamination shower covered in radioactive hazard warnings. Patients and their families also quietly encountered two vacant registration desks. Both of these clues, although fairly benign to those who see them every day, provided an immediate source of confusion and anxiety for outsiders at a time when the emotional costs of wasted energy and anxiety were particularly high.

Reviewing observational video led to another troubling discovery. As hospital staff members well knew, there were two emergency entrances at UH, one for ambulances and the other for the public. Over the ambulance entrance on two sides of a portico were backlit signs that said "EMERGENCY ROOM" in huge, two-foot, bright red letters. However, the walk-in entrance was not designated at all.

Video footage captured automobile after automobile pulling up under the portico, stopping to read the "ambulance entry only" sign on the set of doors, then trying to figure out where the drop-off entrance was for them. Without the knowledge insiders took for granted, how were stress-rattled family members supposed to know where to go? New signage now provides the proper clues.

Some of the observations that result from auditing experiences can be as obvious as the need for better signs and wayfinding. Others may be more subtle, even humorous. At one point, the UH audit team discovered a kidney-shaped plastic vomit tray being used as a candy dish. Seeing the experience through the eyes of their customers, emergency department staffers recognized the negative clue . . . and swiftly moved the sweets to a more appropriate container.

Customer experiences don't recognize physical or geographic boundaries. Clues continuously add up, wherever and whenever they are picked up around the Experience Ribbon.

Stretching Physical Boundaries

As Avis discovered, customer experiences don't recognize physical or geographic boundaries. Customers were anxious over what happened before or after their rental experience as much as the rental experience itself. Clues continuously add up, wherever and whenever they are picked up around the Experience Ribbon. For some businesses, that can have serious consequences.

In suburban Minneapolis a few years ago, the cross-functional experience auditing team for Allina Healthcare's Unity and Mercy Hospitals didn't confine its Clue Scanning to sensory and environmental inputs from just the confines of the hospital property. To more fully explore the Experience Ribbon and the emotional needs of emergency department patients, the auditing and Clue Scanning effort went "outside," staging an accident in a park about five miles from the hospital, then recording the clues that patients and their families encountered long before entering the hospital itself.

From a rational or operations-oriented standpoint, such an extended approach wasn't strictly necessary. But considering the emotional highs and lows of patients and family members from the point of injury proved to be an eye-opening exercise. Adopting the vantage point of a child hurt at a playground in the park, audit team members looked for the clues that would be sensed not only by the victim but also by the family, others in the park, and people offering impromptu medical assistance.

As the team charted the route from the playground to the emergency department, members were shocked to find very few directional signs in the blocks surrounding the hospital. Out on the freeway, a generic "Hospital" sign was indeed in place, but it had been located at a confusing fork between two major exits. On surface streets, some signage gave no indication of how near the hospital was or which direction to turn. The difference between two blocks and three miles or making a wrong turn could be agonizingly significant to an anxious parent or caregiver. Typically the signs are not reviewed or monitored very consistently

Allina's auditing team emerged with a new appreciation for the experiential topography that staffers had simply (and understandably) grown accustomed to over the years. They realized that the patient experience does not magically start at zero when the hospital doorway is crossed.

Both UH and Allina, auditing experiences from the customer's point of view, exposed blind spots in the way Experience Clues from the critical to the simple had traditionally been viewed and managed. The broadened perspective helped identify actions that could be taken immediately and longer-term challenges that would require a phased approach. Importantly, the involvement of each organization's people involved in the auditing effort itself provided an immediate impetus for taking action.

Everything Counts

Like discovering a salt shaker behind a napkin holder, auditing sometimes results in unexpected discoveries and connections. A few years ago, researchers walked through the rental experience side by side with customers in an Avis audit and elicited thoughts, feelings, and impressions about the many aspects of the experience, including car cleanliness. Through that effort, an important discovery was made.

Avis and the car rental industry in general traditionally viewed the cleanliness of cars as an important lever to customer satisfaction and loyalty. From years of focusing on its own processes rather than its customers' experiences, Avis had understandably always assumed a cause-and-effect relationship between vehicle cleanliness scores and giving cars a more thorough wash and vacuum.

The Experience Audit discovered that customers appreciated washing and vacuuming but understanding their thoughts and feelings around cleanliness itself provided a new perspective. On deeper examination, it turned out that customers based their feelings about cleanliness on a variety of other things, as well—subjective observations that seemed to have little or nothing to do directly with clean cars.

It was revealed that long before they got to their cars, customers were already forming powerful judgments about cleanliness. For instance, the way infant seats were stored and distributed, the appearance of the windows in the rental area, and the occasional overstuffed trash can or wilted plant in the rental office all had the power to outweigh a tag hanging from the mirror affirming that the car in fact had been freshly vacuumed and washed.

This insight helped Avis realize that washing and vacuuming wasn't enough. If it stayed focused on tweaking the cleaning process of its cars alone, it likely would continue to fall short of its targets in the "clean vehicle" category. On the other hand, those rental locations that put the infant seats in poly bags, placing them neatly on shelves within customer view (previously, they had been piled on an oil-stained floor) and put their rental facility on a regular "hygiene" schedule very quickly found themselves being rated higher—*for the cleanliness of their cars.*

What's more, overall comparative tracking showed an interesting quirk: Even though Avis's cars weren't being cleaned any more often than anyone else's or any more intensively than before, customers started to give Avis higher marks than its competitors for the cleanliness of the cars on the lot.

Ronald Masini, the Vice President of Product Development at the time, remembers that Avis had been going crazy trying to raise its clean car rating. "If we washed them any more, we'd have washed the finish off the cars," he says jokingly. "It was astonishing that you could move perception of the cleanliness of the car without touching it. The actions we took kept the competition scratching their heads trying to figure out what we had done." [3]

Think about experience management as a total system. Each integrated and aligned part of the system creates greater value as a whole.

That's why it's so important to view the experience through customers' eyes and from inside their heads. The impression of how clean Avis cars were didn't start when customers first saw and got into the car. They processed cleanliness clues all along their Experience Ribbon and transferred them to clean vehicles.

The Avis audit underscores the importance of thinking about experience management as a total system. Each integrated and aligned part of the system creates greater value as a whole. As Avis learned, it had to manage the total experience better to move the needle on customer preference. Without the insights gained by auditing from the customer's vantage point, Avis might still be trying to devise intricate new ways to improve its car-cleaning processes. It would still be receiving customer ratings stuck firmly in the neutral zone. And the company still wouldn't have a clue as to why.

Gaining Emotional Insights

As noted, much traditional research has been blind to the emotional nuances in the customer's total experience. In part, this was because scientific insight into how the brain works—and, thus, how customers think and make decisions—was lacking. Further, research often has focused too narrowly on operational and functional subjects. As a result, researchers regularly have employed what turns out to be misguided rigid questioning techniques. Letting customers go where they want to go and following them through their unconscious thoughts and feelings turns out to be more potentially useful than leading them toward responses that emphasize their purely functional reasoning.

For their part, whether being interviewed with short surveys or through in-depth sessions, customers tend to provide seemingly insightful, rational answers that do not on closer scrutiny reflect their true emotional reality. Does this mean customers lie? No, not intentionally. But there is a natural human tendency to try to be helpful or to create intellectual alibis based on how people think they *should be* answering the questions. There is also the fact that customers simply aren't able to articulate many of their feelings due to their subconscious origins.

Remember that much more is going on inside your customer's mind than simply a rational quest to satisfy a functional need. Conscious thought is the tip of a very large iceberg. As much as 95% of thinking takes place in the unconscious mind, which according to Zaltman is "that wonderful, if messy, stew of memories, emotions, thoughts, and other cognitive processes we're not aware of or that we can't articulate." [1]

Zaltman's patented consumer research technique, ZMET, surfaces unconscious feelings. It begins with the premise that the reason customers can't adequately describe what they really want and value is because they haven't had a consistent communication bridge to their deeper emotional values and needs. For Zaltman, if 95% of what is going on inside the customer is unconscious and decisions actually *happen* before they are *made*, any research founded on mostly conscious rational thought is certain to have some major blind spots.

Auditing of experiences has to take this into account. Office Depot, for example, wanted to gain insights for developing better relationships throughout the store and around information technology products and services in particular. So Office Depot used in-depth Experience Reflection Interviews focused on uncovering the unconscious emotional aspects of the customer experience.

A consistent thread—and an unexpected opportunity—turned up around customers' technology experience. In the industry in general, research found that it is common for customers to feel talked down to and even put down when asking questions about computers and technology. The image customers used to characterize such interactions was of a stern, all-knowing parent talking to a child. In this context, parent-to-child language and conversation generated unconscious feelings of inadequacy and insecurity.

One of the essential findings of the Experience Reflection Interviews was that customers did not lump Office Depot into that category. Instead, the alternate image they used to characterize their Office Depot experience was of a young child helping a sibling cross railroad tracks. In stark contrast to the parent-child dynamic, the image of the siblings evoked feelings of helpfulness, trust, and partnership.

Office Depot used these insights in experience management efforts as well as store designing, staff training, and advertising. Relevant clues help communicate that Office Depot stores and staff are nonintimidating and trustworthy, and that no one will be put down for asking even the most basic of questions.

Staying on Target

The depth of insight that today's sophisticated interpersonal research techniques can yield is vital to gaining a deeper understanding of customers' critical needs and desires. They allow you to move past superficial reactions and top-of-mind associations to probe for the unconscious response *feelings* that an experience elicits. Don't stop your probing at a simple reaction. Keep digging for the critical emotional insights.

For Northcentral Technical College (NTC) in Wausau, Wisconsin, digging deeper in interviews provided a way to get at the role of lifelong learning in students' lives. Most of NTC's students have chosen to come back to school later in their lives (average age on campus is 33) to address specific goals, many of them career-oriented. Rather than simply something to do, these students see NTC as providing hope that can lead to lifelong benefits.

Such emotion-laden objectives opened the school's eyes to realities it hadn't previously appreciated. As NTC's administrators learned to see their college from the vantage point of experience and gained a heightened sensitivity to their student's Experience Ribbons, they were struck by how many trying conditions students were expected to endure.

Auditing can examine virtually any aspect of the way a business is currently doing business.

One of the most indelible was registration—an early experience that sets initial expectations and feelings that will be packed along to the classroom for months or years. With NTC classes on a first-come, first-served basis and registration hours limited, lines often started to form at 5:30 A.M. on registration days. And because it has a mature student body, it wasn't uncommon to see parents waiting in line with kids in tow.

It was a simple but meaningful "fix" to expand registration hours and computer interfaces. Adding a low-key children's play area to keep kids occupied was also an easy enhancement. But though the changes themselves appear simple, NTC's research shows they are having an immediate positive impact on the student experience that the college is providing.

Insights Through Communication

Auditing can examine virtually any aspect of the way business is currently done. Through the science of linguistics, studying communication exchanges can yield subtle insights that can have significant impact.

Dr. Charles Cleveland, who has developed text-processing software that compares the language of one context (or group) with another, cites this example to illustrate the differences in word context. [4]

Consider a car rental counter. People are waiting for cars. The counter staff is competent. Everything is routine.

Or is it? Little words can make a big difference. What differences do you see in these three simple statements?

- "I will have *a* car ready for you in five minutes."
- "I will have *the* car ready for you in five minutes."
- "I will have *your* car ready for you in five minutes."

Only one word has been changed in these statements. The word changes are very simple, yet each statement has a different emotional impact. The first conveys nothing definite: It could be any car, just as it could be *anyone's* car. The second implies that at the least, a specific car has been allocated to the customer. But notice that control of it has not yet begun to pass. The third example says that not only has a car been identified for this particular rental but also that, in effect, it already *belongs* to the customer. The only issue remaining is how long it will take to have it ready.

Little words can mean a lot, which means that being aware of the language that your organization uses can have a significant impact on how customers feel and what they remember.

Suppose that at the rental counter above, the employee had said "a few minutes" instead of "five minutes." What effect would that have had? From the employee's point of view, very little. From the customer's point of view, however, perhaps a lot. Five minutes has the exactitude of a promise. It conditions the customer's expectation of time and provides a clue to how proficient the experience will be. It also acknowledges that the customer is a co-creator of the value experience.

Obvious and Subtle

Back in the early 1990s, Ritz-Carlton Hotels made a very subtle adjustment in the way it wanted its people to connect with customers. Instead of saying, "You're welcome," Ritz-Carlton people from the front door to the housekeeping staff were encouraged to say, "It is my pleasure." The change reflected the character of the establishment as well as the expectations customers have in it.

For many years now, Ritz-Carlton has focused on creating an experience of "ladies and gentlemen serving other ladies and gentlemen." The clues woven throughout both the physical environment and the way the staff interacts with the clientele have been carefully managed to support that feeling.

Auditing experiences can reveal where to fine-tune the words your people use to bring better alignment and authenticity to interactions. A financial services firm recently explored the language effectiveness of its call centers. By monitoring several hundred random conversations between CSRs and customers, it was able to isolate words that conveyed information in the most user-friendly contexts for customers. After training its CSRs to use those words and phrases, customer satisfaction scores rose 12% for the company, and employee retention increased by over 20%. [4]

As Mark Twain put it, "The difference between the right word and nearly the right word is the difference between lightning and a lightning bug."

Audit the Full Spectrum

To repeat an earlier admonition, you can never and will never know enough when it comes to managing experiences. Customers change. Conditions change. The shelf life of knowledge in modern business is distressingly short. The more you know and the more you continue to learn, the better.

By auditing the full spectrum of its customer experience, Avis once again turned up an important fact for its subsequent experience designs. Like most rental car companies, Avis spent the bulk of its humanic training dollars on the people staffing its counters. But also like most rental companies, it had created and deployed automated systems that allowed many of its best customers to bypass the counter entirely and go directly to their cars.

The learning: The majority of Avis's training dollars were being spent to train the people at its rental counters. But the majority of the humanic interactions of its most frequent (and valued) renters were with its shuttle van drivers, the people on the lot with the handheld roving-return computers, and the security guards at the gates.

Those individuals' roles in the customer experience had never been fully acknowledged, let alone deemed important enough to devote very much training to. What attention they received had focused purely on function: how fast the roving-return operators could spit out a receipt, how thoroughly the security guards handled the paperwork before letting a car into or out of the lot, and the like. As a result, many of Avis's best customers were leaving the lot having had no contact with the counter people who had been so painstakingly trained in customer interaction.

On the basis of auditing its customers' experience, that has changed at Avis. Now, roving-return operators are trained to make sure customers have taken their bags, coats, and sunglasses; to ask whether there were any problems with the car; and to answer questions about flight departures and shuttle schedules. (Helpfully, their handheld computers contain flight times.) Meanwhile, security personnel are equally prepared to make sure customers know how to operate the lights and radio if the car is unfamiliar, can help them figure out how to open the fuel door or engage the cruise control, and can provide the directions they need to get off the lot and onto the freeway or into town with a minimum of trauma. Shuttle drivers announce where to go and how renters get their cars, then wish them well on their journey as they are returned to the terminal.

Auditing the current experience is the most critical discipline in creating the foundation for a full-featured experience management system.

Moving away from a traditional process focus, auditing helped Avis to identify and develop roles around the customer, then to educate its work force accordingly. It's the difference between making sure the contract is in order (process orientation) and making sure the occupants of the car leave the lot safely and feel in control (customer-back orientation). Customers perceive the difference, and so do employees.

For Avis, the needle on preference has been moving accordingly in both areas, The company has been recognized for the past four years as the brand with the highest customer loyalty in the car rental category, according to a rigorous annual customer loyalty survey conducted by Brand Keys.[1] And for much of that time it ranked number one in the closely watched J.D. Power rental car customer satisfaction study. In a 2002 article, Business 2.0 [5]noted that Avis has created its impressive record of brand loyalty, "certainly not by throwing money at the problem: it spent just $9 million on advertising last year—a fraction of Hertz's $53 million. Instead, [the company] focuses with single-minded intensity on how customers feel about each step of the car rental process and applies that knowledge to the day-to-day running of the company. Avis manages its customers' total experience from the moment they walk in the door until they hand in their keys at the end of the drive."

Avis also experienced a considerable increase in front line employee retention according to Ron Masini.

---

1. *Brand Keys Customer Loyalty Award, 2000, 2001, 2002, 2003, Brand Keys, 9 West 29th Street, New York, NY 10001; keys@brandkeys.com*

Expect More

Auditing the current customer experience is the most critical discipline in creating a foundation for the experience management system to come. This is because it reveals what your customers' deep needs and desires are and underscores where they are and are not being met in the current experience you're delivering.

Even for the most clue-conscious people among your ranks, this can be a life-changing undertaking. It also can be a culturally jarring experience for an organization. There's a definite letdown when discovering that the reality of the experience you think you have been creating doesn't align closely with the experience your customers actually need and desire.

In auditing, your priority should be less what kind of research you do and more what kind of discoveries you can make. Sometimes, like the treatment of infant seats at Avis, the unexpected insights that turn up are the most important outcomes of the effort. Expect the combination of assessing and auditing to have far-reaching effects as they help uncover insights into the needs and desires that customers find most meaningful.

With that perspective, you can begin to think seriously about designing experiences to fulfill the specific emotional and functional needs of your customers.

References

1. Gerald Zaltman. *How Customers Think: Essential Insights into the Mind of the Market*, pages 5-6 (Cambridge, MA: Harvard Business School Press, 2003).

2. Laurence J. Peter. *Peter's Quotations: Ideas for Our Time*, page 37 (New York: Morrow, 1977).

3. Ronald Masini, personal communication (2003).

4. Dr. Charles Cleveland. "The Little Words in Life," presented at the Distinguished Fellow Series, University of Toronto (April 2001).

5. Thomas Mucha. "The Payoff for Trying Harder," *Business 2.0*, pages 84-86 (July 2002).

9

THE DISCIPLINE OF
DESIGNING EXPERIENCES

Designing experiences is not new. From social settings to religious cere-
monies, and from architecture to entertainment, experiences have been
designed for centuries. But the concept of purposefully designing customer and employee experiences, with the discipline of blending clues
into a system that manages the value created, is new.

The discipline of designing experiences blends creativity with strategic
rigor, enabling experiences to connect on a customer-defined value in a
manageable and sustainable system. Clues are the heart of the system
that manages experience, and creating and integrating clues are at the
heart of designing experiences.

Illusions and Realities

Systems thinking is central to designing experiences. Each and every
clue must be meshed with other clues to form a mosaic that will be valued by the customer and that can be managed by the organization.
Clues cannot be thrown out in a tangle, like loose threads. Rather, they
must be woven together into a tight fabric that by its nature offers
greater strength and flexibility than any of the individual strands would
on its own. Knowing what an organization's capabilities are (as a result
of assessing) and what the customer's needs and desires are (as a result
of auditing), Experience Design requires a set of design filters that constantly aligns your efforts to maximize effectiveness.

Clues cannot be thrown out in a tangle, like loose threads. Rather, they must be woven together into a fabric that by its nature offers greater strength and flexibility than any of the individual strands would on its own.

As much as anything now on the planet, the Walt Disney Company theme parks represent a functioning experience management system. "Guests" are carefully integrated into a world in which mechanic and humanic clues combine to deliver meaningful experiences day after day, generation after generation. Not every inch or minute of Disney's experiential world is accessible to its customers, yet every aspect is engineered to create the Disney experience. In the Disney vernacular:

- *On stage* refers to the times and settings in which guests encounter the people, places, and things that add up along their Experience Ribbons to become memorable experiences.
- *Off stage*, on the other hand, refers to the parts and people of Disney that guests never see—from which, in fact, they are scrupulously excluded: the times and places where systems are maintained, where cast members get into and out of character, and where the park's administrative professionals work to keep the world outside the gates from intruding on the world within.

Through constantly maintained customer-back filters, the off-stage keepers of the Disney experience design integrate all of the on-stage parts. The on-stage experience is freshly painted and scrubbed, and hardly any detail is overlooked; off stage, dumpsters get dinged, materials get stacked, and people get sweaty, just as they do in the real world. But that is not the world that Disney's experience designers (imagineers) intend for guests to see and interact with.

From day one, Disney cast members—whatever their roles—are taught the importance of maintaining the difference. Off stage, you can be who you are in your everyday life. On stage, you are expected to be in character, whether that character is identified by an oversized Goofy costume or a broom and a dustpan.

Although some aspects of the Disney design are obvious, others go largely unnoticed. On Main Street, at the Magic Kingdom, and at EPCOT's World Showcase, buildings appear to be larger or smaller, closer or farther away, depending on where the guest is standing. On Main Street, the Disney core, the buildings are actually two stories high but are designed to look three stories high. It's a function of scale: The first level is designed at seven eighths of full height, the second is a little more than half scale, and the top level is a little less than a third of full height. [1] The buildings feel small but look large—the change in scale affects how guests perceive the "impact" of the building.

Disney uses buildings as Mechanic Clues to enhance what people are feeling. Main Street appears to be a bustling downtown mall but actually consists of only a few buildings in a small space. The path between the railway station and Cinderella's castle encompasses two city blocks, two squares, and two waterways, yet it is only 900 feet long. In addition, the street is narrower, and door and window openings are smaller than normal to enhance the intimacy and create an effect. That's especially important for children, who find the reduced size reassuring and easy to comprehend. [2]

Emotionally, the effect created is one in which large seems small, and guests feel more important as a result. For children, it makes the adult world seem smaller and less foreboding. For adults, it enhances the intimacy and charm of a place they may never have been. No single clue, considered by itself, is that significant. But once woven together, the design gains a power and coherence that transcends ages, languages, and other demographic differences.

Experience Design Practices

A systematic framework is needed in the discipline of designing experiences. The process involves five distinctive practices:

1. Build a Diverse Design Team

2. Drill Down to the Experiential Core

3. Focus on Clues, Clues, Clues, and More Clues

4. Develop the Experience Narrative or Story Line

5. Prioritize Experience Implementation Opportunities

Practice 1. Build a Diverse Design Team

Designing experiences is best mastered as a collaborative effort and will greatly benefit from a combination of diverse talents and perspectives. What's more, the use of a cross-functional design team helps encourage broad-range buy-in to an Experience Management System. Designation of the team leader or director is critically important. This person should be an experience champion in every sense of the word—someone with a full understanding and appreciation of experience as the value proposition; someone who actively and enthusiastically participates in the disciplines of assessing and auditing; someone with stature and respect within the organization; someone with passion. Once that leadership is identified, it's appropriate to establish the team.

In assembling a design team, the first question to ask is, Where will you find people who generate great insights and the most creative and disciplined minds? Within the organization? Among outside specialists and subcontractors? From a mix of insiders and outsiders? Successful teams usually reflect what works best in a particular organization's corporate culture. As a rule, however, diversity produces better results than homogeneity. Over some 20 years, I have seen design teams that have incorporated patients, students, customers, board members, industry experts, interior designers, architects, and ad agency personnel, as well as people from within the organization.

A team whose members have never worked in design or even worked together before can indeed develop a highly distinctive character. Some years ago, the Cadillac Division of General Motors assembled a special group that included Bill Booziotis—retail legend Stanley Marcus's personal interior designer and architect, widely respected for his planning and architectural design services for art museums and galleries—and Andrée Putman, an interior designer recognized for leading the minimalist "less is more" movement. Together we worked with Cadillac's own experience design team to pull together the clues, ideas, and concepts that best portrayed the notion of "art and science" in a retail atmosphere.

Some organizations have even used psychological profiling to assemble the team on the premise that understanding people's styles, emotional intelligence, and other factors increase the odds of successfully "engineering" a high-performance design team.

The most effective Experience Design teams include participants representing both mechanic and humanic perspectives and expertise.

Whether they come entirely from within or include external specialists as well, the most effective experience design teams include participants representing both mechanic and humanic perspectives and expertise. Inside your organization, you'll find qualified candidates at different levels and areas throughout the organization:

- Operations people bring a logistical perspective and a predisposition to thinking in terms of process consistency and reliability, which benefits the design of mechanic clues. Generally, they have a good sense of the reality and everyday challenges of implementation, as well as strong intuitive insights from being close to the customer in the field.
- Human resources specialists, whose jobs rely on an appreciation and mastery of people skills, are more likely to contribute a deeper understanding of the psychology of human nature. They tend to be more in tune with humanic clues and the emotional values of customers, as well as the needs of the organization's own people.
- Marketing and marketing research staff are typically sensitive to customer needs and desires and are practiced at building communications story lines that work in competitive marketplaces. Their efforts will become even more effective as they become more cognizant of the customer's Experience Ribbon and their evaluations of current experiences. Good marketers know how to encourage thinking outside the box to enhance the creative process.
- Finance professionals offer a resource-sensitive reality check and tend to appreciate the long-term economic value of customer loyalty. Their involvement can help you assign tangible value to the intangibles as they relate to customer value creation.
- Customer service specialists typically are close to the customer and can help interpret information on both customer accolades and customer irritants. They are more aware of the things an organization is doing that consistently impress customers and some of the things that exasperate customers and employees—those on whom the business depends for its very future.

Although eventual consensus is important, avoid believing that the team will benefit from having everyone on the same page all the time. What happens if the *same* page turns out to be the *wrong* page? There are countless examples of the fatal flaws in "group think" where the consensus leads to serious consequences. The most significant of these recently was the NASA disaster of the foam heat shields breaking off the spacecraft Columbia. Even as the shuttle orbited the earth and e-mails bounced from department to department, some expressing concern that re-entry could be fatal, complacency and fear of bucking the group's consensus thinking was the mindset—leading to disastrous conclusions.

Unless you encourage and allow acting on differing opinions and opposing viewpoints, you may not recognize some of the many false starts and blind alleys out there. You need people who can think individually and be bold enough to express their thoughts but who also can discuss, debate, and build on ideas as a group. Nothing stimulates the creative process more than a little dynamic tension.

Without a doubt, the most valuable "hidden" benefits to the designing process are the cross-functional viewpoints and energy brought to bear toward realizing one overarching goal.

Learning from Participation

One almost constant benefit of designing experiences with cross-functional teams is the way the individual personal benefits develop for participants. When exposed to customer-centric design activities, even people who traditionally see the business as purely functional and numbers-driven can become zealous and knowledgeable advocates of experiential value.

Exposed to customer-centric design activities, even people who traditionally see the business as purely functional and numbers-driven can become zealous and increasingly knowledgeable advocates of experiential value.

Ron Floto, the visionary CEO of a Florida-based grocery chain when it was an early adopter of managing experience as a value proposition, pushed to have one of the most skeptical and cynical individuals in his organization put on the design team. Having him intimately involved in the project nurtured a keen awareness of the power of experience—and this individual's conversion to an experience evangelist was remarkable.[1] By the same token, when the idealists and dreamers have a chance to spend some extended time with more detail-oriented colleagues with whom they seldom mix, they also often gain a greater appreciation for their perspective.

What size team will be most effective? There are no magic numbers or formulas, but between seven and 11 members comes close. Three to five members is probably too small or too narrowly focused to achieve broad-based critical mass. Once a group grows beyond 10 participants, it can start to lose productivity and become unwieldy.

Sometimes, of course, you will need to balance practicality with politics and include representatives of key constituencies. To keep everyone invested in the process, an oversized team will often function better if split into two parts: a larger group whose members participate on a periodic basis or take on more high-level issues and a smaller core team that can provide continuity and move things along day to day.

Practice 2: Drill Down to the Experiential Core

Once you have your design team, you'll need to ensure that members are fully up to speed on two high-priority areas.

- They will need a deep sense of clue consciousness—knowing what experience clues are and what they communicate to customers on a rational and an emotional level.
- They also must grasp the importance of understanding how customers desire feeling in the experience, which is the emotional end frame you hope to create so that they will keep their eyes on the ball.

Designing is less a matter of bold, broad brush strokes and more a commitment to creating and then managing individual experience clues that, when integrated, combine to deliver the desired emotional end-frame that will create preference and commitment. It's one thing to say, "Let's dazzle the customer" or "Let's delight the customer." You might as well say, "Let's give the customer a *supercalifragilisticexpialidocious*

---

1. I remember Floto wondering, "What in the world did we do?" after a meeting in which the individual in question had advocated—persuasively and with well-grounded experience reasoning—putting *a fountain* in a store, much to his CEO's surprise and the amazement of his colleagues.

experience." But saying it doesn't make it so, let alone make it meaningful to the customer and even more important, to employees. Employees need a clear and articulate understanding of the feelings their customers desire to experience. To deliver *supercalifragilisticexpialidocious*, you have to know what it means[2] and why that's significant from the customer's point of view.

If "God is in the details," as the world-renowned designer Ludwig Mies van der Rohe once noted, you're taking on a challenging task. For example, think about something as simple as the "correct" way to shake someone's hand. It's more than simply a matter of grip. Posture, eye contact, how long you maintain the grip, how much pressure you exert, what you say, how you perceive skin-on-skin elements (warm, cold, dry, sweaty, hard, soft), what you do next, and so on—all are details, and any and all can be significant clues in the overall encounter. Because clues are the atomic structure of experiences, no clue is too small or too insignificant.

It's also valuable for the leader of the design team to continuously manage the experience of the team members involved in designing the experience.

Defining Your End Frame

So where do you start? Start where you want to finish: Whether you have defined the emotional end frame in terms of an Experience Motif or are using some other technique for alignment and focus, your goal in designing is to generate clues that fit and will contribute to that clearly stated end frame. This is where an Experience Motif starts to prove its worth as a touchstone and guide to "true north." It represents a distinctive summary of the customer's deep emotional needs, typically in a creative combination of just three words that articulate the feeling customers desire.

It will be much easier to keep working sessions on track if the team always keeps the customer and the experiential end frame in mind. Each idea for an individual clue suggested throughout the design pro-

---

2. In case you are wondering, this is from *Mary Poppins* (Walt Disney: 1964). According to the Web site Gibberations+ (cyber-gish.com), it means "atoning for extremely delicate beauty while being highly educable."

cess has to be evaluated on whether it contributes or conflicts with that desired end frame.

The power of an effective Experience Motif is highly visible in the work done at the Health and Wellness Center by Doylestown Hospital in Warrentown, Pennsylvania. The Center's motif is "Understood, Strengthened, and Renewed."

Initially, the words the design team landed on were "important, healthy, and comfortable." But by drilling down deeper, the design team became progressively more focused on creating distinctive value and the words changed.

The differences in the words may seem subtle, but as the team found, they led to far more creative and distinctive outcomes. Which organization would you feel a greater bond to, one that left you feeling *understood, strengthened,* and *renewed* or *important, healthy,* and *comfortable*?

- Feeling *healthy* is a minimum expectation in medicine—albeit one not always achieved. Feeling *important* is nice for the ego, but what health benefits does it imply? Feeling *comfortable* could be a superficial state and may infer that the care provider is content to overlook your deeper, more serious health issues.
- But feeling *understood* says that the care provider has listened to you and engaged your health issues on your terms. Feeling *strengthened* means that you are in better overall health. And feeling *renewed* suggests that you are tuned up and ready to re-engage your world.

Pat Vida, Vice President of Health Quality Partners, Inc., one of the tenants in the Wellness Center and operator of its Health Design Center, saw the power of the motif in practical terms one day while working out on a treadmill, of all places. After a day of intense work in an experience motif facilitation workshop, in which the team had made the breakthrough of arriving at their three-word motif, Pat went to do her regular workout. She mentioned to the woman on the treadmill beside her that the Wellness Center had just created an extraordinary mandate to manage every experience clue toward support in making patients and family feel "understood, strengthened, and renewed."

Even if you know nothing about an organization, a strong motif can give you a visceral sense for the kinds of experience it has committed to deliver to its customers.

As she talked, she was startled to find that the woman had tears in her eyes as she listened. When Vida inquired whether something was wrong, the woman said that her mother had just passed away after a long battle with cancer. She told Vida that being understood, strengthened, and renewed was all that she wanted to feel and that she wished her mother could have felt that way during her cancer treatment. Right then and there, Vida knew the team had identified an extremely powerful tool for focusing their experience management efforts.

Even if you know nothing about an organization, a strong motif can give you a visceral sense for the kind of experience it has committed to deliver to its customers. On the inside, such a consensus-building alignment tool can have far-reaching ripple effects with the clarity it creates.

At Doylestown Hospital, the Wellness Center's motif cast the organization's vision statement in a new light. Previously, the vision was to "Create a world-class health care experience for the community." What exactly, or even approximately, makes a health care experience "world class"? And how operationally would that distinguish Doylestown from others? Today, the Center's vision statement is "to create unparalleled health and wellness experiences by understanding, strengthening, and renewing one individual at a time."

Vendors, independent contractors, and tenants of the Wellness Center have all been enlisted in the effort to deliver on the Center's motif. According to Bob Bauer, Doylestown Hospital's CFO and the visionary project leader for the Center, alignment around delivering customer values has led to great efficiencies and avoided some of the costly missteps that commonly occur in architectural design and construction.

Divide and Design

Just as in the art of cartooning, designing an experience starts with the end frame, then works backward, laying out the preceding panels that will lead the customer to the desired outcome. Having identified the emotional end frame, you can begin to address the specific clues involved in various layers or component parts of the experience. Knowing the end frame constantly reorients you to how the customer wants to *feel* at various points around the Experience Ribbon, as well as at the end, which helps you keep the design process on track.

The best way to manage a process that can be so wide-ranging is to break the experience into logical sub experiences and psychological pathways. Then you can create clues and clue clusters within and around each one. Since the goal of experience management is to systematically create emotional value for the customer, when designing, you must go beyond simply mapping points of interaction or process. A customer's experience contains multiple sub experiences, each created by the psychological pathways of what the customer is feeling. Each of these must be mapped. Once charted, the sub experiences and the psychological pathways are used as the context for clue and role development as well as language and behavior guidelines for the organization.

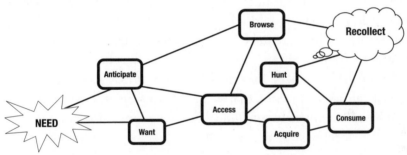

Figure 9.1 Illustration of sub experience or psychological pathways in the customer's mind.

The psychological pathway illustrated in Figure 9.1 is of a buying experience. For the purpose of this illustration, 9 sub experiences have been identified. Because the human mind does not think in a linear fashion, we must chart the many ways the experience of "buying" might organize itself from a psychological and emotional standpoint. Through this schematic we can see the different emotional patterns and determine which sub experiences to design around.

For Buick's Flagship dealerships, experience designers broke each aspect of the customer's buying experience into sub experiences and addressed each in turn. The experience of arriving at a Flagship dealership is the focus of one entire sub experience of the Experience Design, as are the experiences of parking, entering the building, financing, and taking delivery of a car at the dealership. For example, Buick's team put concentrated effort into the shape and profile of the facility, how customers would approach and navigate the location from a sensory and psychological perspective, and what humanic and mechanic clues they would encounter: where and how they would park; what they would see on the building's façade; what they would experience in the entryway to the showroom; what they would hear and be able to touch; and the look and feel of the windows, signage, and so forth.

Traditionally, for many organizations, Experience Design, inspired primarily by the designer's creative intuition, will be subject to criteria regarding cost, implementation time, and resource allocation. Effective experience design and management mandates value creation around what customers feel about the experience using a motif as a critical design filter.

Remember Avis and the infant seats? Looking at the issue of the cleanliness of its cars, Avis would understandably have focused on what was happening not in the rental office but rather out on the lot. By doing so, it would have missed the importance of what was happening along all stages of the customers' Experience Ribbon. It may seem random and almost capricious to think that seeing infant seats stacked on the floor could lead customers to conclude that there's something not quite right with the cleanliness of the cars. But it's precisely that kind of unconscious connection-making that makes taking a multilevel approach to design so mandatory.

For RBC Financial Group, Canada's largest financial services provider, focusing on psychological pathways, in what they refer to as the "customer corridor," has allowed designers to break the larger experience into such elements as anticipation, access, information exchange, and resolution. When RBC worked its way through experience design recently, each of these elements was addressed individually but always with an eye toward how they would impact the other psychological pathways and the desired emotional end frame. The foundation for these robust insights came from Metaphor Elicitation Research conducted by Innerviews, Inc., a licensee for ZMET research methodology in Canada.

> *You can't literally control what the customer thinks and feels about any given experience. But when you focus your efforts on creating clues there is a demonstrable ability to move the needle.*

Practice 3: Focus on Clues, Clues, Clues, and More Clues

Sooner or later, of course, it all comes down to clues. In the end, it's those clues customers absorb and digest that bond them to an experience. You can't literally control what the customer thinks and feels about any given experience. But when efforts are efficiently focused on centering all clues on the same customer-back emotional end frame, you will have a far greater ability to create consistent emotional value for the customer. Remember: Clues are sensed not just by seeing and hearing but also by smelling, tasting, and touching. Take creative advantage of all of these opportunities as you conceive your experience designs.

An organization that succeeds in effectively leveraging sensory clues along with strong humanics is a barber salon called Truefitt & Hill [CQ]. Currently, there are just three Truefitt & Hill shops in the world, but once experienced, you will not forget them. There is one in Toronto, Canada, another in the Bloomingdale's in Chicago, and the original in London. In England, Truefitt & Hill has been the official purveyor of haircuts to the royal family since Charles Dickens' time. In fact, each week, one of their barbers still goes to Buckingham Palace to cut Prince Phillip's hair.

When you're in Truefitt & Hill, you feel like royalty. The interior is designed in rich greens and furnished with antique chairs. The barbers wear starched white coats and bow ties and exude pride and knowledge in their craft. If you get a shave it will include at least nine hot towels, three passes with a straight razor and a facial massage. Everything, from badger hair shaving brushes to their signature scents, resonates with the sights and smells of barbering, not the utilitarian splendor of synthetic countertops, cleaning chemicals and take-a-number efficiency.[3]

As you proceed with the discipline of designing, a deft touch will be needed to nurture design teams in which creativity can flow—and sometimes play—freely. Idea-generation sessions should unleash rather than leash creativity.

There are countless ways to stimulate creativity in the design process. The green field perspective has been mentioned already: If you were starting over today with none of the accumulated baggage of past experiences to hinder your efforts, what would you do? Your design team might also find it productive to think about familiar aspects of your business in unfamiliar ways. If Disney, Mayo, Harley, or Krispy Kreme experience designers were represented on your team, what might they contribute? Stretching our strategic perspective to "explode" the depth and breadth of experiential perspective leads to interesting opportunities.

The University of Minnesota's Carlson School of Management broke new ground when they conceived an innovative clue-laden flagship experience program to help MBA students bridge classroom theory and real-life experience. Many MBA programs include competitive one-term internships for credit, but the school imagined the concept at an entirely new experiential level for students and the community. Ultimately, four student-run businesses were established—one in consulting, funds management; venture capital and small business start-up. Each offers two and a half semesters of real-business experience to students—as either money managers or consultants. Carlson now boasts the largest student-managed fixed income fund in the United States and the first student-run consulting business that has engaged with Fortune 500 companies as well as small- to medium-sized businesses. The enterprise has executed consulting contracts generating several hundred thousand dollars per year. The program itself generates a clue that students have real-world experience when they graduate.

Beyond encouraging fresh thinking in clue design, you need to make sure participants will see progress and understand the role and orientation of their efforts. Stimulate the ideas first. Worry about sorting them

3. A few years ago, with a few hours to kill before a meeting, I was wandering through Scotia Plaza in Toronto when I was attracted by a distinctive perfumed scent—one that was both inviting and reminiscent of the scents I recalled from the barbershops of my youth. I tracked it down to Truefitt & Hill. Even though I live in Minneapolis, Minnesota, I will time my haircuts around business engagements in Canada just to go back to that shop. And it is primarily the result of the great feeling of having a distinctive experience which left me feeling extraordinarily confident and absolutely connected—feeling really good about myself. Interestingly, my first Truefitt & Hill haircut was not a perfect one. Like the first haircut we get from a new barber or hair salon, the individual has to learn how we like it cut. My willingness to go back, however, despite a less than functionally pleasing haircut, reflects the way I felt emotionally—the clues provided by the experience surrounding the haircut overrode the functional clues of the haircut itself. I've been back again and again.

into usable and unusable categories later. If people self-edit themselves for fear of criticism, the design elements that result will tend to be safe and bland. The idea is to generate volumes of ideas first and narrow down the range later.

Sorting and Filtering

Inevitably, you will need to sort through and bring order to your clue generation. Designing experiences involves a number of activities to ensure that depth and breadth are being capably addressed with effective clue generation and evaluation. For example:

You can map sub experiences on one axis and clue design categories—such as humanics, mechanics, the different senses, or other organizing principles or criteria—on the other (Figure 9.2). As ideas are generated and then evaluated, they can be apportioned and mapped appropriately, so the overall effort can be scanned at a glance to quickly see whether there is consistent concentration of clues.

Clue Grid

	Anticipate	Want	Access	Browse	Acquire	Recollect
Humanic Conscious Unconscious Sight Sound Touch Taste Hear						
Mechanic Conscious Unconscious Sight Sound Touch Taste Hear						

Figure 9.2 Mapping Experience Clues on a grid.

- Clues can be refined and sharpened by applying filters such as the experience motif or special research insights. How does a given clue "sync up" with known emotional needs? Do some clues contradict one another or work at cross purposes? Do they sharpen the experiential focus or, like towel swans, miss targets in distractingly innovative ways?

- And you can continually challenge the team to identify enough clues that are truly distinctive, unique, or differentiated from what competitors are doing.

No matter how much you may be impressed by any particular Mechanic or Humanic clue, the real power in an Experience Design comes from weaving clues together that span the entire breadth of the Experience Ribbon and relentlessly probe for deeper emotional relevancy.

The emergency services department at University Hospital (UH) in Augusta, Georgia, experienced this after designing new signage based on their motif both inside the facility and outside. The value of the effort was underscored when a nursing candidate (a very valuable resource in the nursing shortage in health care today) completed an interview at a competitor's facility a few blocks away, then arrived at UH. Upon completing her interview, she reported that she knew she wanted to work at UH the minute she drove onto the grounds. When asked why, she said "Well, your competitor's ER sign read 'Trauma Center—Emergency Entrance,' yours read 'Emergency Care.'" Vice President George Ann Philips responded by saying, "Our experiential signage is doing more than giving directions. It's sending a message about who we are as an institution."

Creating and managing clues isn't about counterfeiting emotional markers that try to manipulate customers. Effective experience design is about determining how to elevate clues to resonate more powerfully and authentically. Whether you're designing a brand-new customer experience or redesigning an existing one, the imperative is the same: Eliminate negative clues, overhaul neutral ones to enhance and telegraph the emotional end frame, and create highly differentiated positive clues that reflect the same end frame.

Blueprinting the Experience

Bringing individual clues to life in a manageable system requires an understanding of what the pieces are, what feelings they are designed to create or reinforce, and how they integrate into the whole. A literal way to depict various clues, their place along the Experiential Ribbon, as well as illustrate their interrelationships, is to create a set of Experience Blueprints like the one illustrated in Figure 9.3.

Just like their counterparts in architecture, Experience Blueprints articulate the structural support system for what you are trying to build. They're a way to help the design team and the people who will have to bring the design to life and manage it over time to integrate clues into the daily life of an organization.

Experience Blueprints provide a robust and user-friendly style of visual storytelling, presenting the integration of clues as a system.

Developing these distinctive visuals provides a way to illustrate a wide range of sensory details. Figure 9.3 illustrates one exterior page from a hospital client's Experience Blueprint. Note the articulation of sensory and emotion-based clues even in an area of the experience generally devoid of those kinds of signals.

Experience Blueprints provide a robust and user-friendly style of visual storytelling, presenting the integration of clues as a system rather than a strictly linear flow of ideas. Illustrating clue designs as integrated schematics helps focus awareness on the wide variety of stimuli customers are sensing.

Experience Blueprints also provide an important orientation and learning tool as you spread experience management through your organization. In recent years as brain science has advanced, the way that businesses and educational institutions alike approach adult learning has become more visually sophisticated. Although most traditional education and training is still word-based, we now better understand that people don't all learn the same way. Some work best from verbal information, others from visuals, and still others from doing.

Experience Blueprints present an opportunity to literally "make clues tangible" in a way that leverages all three learning styles. As designs are firmed up and rolled out, and your design team begins to bring others in the organization up to speed, Experience Blueprints serve as a quick, direct, and effective way to show everyone what the experiential superstructure will look like. Updated periodically, they will continue to serve as a practical visual guideline for ongoing efforts.

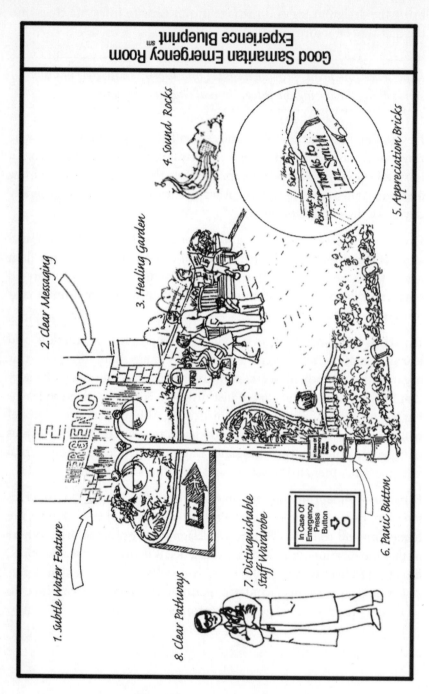

Figure 9.3 Experience Blueprint.

Practice 4: Develop An Experience Narrative

The discipline of designing also involves a specialized form of storytelling. Just as an Experience Blueprint helps people visualize the placement and positioning of clues, humanic roles describe characteristics and primary and secondary roles. An accompanying experience narrative tells a story of the entire experience, in detail from the customer's perspective. In story form, it relates how customers should feel and react because of the more emotionally defined physical clues and human encounters they will be exposed to in the new experience design. Jim Nortarnicola, former Chief Marketing Officer at Blockbuster International, found Humanic Roles and Experience Narratives helpful to both executive leadership and front-line employees. "Much of the value and impact of 'experience engineering' comes from getting the organization to see its work in a different way. The experience story and narratives allowed our executive leadership to visualize the transformation that experience initiatives would create," he said.

> "The narratives supported HR's efforts in helping store employees better understand their role in creating customer experiences. They allowed the traditional training generalist to see the employee's role as a dynamic one, freeing them from the constraints of a traditional HR view of 'job descriptions'."[4]

Experience Narratives lead naturally to explorations of the Humanic Roles that must be fulfilled in managing an experience Both narratives and role depictions are proven elements of stagecraft. In stage and cinema, actors often rely on a "bible" that defines important characteristics in helpful detail. Knowing the dimensions of the role helps them fully understand key characteristics critical to their performance. It also helps others relate to them in consistent ways throughout their performance. The vernacular of Disney is instructive in this regard. The world of Disney consists of cast members and guests. You're either one or the other. If you're a cast member, you have a role whenever you're "on stage"—Goofy is Goofy whether he's greeting guests on Main Street in the Magic Kingdom or taking part in the opening pitch ceremony at a baseball game. The context provides an experiential richness

---

4.   Jim Notarnicola. Personal communication, December 2003.

for both the individuals in the role and the customers who encounter them in the performance of their role.

Articulating Effective Roles

As part of its Buick Flagship design work, General Motors recognized that it had to prepare its people for roles with more definition and articulated characteristics in the new dealership environment: the role of a sales consultant, the role of a finance specialist, even the role of a person cleaning the cars on the showroom floor, among others. In some cases, new roles such as welcomer (note that it's not a "greeter") had to be created so that a greater sensitivity to how customers wanted to feel would be conveyed.[5]

The implications of people understanding what they do in the context of their role in a customer-focused experience are enormous.

Ed Petrowitz (then the national sales and service manager for the Buick Motor Division), who helped manage the effort, has a unique way of expressing the importance of articulating roles and the melding of mechanic and humanic clues. Noting that the auto industry had traditionally spent a great deal of time, money, and creative talent on improving the physical design of its dealerships but hadn't taken similar care to fuse clued-in roles for its people, he pointed out that it could be likened to moving the *Beverly Hillbillies* into the mansion. Employees were being moved into new surroundings without any knowledge of why certain experiential design choices had been made or how those choices would enhance their individual interactions with customers— much as the Clampetts remained oblivious to the purpose, esthetic design, and personal enjoyment that the "cee-ment pond" offered.

---

5. I remember attending a customer recognition cocktail party at Carl Sewell's outstanding Cadillac dealership in Dallas, Texas, and noticing that during the party, uniformed porters were actually cleaning the cars. If someone walked by and leaned on a gleaming quarter panel, their fingerprints had a life expectancy of about a nanosecond. Overzealous? Hardly. The people attending the reception were Sewell's customers and prospective customers. At the moment, no one was trying to sell them a thing. If Carl Sewell had people cleaning up at such an "off-duty" time, how could you not get the impression that cars were always treated like pieces of fine art at Sewall Cadillac?

Fusing Mechanics and Humanics

The implications of people understanding what they will have to do in the context of their roles in a customer-focused experience are enormous. Although reams have been written about customer service and the importance of human behavior, much of what has been missing up to now is the idea that these behaviors are part of a system that integrates both mechanic elements and humanic elements into a performance that the customer evaluates.

Consider the role of the *barista* at Starbucks. By definition, a *barista* is someone who has been professionally trained in the art of espresso preparation. In Italy, the job is given so much respect that the title is earned through proven skill and experience and is considered an honor when achieved. Starbucks has continued this tradition by ensuring that the role of *barista* encompasses far more than simply making coffee, waiting on customers, or busing tables. The *barista* orchestrates and celebrates the Starbucks experience for customers with enthusiasm, skill, energy, and flair. You can get a cup of coffee anywhere. The Starbucks experience is multi-layered from both a humanic and mechanic perspective.

By the same token, if you think about experiences that clang discordantly when you're the customer, how often is it because the individual you're dealing with slipped out of character? The health care provider who wouldn't take the time to listen to your symptoms. The car salesperson who tried to pressure you into the wrong model. The hair stylist who was more focused on personal problems than you cared to know about. The stereotypical gum-snapping, private-phone-call-absorbed counter clerk who couldn't be bothered to wait on you.

There's a valuable richness in understanding the distinctiveness of a role compared with mastering the straight skills and functions of a job. And it can be tremendously motivating for employees as they come to realize that they are being empowered to do much more than simply repeat a few rote-learned phrases and behaviors. They are encouraged and supported to deliver great performances.

For the experience-driven organization, defining and managing experiences in the context of roles requires fleshing out the characters involved, just as you would if you were directing them in a performance, then helping people understand what they must do to portray the fullness of their particular character. It's not something to be left to chance—any more than the cast of a performance will simply show up on opening night.

It follows that the nature and demands of the role involved must be woven into the company's selection, orientation, education, and training activities. Defining roles provides an essential form of clarity. Companies will have a better idea of the characteristics they need in new hires. And from the start, employees will take pride in knowing that their personal characteristics will have tangible impact on what they do professionally. That helps reinforce the authenticity and effectiveness of their performances.

Performing the Role

It is possible for people to perform more than one role in an experience. In designing, the trick is to resist defining roles rigidly for employees. Rather, role descriptions should guide their performance and consider how they will mesh with the environmental clues that you've determined will have impact with the customer.

The same basic role may take on different characteristics in different business settings. Consider the subtle differences between a greeter and a welcomer. The former is simpler, a largely mechanical role in which the emphasis may well be primarily on function (to say hello and maybe goodbye to customers). The latter, on the other hand, implies a greater depth of personal involvement in the customer's experience. It has elements of hospitality, comfort, care, and responsibility in helping customers navigate where they need to go in the organization.

Sales roles are often difficult to align smoothly with experiential values, particularly in industries where maximizing short-term volume has been given precedence over anything else. In the automotive industry, some organizations have decided to compromise. They've concluded that selling skills that have worked for their sales staffs in the past can't be totally scrapped on a moment's notice. Although they're expecting more attention to be paid to customer expectations, they're also being realistic about the established practices of their businesses and the time-honed skills of their people.[6]

On the other hand, some automobile organizations have said, "Here's where the long-term value is, and here's how we're going to expect our people to engage the customer." That's what Saturn and Lexus did. It helped that both companies started with a green field—customers had no previous experiences with the brand, so the desired experience could be created from scratch. But inevitably, many of its salespeople came from elsewhere in the industry and had to learn the dimensions of their new roles in the new setting, much like an accomplished actor learns to perform Neil Simon differently than Shakespeare.

Make Sure the Shoe Fits

The temptation will be to create idealized roles and expect people to bend and shape themselves to fit them. A more effective approach is to start by finding a fit between the role and the personality traits of the people who will have to fill it. Ritz-Carlton does this exceptionally well by having prospective co-workers interview job candidates. Because they already are performing in the roles, they know what's involved and often display a great deal of perception in judging who could or could not be a match-up to the demands.

Office Depot reinforces the conceptual side of the role it expects its store personnel to play through the simple device of nametags. Each frontline worker is now a CEO—a customer experience officer. The title encapsulates the idea that the role is one of actively managing each customer's experience, not merely answering questions when someone interrupts an employee who is stocking shelves. The nametags serve as constant reminders that everything they do should support how customers feel when they leave the store.

For some organizations, this may be a revolutionary concept. For many, it will be more of an evolutionary step. Either way, roles can

---

6. The problem was authenticity: How do you take a pack of wolves and turn them into sheep? They couldn't do it. They could, however, tone down the more aggressive behaviors as salespeople became better aware of the previously unremarked experiential dynamics involved. Roles need to be fused with the people placed in them and that in the employee education process, companies have to uncover ways for their people to discover the needs of roles without losing the authenticity of who they are.

serve as a kind of Global Positioning System for humanic behaviors by providing a reliable way for employees to constantly reorient themselves to the experience they're creating.

A final note on roles: Education is often needed for an individual to understand a role in its full depth and how the role fits him or her. Organizations are prone to view this as training, but education and people skills may be the more apt terms. As the late Stanley Marcus, the renowned retailer who guided Neiman Marcus for decades, emphasized, you train animals—you *educate* people. Skills can be trained, but behaviors are learned.

Practice 5: Prioritize Experience Implementation Opportunities

As both Mechanic and Humanic Clues begin to gain cohesion in your Experience Blueprint, you'll naturally start prioritizing implementation based on market opportunity and your organization's capabilities. Few organizations can do everything at once. An important part of the discipline of designing experiences is establishing priorities for eventual rollout.

An important part of the discipline of designing experience is establishing priorities for eventual rollout.

Consider an automobile dealership. Visitors wandering the showroom floor and the parking lots are primarily concerned with the gleaming models arrayed for their consideration—the products. If they were looking for a loaf of bread or a DVD for the weekend, they'd be somewhere else.

But parking cars in a building and posting people ready to pounce on customers around the periphery does not create a satisfying car-buying *experience*. Some customers need to wander and browse; look and admire; kick the tires and slam the doors; and interact with salespeople, support staff, mechanics, and even other customers at their own pace in seeking answers to their questions.

That's all part of the experience. All the senses are in play, processing the sounds of music, ringing phones, and animated conversations; the smells of new "leather" or old coffee; the condition, style, color, and texture of the furniture; the lighting; and the calculators, awards, and family pictures on the desks.

To design experiences, those clues should not be left to chance. However, a dealership that chooses to manage experiences needs to prioritize and decide where to invest first. For example:

- The smell of a new car qualifies as something close to an aphrodisiac for some people. That's a positive. No smell at all is a neutral. The smell of a pizza box from lunch is a negative. It's relatively simple to accommodate or eliminate such simple sensations in the design and management of experiences.
- A salesperson who can accurately sum up the pluses and minuses of competing models based on current information from *Consumer Reports, Car & Driver,* and Internet buying services most likely will be regarded as a positive. Someone whose energy level and personal interest seems stuck in low gear will come across as a neutral at best. Those who seem to have trouble answering a question in other than programmed and scripted sales-speak will earn negative marks.
- In many traditional auto dealerships, consumers feel like helpless prey. The desks are often placed around the cars like hunting stands, just waiting for the unsuspecting victim. And when the sale is made, a check mark goes on the sales scoreboard for the month, not unlike a set of antlers on display in a hunting lodge. Such dealerships might just as well put the sales staff in orange vests and waders so that there's no doubt of their role in the experience.

This is not an overstatement. Research validates that in such physical layouts, the humanic and mechanic clues have been so negatively created that they engender a very real emotional feeling of being hunted in the customer's unconscious. No wonder so many people find car shopping such a stressful experience. And no wonder that the repurchase rate in the typical dealership often is in the 30% range.

Experience Harmonics

Designing experiences begins with the customer and ends with the customer. When clues are aligned with the customer's known desires and emotional needs, distinctive experiential value is being created. When they're not in harmony, conflicts occur.

A common scenario that depicts this dissonance in call centers, for example, is telling customer service representatives to ensure that customers are treated well, to make the interaction more like a relationship than a transaction. Yet the primary measurement of performance is "talk time"—the average length of time that calls take. In an experiential context, the measurements must reflect the desired experiential value measure you want to establish.

Similarly, a grocery store chain may insist that it wants its cashiers to be more involved with customers, yet it measures their performance in terms of electronically tracked scans per second. This is not aligning employee performance measurements in a way that is harmonious with improved customer experiences.

When people are anxious or stressed and they're trying to interpret what they think needs to be done without the benefit of experiential direction and standards, the customer's Experience Ribbon will start to fray. When the organization, its employees, and its customers are co-creators of value, they're more likely to be working in harmony.

Designing experiences begins with the customer and ends with the customer. When clues are aligned with the customer's known desires and emotional needs, distinctive experiential value is being created. When they're not in harmony, conflicts occur and the value created is eroded.

Experience Management Systems span the spectrum from simple to complex. In many ways, it's like playing a video game: As quickly as you master one level, your improving skills immediately take you to more involved and challenging tests. But as you master each successive level, your system becomes increasingly robust and resilient.

Don't be reluctant to start at a basic level. But do start. Until you get in the game, you can't begin to build the skills that will lead to experience management systems that effectively connect with the breadth and depth of customer desires. Your customers will notice. And so will you and your bottom line, as a result of more fiercely loyal customers.

References

1. J. Pastier. "Architecture of Escapism: Disney World and Las Vegas," page 27, *AIA Journal* (December 1978).

2. Alan Stone. *Delusion by Design: Architecture and Manipulation at Walt Disney World.* Study project (New College, January 1993).

10
THE DISCIPLINE OF IMPLEMENTING EXPERIENCES

Managing experiences in a systematic way can literally open the eyes and change the mindset of an organization. You can feel the buzz. People at every level can see how powerful well-managed customer experiences can be in building customer preference and loyalty.

Dr. Robert Ernst, President of Northcentral Technical College (NTC) in Wausau, Wisconsin, explains, "I knew immediately when I first heard about managing the customers' experience that it would enhance the value, loyalty, and commitment our learners feel about the institution. The idea of managing experiences systematically is so logical and such a powerful source of value for the institution and its employees and students or customers. Yet it's seldom the focus of staff, faculty, and administration." [1]

Which brings up the real question: How do you actually make it happen? How do you implement a system that will equip and transform an organization to consistently manage the creation of customer value that is generated through experiences?

Experiential Leadership

Up to now, the focus of this book has been on gaining critical customer insights and understanding, then incorporating this knowledge into an Experience Design that integrates humanic and Mechanic Clues that resonate authentically with customers. The discipline of implementing brings the effort to life in the day-to-day operation of the organization in two ways. The first is concerned with embedding and integrating the Experience Clues throughout the customer's Experience Ribbon. The latter is concerned with the alignment and integration of organizational competencies and capabilities to manage the experience and fulfill the customers' needs and desires. Implementation can generally involve changes large and small throughout all levels of the environment, processes, promotion, and people strategies of the business.

It's common for people to prefer maintaining the status quo to the discipline that change requires. Change represents risk and the unknown. Change can be scary, which is why passionate, supportive, and involved senior leadership is a prerequisite for successful Experience Implementation.

Leaders can't make organizational change happen by themselves, but they can cause it to fail. Senior teams must demonstrate a clear commitment to experiential change so the entire organization can take cues from them. They must convey through the clues they emit that experiential transformation is a priority. Otherwise, the effort will be doomed to eventual stagnation and failure.

The leadership of any organization embarking on experience management implementations must have a solid grounding in the theory of experience management and an unwavering belief in the impact that experience can have on their organization.

In 2003, Blockbuster demonstrated intelligence, sensitivity, senior vision, and commitment to creating greater experiential value upon completion of a systemwide examination of the Blockbuster customer experience. Although the company's ambitious Experience Design and implementation initiatives will eventually be felt in all reaches of the company through a systemwide rollout, senior leadership realized that experiential commitment had to be nurtured and conveyed at the highest levels of the company.

Blockbuster's middle management was highly motivated, and their commitment was reinforced by the involvement and leadership of CEO John Antioco, President and COO Nigel Travis, Executive Vice President of Marketing, Merchandise and Concepts Nick Shepard, and EVP and COO North American Operations Mike Roemer.

Familiar Approaches: A Clued-in Team

Implementing the Experience Design means embedding the Mechanic and Humanic Clues that have been designed into an existing customer experience (or sometimes creating a new experience that did not previously exist) to create a more differentiated and valued customer experience. Once embedded, the clues must be supported by a system for continuously managing their integration and for constantly fine-tuning the total effort.

Because the implementation of clues is process-driven, and depends on more traditional project management strengths, organizations will find they have a natural propensity to apply energy in this area. The enhanced project-management skills developed in so many businesses and industries over the past two decades can be readily adapted for experience management purposes. But on a broader scale, there are still some challenges to be faced and new skills to be mastered.

The Team

The heart and soul of implementation, just as it was in design, is the team you put together to make it happen. Identify members whose skills, understanding and dedication are valuable for both the initial effort and the long-term management of the system. Even if you don't need them initially, you should also identify any outside resources your team may require. Finally, determine who should play the critical role of implementation team leader and ensure that the person you select has critical senior-level support.

Experience Implementation involves five broad activities:

1. Aligning resources and opportunities
2. Educating the organization
3. Orienting and immersing people in their roles
4. Rolling out the design itself and embedding Experience Clues
5. Establishing accountability and performance

Aligning Resources and Opportunities

A variety of resources—financial, human, and psychological—will be necessary to implement your design over time. Your first challenge is to plan the implementation realistically, accepting the opportunities and limitations imposed by the resources you have available.

When people "get religion," there's a natural tendency to rush right in and start painting with a broad brush. Beginnings have a way of immediately elevating expectations all around.

Good launches, however memorable, need to mature into sustainable systems and practices. There's no point ratcheting up expectations and trying to achieve new levels of performance that you can't sustain.

Focusing attention on high priorities and making sure everyone knows where the bar is being set help generate enthusiasm and put everybody on the same page. Some organizations have found it effective to create a Customer Experience Department and even to designate a Chief Experience Officer (CXO) to lead the implementation team and efforts. Giving someone the mantle of leadership conveys a sense that this initiative has high-level corporate support in the same way that the designation CIO testifies to the importance of information in modern business.

But good launches, however memorable, need to mature into sustainable systems and practices. There's no point ratcheting up expectations and trying to achieve new levels of performance that you can't sustain. Too many of your people have likely seen too much of that in recent years. Accept the fact that some continuing "experience evangelism" will be needed to permanently ingrain the approach in your organization.

In a way, you're attempting to restructure your company's genetic code. Up to now, people and processes have been programmed to operate in certain ways—and most of them probably have not placed a priority on managing all the various elements of the customer experience. Synchronously, by implementing the Experience Design, you are essentially working to produce a healthier, more experiential DNA for your organization to make it more genetically capable of creating and managing a more preferential customer experience.

To do that, you must spread this new operating code throughout the body of the organization, getting it into the nucleus of the cells where fundamental change will take place and nurturing that graft until it is accepted and becomes both self-sustaining and self-replicating. One of the roles of the implementation team is to be the "scientists" for change within the organization.

In the discipline of assessing, your organization gains useful insights into many of the global alignment issues within the company. These, of course, do not go away with the proclamation of experience as a value proposition. To the contrary, they challenge the team to make informed and prudent choices relative to the investments of time, effort, and organizational resources.

Operationally, one of the first activities for the implementation team should be the simple act of mapping all existing and planned major programs and initiatives across the organization, according to their potential impact on the Experience Design that you will be rolling out. It's best to know up front all of the forces currently or soon to be in place that can send conflicting messages, as well as those initiatives that may synchronize well with experience management efforts.

As you identify the most glaring misalignments and get the organization thinking about timelines for change, you will raise some provocative questions. Among them:

- How much of what we have been working on in recent years is geared more to short term and may actually inhibit building customer equity for the long haul?
- How many current and planned activities give employees an incentive for outcomes that may contradict creating experiential customer value?
- How many practices (even those at one time accurately labeled "best") have plateaued and taken on lives of their own, yet now have little relevance to creating a preferential customer experience?

As you move into implementation, it's time to resolve such conflicts to the extent that you can and create a more seamless alignment. As you do so, the good news is you should expect two positive outcomes. First, an enhanced sense of simplicity and natural momentum develops as overlaps are eliminated and the familiar spaghetti-like tangle of legacy programs is simplified. Second, identifying and eliminating duplication and off-target efforts may reveal "new" budget dollars and employee hours that become available to your organization.

Making the most of limited resources adds to the pressure to pick your spots carefully when moving into implementation. Reality suggests that most implementation efforts will need to be incremental, taking advantage of circumstances of time, place, and market opportunity.

Consider North Central Technical College (NTC). Established in 1912 in a small, two-story building as the Wausau Industrial School, NTC today offers more than 40 one- and two-year programs, many involving health care, through its Wausau hub and five satellite campuses in northcentral Wisconsin.

In 2005, a new Health Sciences Center will open its doors, tripling classroom space, doubling the number of graduates from the nursing school, and allowing the addition of a variety of new programs in new occupational areas, including cardiovascular technologists, medical assistants, respiratory care practitioners, and medical lab technicians. Rather than simply put up a new building to house these classes, NTC has chosen to use the new facility as a place to introduce a more experience-oriented approach to the adult learning it provides to 18,000 students (average age: 34+) each year.

At NTC, about a quarter of the school's 400 full-time employees were involved in the school's experience assessing, auditing, and design efforts. Initially, teams focused on the design of the new Health Sciences Center as well as the need to revamp registration procedures, but preliminary clue-scanning exercises took place all over campus. After teams visited the school's bookstore on half a dozen occasions, the bookstore manager became intrigued enough to make inquiries on his own—and ultimately volunteered his operation as the third phase of NTC's Experience Implementation. As the Health Sciences Center came online and registration processes were fine-tuned to be more experientially satisfying, a new team was formed, and the bookstore experience became the next target of experiential opportunity to be addressed.

Sometimes, the scale of an experiential implementation will be dictated by competitive circumstances. At other times, it may involve a circumstantial opportunity.

Sometimes, the scale of an experiential implementation will be dictated by competitive circumstances. At other times, it may involve a circumstantial opportunity.

One of North America's leading diversified financial services companies, RBC Financial Group (formerly known as Royal Bank of Canada) is Canada's largest financial institution as measured by market capitalization and assets—and one of its most respected brands. With 60,000 employees, it provides personal and commercial banking, wealth management services, insurance, corporate and investment banking, and transaction processing services on a global basis for more than 12 million personal and business clients through offices in North America and some 30 countries around the world.

As it charts its course through the early years of the twenty-first century, RBC is working to build enhanced experiential relationships based on better fulfilling individual customer needs at different stages of their lives: as singles, young marrieds, young families, parents dealing with college funding needs, and active seniors. Toward that end, RBC has been delving more deeply into understanding customers' needs and values at each life stage while also laying a foundation for transitions to later stages.

To succeed, RBC realizes that its people must grasp that the Experience Clues to establish value will change as the customer's life stage evolves. So RBC is working to broaden and deepen its creation of experience designs that will resonate with customers at different stages of their lives while proving to be operationally manageable—and profitable.

For Bremer Financial Corporation, a much smaller, regional, privately held banking institution headquartered in St. Paul, Minnesota, the focus was on immediate needs. Bremer may one day aspire to the same level of system-wide implementation as RBC. But for the time being, it has chosen to implement and align experience designs for one impor-

---

tant if sometimes overlooked target audience—its own employees. About 300 of them are now working in a new operations center that opened in late 2002 in an outer-ring suburb of St. Paul. The old center was originally designed to accommodate less than 90 employees. But nearly 175 were shoehorned into the old center when the new center was commissioned.

Believing that customers would not notice an experiential difference if the employees with whom they interacted didn't have a good experience, Bremer opted to put a concerted effort into designing the experience its operations and training staffers have.[1] The investment wasn't free. Measured strictly in dollars, it may have added 3% to the cost of the facility. But the results of the investment are expected to become measurable over the life of the facility, with payoffs involving not only more proficient customer transactions, but also greater employee retention.

Educating the Organization

An important challenge in implementing an Experience Design is delivering the specific people strategies that support implementation. This requires embedding an appreciation for the value of experience management and experience design into the DNA of the organization. Companies that "bolt on" experience programs without thinking through and planning their approach to changing organizational behavior will find that their efforts will fare poorly.

Many change efforts fail simply because the elements needed to sustain the change—the new DNA—are not integrated into the heart and soul of the organization. Despite the best of intentions, simply painting the new DNA onto the outside of the cell wall in superficial ways that don't penetrate won't survive. Big meetings and bright banners without relevant concepts for the people side of experiential transformation are sure to disappoint. Unless and until the DNA of experience management is spread throughout the organization (Figure 10.1), even the most promising efforts will produce only fleeting benefits.

1. "Customers won't feel it if the employees don't," explained Executive Vice President and Chief Information Officer Grenville Blackall during a guided tour of the new facility in early 2003. "We feel the quality of the customer experience comes from the quality of the employee experience."

Infuse Experience Into DNA

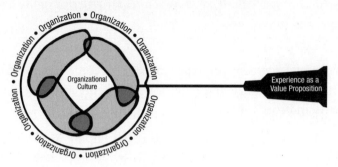

Figure 10.1 Infuse experience into the organization's DNA.

Committing to improve the customer experience demands that you make sure you can deliver on the promise. It's easy to underestimate what it will take for your organization to *truly* sense and respond to customers. Traditional command-and-control leadership can't make it happen, and traditional training can't teach people how to do it.

A framework I've found for strategically addressing the people changes associated with experience management is a perspective we developed with my colleagues, Erika Andersen and Jeff Mitchell.[2] The key is to drive the transformation to an experience management system on three levels: vision and strategy, leadership, and skills and knowledge.

Vision and strategy are the outward manifestations of the new DNA, and it falls to leadership to incorporate experience values into them. Earlier, the idea of an Experience Motif prompted you to try to sum up the way you want customers to feel in three meaningful words (to the customer). Now set those words side by side with words that articulate your brand values. The closer the alignment between the expressions, the deeper the experiential DNA has already started to embed itself in your organization. The wider the gap, the more nurturing you'll likely have to do in order to sync the organization with customer experience value.

---

2. Erika Andersen and Jeff Mitchell, principles with Proteus International, Inc., have been instrumental in strengthening Experience Implementation tools and approaches. Proteus is a certified partner of Experience Engineering.

Experience management principles need to become basic elements in all visioning and strategic thinking, as well as being reflected in mission statements and core values.

Experience management principles need to become basic elements in all visioning and strategic thinking, as well as being reflected in mission statements and core values.

Leaders who have spent time and effort developing an organization's current vision and strategy may be surprised to learn how they might be altered to support a customer experience outcome more powerfully. The process of creating an Experience Motif itself and comparing it with values very often can unfreeze such resistance.

A common pitfall in implementing experience designs occurs by not educating up as well as down to help leaders become increasingly aware of what's at stake and how important it will be for them to truly get out front and lead the changes required.

At RBC, the concept of managing the total client experience came squarely to the forefront almost five years ago while a marketing team was working on a North American branding effort. Under the leadership of Anne Lockie, Executive Vice President, Marketing and Sales, Judith Hatley, currently Senior Vice President of Client Experience, RBC Royal Bank, and Shauneen Bruder, currently COO of RBC Investments, the team began researching the gap between the experience customers desired and the experience being delivered.

In the 18 months following their initial work, Hatley worked tirelessly with others to enlist the support of the bank's top management in closing the gap. The response from the management council—and particularly from Jim Rager, Executive Vice President of RBC Banking, and Gordon Nixon, the CEO and Chairman of RBC Financial—took tangible form in the creation of the Office of Customer Experience, with Hatley named Senior Vice President of Client Experience, and given responsibility for leading one of the largest and most widespread efforts RBC has ever undertaken.

Every critical management area now is deeply engrossed in enhancing the RBC experience on a broad basis, and "superior client experience" has been adopted as one of RBC Financial Group's strategic priorities across all operations. When senior management put its backing behind focusing on the client experience, the initiative moved to the central core of the customer value proposition.

To prevent company leaders from becoming unwitting impediments to the new experience management system, they must know how to make experiential perspectives visible day to day—--in the way they speak to employees, in the way they act to support the big-picture changes, and in the way they reinforce the actions and commitment of people throughout the organization.

It's more than a matter of lip service. Actions do indeed speak louder than words: Others will take their cues from what they see leadership doing, not simply from what they are saying. Leading by example, those at the top must clearly demonstrate their commitment to and belief in the value of experience customer value creation and its contribution to competitive advantage and company performance.

At the Buick Division of General Motors, senior leadership realized early on that if middle managers weren't fully grounded in experience management disciplines and involved in the process that was to create Buick's customer experience, extending the concept into the hearts and minds of frontline employees would be impossible. As a result, Buick's initial Experience Education focused on middle managers, who in turn were charged with coaching dealers and monitoring their ongoing individual efforts when the actual design was rolled out.

Employees, for their part, face an immediate and continuing learning curve in building experience skills and knowledge. If they don't fully understand the experience management system—what it is, why it's beneficial to the customer and the organization, and how it can make their own jobs more interesting and rewarding—then the best the company can hope for is that they will simply comply with what's being asked of them. Behavior born of compliance feels hollow to the customer. Commitment is the only reliable standard for delivering an honest customer experience.

That starts with comprehending the benefit of doing something, grows as the individual feels capable of doing it, and is eagerly supported when employee behaviors are reinforced for doing it well. How employees feel about themselves and how they experience *their* experience performance is a vital element in the discipline of implementing.

It follows, then, that experience-based performance requirements are essential aspects of recruiting and selection; education, coaching, and development; job aids and support systems; managerial and supervisory practices; and employee incentive programs (Figure 10.2). That may call for significant revisions in everything from job descriptions and definitions of core competencies to performance reviews and employee communications and compensation.

Performance Requirements

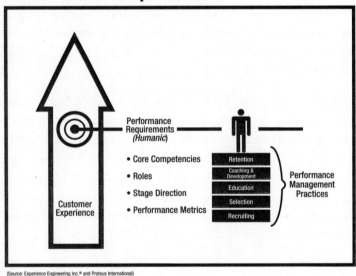

(Source: Experience Engineering Inc.® and Proteus International)

Figure 10.2 Experience value leverage performance requirements.

At Bremer, managers found they needed to do a little experiential evangelism when they asked their people for input on the design of their workspace in the new operations center. Accustomed to making do in a facility intended for less than half as many people, employees wondered just how serious the organization was about using their ideas. To defuse that concern, Bremer recruited "experience captains" who were representative of all of the levels and job functions in the new center and made sure they understood the experience principles and potential benefits at work. Not only did that unleash a flood of input, the way that input was adopted subsequently became a fixture of the new environment—a "Spirit Committee" was created that now works to "keep an eye on the clues" in the new location and keep everybody up to date on progress while also looking for ways to inject energy and encourage camaraderie in the experience for those who have moved to the bank's new suburban location.

In the numbers-oriented RBC Financial Group culture, bankers and financial services people displayed predictable skepticism at first. Leaders of the organization's wide-ranging experience initiatives have spent time to educate bankers and support staff on the importance of understanding how clients wish to *feel* in the interactions they have, not just the financial measures they will use to gauge success.

The results from pilot efforts at RBC have been very impressive. Kathy Haley, RBC's Vice President of Client Experience, says the newly designed and executed problem resolution experience quickly proved itself a success. If, for example, a problem can't be resolved for a client immediately, RBC employee teams now create a "commitment document" for the client that states the problem, the action being taken, and a specific timeline for when the bank will get back to the client. Spurred by a greater understanding that clients need to feel a tangible sense of control and action when they encounter a problem, the document has become a significant clue in redesigning the problem resolution experience. According to Haley, "RBC has leveraged key language and behavior clues we believe will build lasting loyalty. And we're seeing the results in customer satisfaction scores in the pilots." [2]

Orienting and Immersing People in Their Roles

Traditionally, employees have defined their actions on the job in terms of the functions involved—a viewpoint that is actively and passively encouraged in the way they are managed, referred to within the organization, and even compensated. An important step in making the transition up the line from commodity, product, and service to an experiential value proposition is helping people understand that the roles they play in the customer experience are every bit as important as the functional aspects of what they do.

This becomes considerably more critical because of the systems-driven, sense-and-respond nature of experience. On an assembly line, you can train someone to put component A into subassembly B; experiential value as sensed by the customer may never show up on the radar. In service settings, greater acknowledgement has been made of the customer's perspective, but even here most businesses have reduced the behavioral elements to functional or mechanistic process: Make eye contact, smile, find out what they want, fulfill the need, and for goodness sake, tell them to have a nice day. In many service models, if you ask someone to describe the last customer they dealt with, could you count on obtaining a meaningful description?

As people learn to align their efforts with both the rational and emotional needs of their customers, and to perform their jobs as roles, there is genuine opportunity to build strong customer preference. This begins with understanding the dimensions of authenticity in performance of a role as illustrated in Figure 10.3.

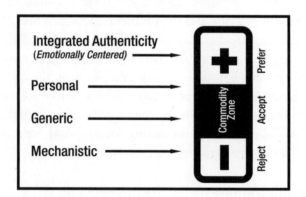

Figure 10.3 Experience Performance Dimensions.

All the clues generated in design sessions can and should be seen in the light of employee roles. An Experience Blueprint offers a way for people to see them within a schematic vision of the intended conceptual Experience Design. An Experience Clueprint moves the perspective from conceptual to a more tangible world, detailing specific clues in terms of the senses involved, implementation specifications, cost ranges, ownership, and other aspects.

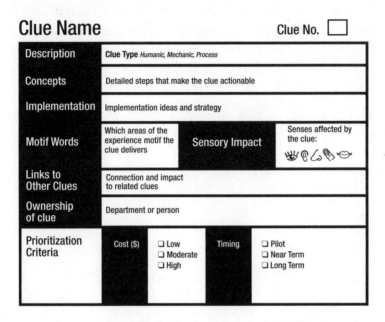

Figure 10.4 An example of a clue in an Experience Clueprint.

Both Experience Blueprints and Experience Clueprints capture Mechanic and Humanic Clues. Full definitions of Humanic Roles, Role Characterizations (Humanic Narratives), and Experience Narratives provide comprehensive descriptions and specific scenarios that illustrate how the Experience Designs are made actionable. All these tangible tools help orient people to their roles in implementing and systematically managing the experience on a continuing basis. Beyond that, experientially designed education activities can hone specific skills and create strong alignment both initially and as implementation efforts proceed.

At NTC, the experience team took the concept of clue categorization and rollout one step further by creating a comprehensive database posted on the school's internal server. This enables all members of the Experience Implementation team—especially those with ownership of clues that depend on simultaneous implementation of other clues—to check on progress, day or night.

Human Resources has a vital part to play in implementation. Incorporating Experience Blueprints, Experience Clueprints, role descriptions, and narratives into employee orientation and recruiting and interviewing will help identify potential employees who have a bias toward creating the desired customer experiences. Appropriate changes in the words and images that appear in recruitment literature and the inclusion of experience-focused customer interactions—either simulated or actual—in the interviewing process are critical.

For both new and existing employees, implementation of Humanic Roles will impact all phases of the human resources function. Humanic Roles will act as an effective integrator for employee recruiting, orientation, education, and development opportunities as well as incentive programs (Figure 10.5).

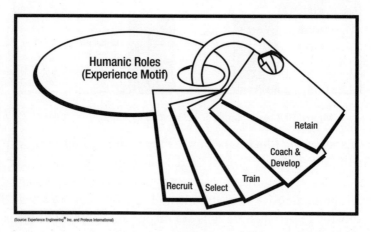

(Source: Experience Engineering® Inc. and Proteus International)

Figure 10.5 Humanic roles as an integrator of human resource systems.

Because experience management represents new ways of thinking and new disciplines, watch out for a common pitfall—allowing instructor quality to be the "weakest link" in the people side of Experience Implementation. Even if the curriculum design is good, educational efforts can still fail to bring about the desired change in employee behavior if instructors are insufficiently skilled as facilitators or don't fully understand the importance of the experiential concepts or skills they're trying to transfer. Make sure instructors have the skills and understanding to develop the people skills that fit the nature of the experience designs you are implementing.

Rolling out the Design Itself and Embedding Experience Clues

Putting the actual design in place can sometimes feel anticlimactic. In some cases, there may be a scale of change so major that customers need to be oriented to it, but often clues can be deployed in low-key ways and allowed to build incrementally.

That doesn't mean that the scale of design and implementing won't quickly reach ambitious proportions. Bremer, for example, started on a small scale in terms of opting initially to implement experiential designs only in the new operations center. But the variety of clues progressively woven in ranges from the simple to the subtle.

For starters, the X-shaped building itself is divided into four color-coded themes, the names for each chosen by the employees who work there:

- *Meadow* for customer-contact areas (most contacts occur over the phone, but ample clearings are provided for face-to-face interactions).
- *Machinery Hill* for mechanical areas, including those where automated systems generate bills and customer account statements (the name comes from the popular location of equipment displays at the Minnesota State Fair).
- *Forest* for operations and filing activities, many of which involve paper.
- *Summit* for the training center, where employees prepare to scale even greater heights.

Employee workspaces are designed so that they can be customized to some degree by their occupants and feature computer workstations whose desks, screens, and keyboard heights can be adjusted to suit individual preferences.

For Thrivent Financial for Lutherans, a diversified financial services firm created by the merger of Lutheran Brotherhood and Aid Association for Lutherans—two once-adversarial and highly competitive membership associations—the blending of formerly separate identities into a unified whole has presented both a challenge and the opportunity for implementing new experiential designs. It's a "green field" chance to show customers what the new entity looks and feels like.

Previously, local offices of the two separate organizations displayed little similarity—not only between the offices of the competing businesses nationwide, but even within the respective organizations. That's changing. A new network of more than 30 regional financial offices was consciously designed to provide consistent clues to the experiences available within.[3]

Customer-Back Implementation

The Rehabilitation Institute of Chicago (RIC) has been recognized as the "Best Rehabilitation Hospital in America" since 1991 by *U.S. News & World Report*. [3] No other specialty hospital has been consecutively top-ranked for so long. Kristine Cichowski, RIC's LIFE Center director, had a sense that the institution's services affected far more than patients alone. Families and care providers also were customers, she reasoned, which made their experiences significant and their input important.

Therefore, a couple of years ago when RIC began development of a new LIFE Center (the acronym stands for Learning Innovation Family Empowerment), she tapped this important source for input on developing clues that would contribute to the new enterprise's success. As part of auditing for the Center, interviews with over 250 people with disabilities, their families and health professionals were conducted and the insights were brought to bear on the way that both the physical and the virtual elements of the new LIFE Center facility would be designed and implemented.

One important insight turned up by Cichowski's research was that patients and their families wanted their physical and virtual experiences to mesh. A clue in the virtual world should have the same meaning as one implemented in the physical plant. Consequently, the LIFE Center's Web site is aligned with the way the physical space in the facility is designed, and clues are embedded there in ways that correspond with clues that patients and their families will encounter at RIC itself.

3. As Cliff Habeck, Thrivent's Vice President of Corporate Real Estate, told us, "An individual who stops by one of our offices should have the same experience, regardless of the location: the same professional feel, the same comfort level, the same service orientation. We think the designs we've chosen will provide a sense of acceptance for members, no matter which organization had served them in the past."

For example, there are by design no hard angles or lines in either place, a significant clue for people accustomed to being constantly aware of snags and obstacles that impede their access. The effect, both real and virtual, is very comforting and inviting, and it contributes an embedded clue to the services that the LIFE Center makes available. Online (http://lifecenter.rehabchicago.org), visitors have access to more than 3000 pages of material and can find links to more than 600 agencies and resource organizations. At the real-world site, which opened in August 2003, the same natural colors and smooth surface treatments make patients and visitors feel equally welcome and comfortable.

Building Designs in

No experiences may be more real and challenging than those in the emergency care unit of a hospital. On August 29, 2003, a little over six years after its first experience management efforts, University Hospital (UH) in Augusta, Georgia, celebrated the grand opening of its new facilities.

UH's emergency department serves more than 75,000 patient visits a year. Through the dedication of Dr. Richard Ekert, Medical Director, and George Ann Phillips, Director of Emergency Services, and the entire staff, the hospital has been working to enhance both humanic and Mechanic Clues for years. But it wasn't until the recent completion of the new facilities that the complete experience design, originally articulated in 1997, reached full implementation.

Throughout planning and construction of the new facility, the team stayed focused on the experiences and feelings of patients and their families. But given the chance to transfer experiential insights to their fullest impact, the new Emergency Care Department was seen as an exceptional opportunity to create a more complete customer-back experience that would support the overall Experience Motif of "making a reassuring, empathetic connection."

One example of this execution was the Pediatric Emergency Care Unit. Here, experience designers considered three potential Experience Designs, but they didn't consider themselves qualified to make a final decision. Instead, they presented them to a true panel of experts—the children of the department's staff—asking them to pick the one that most made them feel reassured and connected.

The top choice, "being inside a treehouse," translates to a secure, empathetic feeling that has been portrayed throughout the department and even the community, and has been enthusiastically embraced by both patients and families, according to Cindy Lundsford, Vice President of Community Affairs. Patients are greeted by a stuffed dog mascot named Jack, complete with black tie and a UH identification tag. In short order, Jack has become something of a local celebrity: A scrapbook records his travels; he appears in countless pictures with patients; he can be seen on pins with his likeness; and he is featured on murals in the examination rooms, complete with paw prints.

The uncompromising dedication to what even the smallest patient feels has become the focal point of a relentless passion. Once UH's team members got clued in, they stayed tuned in, successfully building new and richer experiences on top of established ones.

The discipline of implementing experiences includes not only the clues in the design but also a system of accountabilities that essentially become a commitment management system.

Establishing Accountability and Performance

The discipline of implementing experiences also includes establishing accountabilities that essentially elevate the system to a commitment management system. Encouraging feedback is basic to helping the system evolve. So setting up feedback loops and communication is critical.

As people work their way through the implementation of an Experience Design, there will be a constant need for dialog: to share their thinking, to document their growth, to problem-solve around obstacles, to celebrate their victories, and continually focus on the experiential end frame.

At the Health and Wellness Center, by Doylestown Hospital, in Bucks County, Pennsylvania, the familiar axiom of plan-do-study-act has been tweaked into plan-do-*learn*-act. It's a constant reminder that there's more to feedback and effective communication than simply circulating information. The object of the exercise is to try to use the feedback constantly in improving efforts on behalf of customers.

The prime mover of that approach is Pat Vida, Senior Vice President of Strategic and Business Development for Health Quality Partners, a consortium based in Plumsteadville, Pennsylvania that provides health care quality improvement, health education, public health, and care management in eastern Pennsylvania. Vida has long had a sensitivity to the value of experience as a teacher. Back when she ran Doylestown Hospital's emergency department, she used to set the stage for performance evaluations by having nurses and other staff members go out and lie on a gurney for 15 minutes or so. The objective was to focus on aspects of the patient experience they wouldn't ordinarily sense from their own busy—and upright—posture. After seeing blood in places they shouldn't have seen it and hearing things they never suspected patients could hear, even the most highly focused came back with a new appreciation of the clues being emitted.

To keep experience designs and implementation strategies fresh, an important level of communication needs to be coming continuously from customers, from prospects, even from competitors' customers.

It Runs—Now What?

The underlying principle of any Experience Management System is accountability. Having gone to all this trouble, implementing experiences is not something that can be left to a committee or team. It must become part of the fabric of the organization, with clear lines of accountability to focus on customer-backed based objectives.

And that creates the final, critical test of Experience Value Management as a source of long-term competitive advantage. If you think about implementing experience as a form of strength training, the real payoff for the effort is not in the initial flurry that breaks a sweat. It's in the long-term effort that steadily builds strength and capability. The more weight the more to be lifted, the steeper the incline, the harder you must work—but the greater the payoff will be.

So, too, is the effort required with Experience Management Systems. The organization's increasing experiential stamina and strength begin to create increased confidence. As the results begin to snowball, the challenge evolves into one of system management and growth—making sure the good work launched after so much effort is not left to atrophy or become yet another "flavor of the month."

The long-term test will be to foster a sense of stewardship that will keep the experiential approach evolving and on target. Moving beyond the immediate changes to resilient, long-term organizational practices and strengths is the final step in the transition to total commitment to an experiential value proposition.

References

1. Robert Ernst, personal communication (June 2003).

2. Kathy Haley, personal communication (August 2003).

3. "America's Best Hospitals," *US News and World Report*; July 1991, page 21; June 15, 1992, page 81; July 12 1993, page 66; July 18, 1994, page 54; August 12, 1996, page 52; July 10, 1998, page 65; July 19, 1999, page 72; July 17, 2000, page 75; July 23, 2001, page 44; July 22, 2002, page 66; July 21, 2003, page 51.

11

THE DISCIPLINE OF STEWARDING EXPERIENCES

There's a great sense of ongoing responsibility in the word *stewardship*, which makes it an apt choice to describe the remaining discipline of the practice of experience management. The root word, *steward*, can be traced back to the fifteenth century, where it meant not only a ship's officer "in charge of provisions and meals," but also a trusted and powerful agent in a noble house who acted as a sort of general manager of the lord's manor or castle to keep things running smoothly.

As an experience management discipline, stewarding isn't simply a matter of monitoring and measuring. Neither is it a new twist on the familiar tenets of quality management, although it fosters and embraces continuous improvement. It implies a high level of forward-looking leadership to evolve experiences to create ever-increasing levels of value for the customer, which in turn, returns ever-increasing levels of value to the organization.

Understanding Experience Harmonics

Think of the discipline of stewarding experiences from the perspective of the conductor of a symphony orchestra. The experience that the orchestra delivers is far more than notes on paper or instruments played particularly well. It reflects the way the conductor has rehearsed the personnel resources available for the acoustics of the hall in which the performance will be given, highlighting those performers with real strengths, minimizing the weaknesses of instruments whose players are not as adept and polished, and creating for a broad spectrum of listeners an experience that reflects the creative spirit of the composer in uniquely memorable ways.

A virtuoso conductor can spice up or tone down any part of the system (the musical score) at any time but can maintain stability, staying on track as the piece progresses to create and build an emotional connection with the audience. The performers take their cues from the conductor, managing their specific roles in the context of the greater whole. For the performance to succeed, the entire system and all of the performers in it must be in sync—their instruments aligned, their talents focused, and their energy and efforts neither overwrought nor wasted.

Conducting requires knowing how each part of the orchestra can function (in an idealized sense) and will function (in a realistic sense). It means staying sensitive to any hint (clue) of dissonance, any single note that might detract from the end frame. It requires noticing but moving past the inevitable momentary misplays, never letting such lapses deter or deflect the passion of the performers or the attention of the audience. When the emotional connection is validated by a thunderous, spontaneous outpouring of applause, everyone involved knows that the system has connected and met its objective and reason for being.

Afterward, of course, it's time for the conductor to review the performance, then to get everyone ready for the next performance.

Stewarding experiences will challenge you to continuously examine not only the effectiveness of the experiences you have implemented but also the way they have been integrated throughout the Experience Design.

In an Experience Management System, every individual is a miniconductor, helping to steward the experience which combines various talents and resources in front of an attentive customer audience. Stewarding experiences challenges organizations to continuously examine not only the effectiveness of the experiences that have been implemented but also the way they have been integrated throughout the Experience Design. You will need to constantly update your organization's knowledge of how customers are processing their experiences. How are they interpreting clues? Is perception of the experience achieving simply a commodity-level result or generating real preference? How can you better support your people and the customers with whom and for whom they are working to create ever-more-valued experiences?

Once your perspective shifts to optimizing the customer's experience and the clues that resonate with them, you will never again personally "experience" in the same way. From the vantage point of enlightened clue consciousness, you may find, in fact, that an experiential frame of reference becomes a constant filter in everything you do. Go to your children's school programs or sporting events, and you'll notice that you're thoughtfully judging what's happening around you in the context of your experiential expectations as a parent. Go on vacation, and you'll start sensing systems that do or don't engage your emotional expectations for R&R.

Don't think of this as the curse of clue consciousness because it is truly essential to stewarding. How great would a conductor be if he or she didn't have a deep appreciation for a variety of musical pieces? Clue consciousness is a very good thing. The more conversant you and others in your organization become with the dimensions of experience management in other contexts, the greater knowledge and insight you can bring to your individual roles and responsibilities. In short, the more "experienced at experience" everyone becomes, the more experiential the organization can be in the way it creates value.

In some respects, it's fair to characterize experience management as a virus. Once you are exposed to it, you become a carrier—even if your organization proves initially resistant to its effects. But far from looking for an antibiotic to knock it out, the more others are infected, the more your organization stands to benefit.

The long-term success of an experiential approach to customer value will depend on making stewarding experiences part of the culture of the entire organization. You can't leave it to a committee of just six—or sixty. Experience management needs to be an integral part of *everybody's* job.

Experiential Learning Quest

One of the most important and far-reaching implications of the discipline of stewarding is the commitment to continuous learning that it involves. It's central to an adaptive enterprise model, one that is continually sensing and responding to changes in customer needs and desires, surrounding market conditions, employee attitudes, the communities being served, and tools and approaches that would enhance your experience management competencies.

An airplane provides an appropriate metaphor. Getting the discipline of stewarding airborne is an important event, and its takeoff calls for maximum effort and concentration of all the systems and people involved. Keeping it airborne, by contrast, takes on a different and distinctive degree of intensity—that of routines that can be deceptively simple in their outward appearance but ultimately dangerous if they lure the inexperienced or unwary into a sense of false security.

The systems of the airplane itself are, of course, built to prevent this as much as possible, and pilot training also stresses the need for constant attention to the tiniest details. Just picture the instrument panel in the cockpit. Dozens of sensors constantly sample and read out data on all the different variables that must be successfully managed to keep the plane in safe and stable flight. Larger and more intricate flying machines require more elaborate and complex in-flight instrumentation.

As your experiential efforts shift in similar fashion from the high-stress environment of takeoff to the innocent-appearing calm of extended flight, you will need to develop a pilot's sense for the small, often innocent-seeming changes that can signal everything from simple issues needing attention to very real danger. Toward that end, what kind of instrumentation is in your cockpit? What readouts are constantly in front of you to tell you how things are going? And how reliable are those displays?

A pilot would be foolish to take a compass bearing once and never check it again or neglect to monitor fuel consumption, wind speed, weather conditions at the destination, and the presence of other traffic aloft. As you steward your organization's experiential output, you need to be checking readouts constantly to keep your experiential value creation on course.

The commitment to continuous learning needs to be made on two levels. First, you need to keep learning about experience management in general because the science is in its infancy, spurred by the evolving sophistication of new techniques and tools and by lessons learned from today's fledgling implementations. That doesn't mean you should wait instead of trying to get your own first experiential efforts off the ground. It just means that you can expect many more tools to become available to help you raise the efficiency and effectiveness of the experiential value being created.

Second, stewardship also requires a commitment to continuous understanding of the full breadth and depth of the experiences your customers are having—not just with you but also with competitors and pacesetters in other fields. As the old axiom advises, a rising tide raises all ships. Federal Express and UPS changed the standard reliability expectations of the customers of the U.S. Postal Service just as surely (and profoundly) as Domino's 30-minute delivery guarantee set off ripple effects throughout the service economy.

The clues your customers place in the positive zone today may someday be neutralized, becoming basic expectations that not only no longer provide competitive advantage but eventually become minimum thresholds to be met by anyone with ambitions of competing for long-term customer loyalty.

Sensing and Responding

Stewarding experiences involves four different but related learning activities on both the macro and micro levels:

- *Measurement*, of course, means determining the changes over time that the experiences you've instituted have made on customer value and advocacy. Are customers spending more money, time, and mindshare with you? Are they recommending you to friends and associates? How strong is their commitment to your brand? Do they relate their experience to the emotions expressed in your motif? The experiential metrics you started thinking about during assessing and auditing must be fine-tuned and finalized as your "measurement panel," serving the same function of a pilot's cockpit instrument panel. However, we must go beyond that to understand the total value of experience.

Often executives are concerned about measuring the effect and impact of "the experience" because it feels softer and more intangible. The opportunity experience management presents is to understand the relationship between cause and effect. Most measurements today are based on effect—customer retention, average purchase amounts, complaint resolution rates, unit sales changes, etc. The opportunity experience management presents is to start to understand how they correlate to the feelings and emotions Experience Clues create, the customer perceptions connected to the Experience Motif (the emotional end frame), and the degree of commitment and advocacy customers have for your business. Taking attitudinal, behavioral *and* emotional measurements (Figure 11.1), and analyzing the correlation between them, provides robust opportunities to understand critical cause and effect relationships that organizations often ignore.

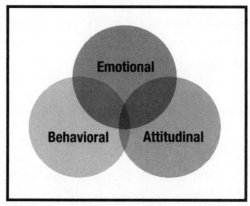

Figure 11.1 Analyzing the correlation provides experiential insights.

- *Monitoring* challenges you to continue to observe in the context of emotional value and experience. You'll find that you can use many of the same tools and competencies you relied on in assessing and auditing—and the results you'll now obtain from them will be even more meaningful because of the foundation of basic learning you've established. In addition, as new tools and skills evolve and current ones are honed, you'll be able to expand your efforts to fill in the subtle details that can lead to major advances.

- *Learning and Refining Intuition* tests your commitment to challenge even your most basic assumptions (see Figure 11.2). As increasingly sophisticated monitoring tools and competencies evolve, an even greater onslaught of data will result, that can induce a sense of analysis paralysis. By making your experiential end frame or motif, a touchstone of your analysis, you'll find richer and more relevant insights because of the consideration for the customer's emotional value that it brings.

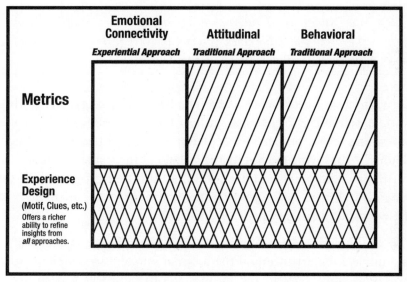

Figure 11.2 Understanding the relationship of cause-and-effect between attitude, behavior, emotional connectivity, and Experience Design.

- *Adapting* is the ultimate challenge. From what you're seeing around you as you're measuring, monitoring, and learning, how can you consciously evolve your experience management system? The goal is to improve the way you deliver on your organization's experiential value proposition

Unless your Experience Management System stays in sync with the way customers are processing and evaluating clues, you run the risk of missing the target of building long-term preference and loyalty.

Stewardship Scale

Just how broad-ranging are the responsibilities that fall under the heading of stewardship? Let's return to Doylestown, Pennsylvania. The Village Improvement Association (VIA) of Doylestown is nationally recognized as the only women's club to own and operate a community hospital. Fourteen women were present at its first meeting back in 1895. More than 400 members are active today in VIA's "third century" of service to the community. The VIA was the guiding force behind the founding of Doylestown Hospital—all eight beds of it—in 1923; these days, it owns and oversees the operations of a diverse and vigorous 500-bed medical complex.

Unless your Experience Management System stays in sync with the way customers process and value clues, you run the very real risk of missing the target of building long-term preference and loyalty.

Throughout its history, the VIA has emphasized looking forward while working to achieve the original goals of the association, which include promoting "every proper means of improving and beautifying Bucks County," "improving the health and welfare of the residents," and "supporting a community hospital and other health care facilities for the benefit of all persons." Each year, members rededicate themselves to these commitments originally made in 1895.

The Health and Wellness Center was completed in the spring of 2001 and marked the expansion of the hospital into a nearby rapidly growing community. Beyond the business motivation was a deep-seated determination by Doylestown's management to continue to make a positive difference in serving the community's modern health care needs. To bring that determination to life, they focused on the integrated experience that the Center could deliver to patients, their families, and the community at large. On the evidence to date, the effort is succeeding on a remarkable scale.

The mandate was to create a distinctive health care experience that would integrate traditional medical services with specialized retail, wellness, and fitness services. As realized in the Health and Wellness Center, this means incorporating medical specialties such as cardiology, orthopedics, dentistry, day surgery, and women's diagnostics with a full spa and fitness center, an interactive learning center, a restaurant, and a bookstore.

The result is a one-of-a-kind health care experience: an integration of clinic, health club and spa, laboratory, restaurant, diagnostic center, along with interactive individual health design services. Patrons just as frequently visit the Center for their daily workouts or to browse the bookstore as they do for outpatient surgery, a diabetes check, or an annual mammogram.

In a field as beleaguered as health care, can an experience-based focus make a difference? Measurements of both dollars and customer feelings say it can and does. Benchmarked against other high-performing health facilities in the national Press Ganey patient satisfaction survey, Doylestown's Health and Wellness Center ranked third of 357 facilities in its first year of operation. [1] The Center scored in the ninety-eighth percentile in overall satisfaction and in the ninety-ninth percentiles for "sensitivity to patient needs" and "explanations given by staff."

Meanwhile, the health design services—many of which are on a fee basis and not covered by insurance—have become one of the most popular offerings of the Health and Wellness Center, with hundreds of customized health designs generated each month. In the same time frame, Doylestown's Health and Wellness Center has well exceeded not only its base financial plan but also the stretch financial plan for revenue and contribution every month since it opened.

Getting Clued In

The results being achieved by the Health and Wellness Center are anything but an accident or a fluke of nature. The hospital's management made a conscious choice to get "clued in" literally before turning the first shovel of dirt for the new facility, and it has continued that theme as the Center has come online. According to CFO Robert Bauer, "We knew that unless we linked everything together holistically, we were at risk of becoming just a mall of health-related businesses, each doing their own thing." [2]

In short, systems-thinking about experiential value was mixed right into the foundation of the facility and the way it is staffed and managed. From the outset, Doylestown went beyond business models and architectural drawings to probe for clues to every facet of its target market's emotional needs and expectations.

- Its in-depth auditing of the nature of health care delivery throughout the country, including far-ranging interviews with the Center's intended customers, provided deep and valuable insights into not just the functional medical needs, but also the emotions that surface in patients' encounters with health care.
- Designers worked hard to fully absorb a multifaceted understanding of the emotional needs that patients, families, and community members would be bringing to the Center.
- Implementations painstakingly followed the design created to meet those needs all along the Experience Ribbon.
- Now, research consistently shows that treating the patient psyche as well as functional medical needs is resulting in better long-term health outcomes—and higher preference levels—than simply addressing medical symptoms alone.

This being health care, there was no honeymoon period. Prominent among the findings of the initial audit was a disturbing insight, although not a surprising one. People felt that in the practice of medicine today, the demands of the medical process almost always take precedence over patients' emotional needs. Based on years of experience, patients—not just in Pennsylvania, but nationwide—we have learned patients feel that the systems and people deployed to serve their needs too often favor *internal* system efficiencies and conveniences. On the basis of the clues they encounter when they come in contact with various aspects of the modern health care system, patients consistently say that the *caring* too often comes up short.

Words and Meaning

During the design process, the findings of the audit, combined with regular internal strategy sessions, led to the development of an Experience Motif that focused on making sure patients and their families feel "understood, strengthened, and renewed" throughout every interaction with the Health and Wellness Center. Thus, the distinctive architectural and landscape design reinforces rather than conflicts with the motif.

The Health and Wellness Center's Experience Design was created from more than 200 Experience Clues. As a result, the Center connects with patients' deeper emotional needs in a variety of conventional and unconventional and/or conscious and unconscious ways:

- A 25-foot interior waterfall and pond
- A unique stone and wood atrium surrounding the waterfall that serves as a central and communal gathering point
- Seasonal healing gardens that surround the building, complete with meditation benches, music, and a healing labyrinth walk
- Availability of Internet hookups, overstuffed chairs, and library-style newspaper and magazine racks throughout the atrium
- A fully stocked bookstore and lending library centered on wellness and linked to the leading recommended Web sites on disease management and wellness strategies
- A full-featured fitness center and spa that provides support to cardiac and orthopedic rehab patients, as well as to the public
- Health design nurses whose sole role is to help consumers create a customized health plan, then to mentor and help monitor their journey
- A guest database (as opposed to the conventional patient database) that maintains individual profiles and, based on information people choose to provide, includes details on the activities and habits beneficial for their age, weight, and physical status, as well as potentially detrimental activities
- Special computers in the spa and fitness center to enable downloading a patron's profile and medical information to assist in creating a truly customized fitness program
- Numerous seminars, symposia, and community events built around health and wellness that include everything from living with diabetes to the principles of Feng Shui (Incidentally, the building design is Feng Shui-compliant.)
- Mammograms and blood pressure checks available without an appointment

- Use of silent pagers so clients can wait for appointments or test results in the atrium, gardens, restaurant, or fitness center rather than being confined to a designated waiting area, however comfortable it may seem
- Educated staff behaviors ranging from voice inflection to gestures, all designed to reinforce the Experience Motif

At Doylestown the decision was made to design and manage experiences that engage patients on multiple levels and serve their needs in multiple ways. The Experience Implementation that resulted was a central component in the planning and development of the facility, and it has continued to serve as an operating blueprint.

Linking metrics to the motif assures that measurements are germane to the indispensable touchstone connected to the emotional as well as the rational elements of the experiences being provided.

To build a long-term base for continuing evolution and improvement, the Center developed a set of Experience Metrics focused on how customers feel about themselves during the experience, as well as how they feel about the people and services with which they interact. These metrics gauge how effectively the motif is being facilitated. Linking metrics to the motif assures that measurements are tied to the indispensable emotional touchstone that drove design and implementation.

Experience-Driven Culture

Ongoing measurement and learning is a significant part of maintaining and enhancing the value of the customer experience. For Doylestown, not only are customer barometers tending upward as the experience design proves its value, but the knowledge of what underlies those efforts is deepening, as well. After just six months, performance measures and motif values of the Health and Wellness Center compared with the overall Doylestown operation showed marked differences:

- Measurements of how well patients feel understood: 9.7 in the Center, compared with 9.0 at Doylestown Hospital in general.
- Measurements of how well patients feel strengthened: 8.6 in the Center, compared with 7.8 in general.

- Measurements of how well patients feel renewed: 8.2 in the Center, compared with 7.7 in general.

Based on national norms, the overall satisfaction scores are excellent. More importantly, the returns from the Health and Wellness Center show a statistically significant difference that is being clearly perceived by customers of the total Doylestown complex. The Center will continue to study the long-term significance of the distinctive experience and its relationship to patient outcomes.

Beyond that, the process of continual probing and fine-tuning has yielded its share of surprises. When the motif was first articulated, those involved in the effort made assumptions about what the terms would mean to patients and their families. In a number of cases, additional learning has fine-tuned some of those perceptions or added subtle shadings that have been integrated into the system.

For example, research has found nearly a dozen supporting feelings that connect to the basic motif value of being "understood"—sometimes in unanticipated ways. The original expectation was that being listened to would be a substantial element of being understood. It wasn't. Instead, patient responses made it clear that being listened to was a given; what elevates the feeling of being understood to a true preference-builder is having a chance to discuss health care findings in meaningful terms and arrive at customized care plans. Listening, in other words, is just a foundation, a commodity. The real payoff comes from listening in order to develop personalized responses.

Similarly, teams originally figured that making patients feel "special" would be an important part of the motif value of feeling "renewed." Special, however, turned out to be little more than table stakes. The higher correlation that research validated was *optimism*. People wanted to feel that they could actually do something to improve their health. The passive feel-good stuff was okay, to be sure. But the prospect of achieving active results was what really made an impact on the preference model.

Start Where You Want to Finish

This intense focus on the motif as the key focus of the experience serves as a gyroscope for the continuous reinforcement of the Center's emotional connections with patients and family. The Experience Motif has provided an extraordinary context for evaluating the effectiveness of the Doylestown experience and weighing all of the elements involved. It also serves as an ever present filter for everything the Center does, from promotional efforts and the creation of special programs to the placement of chairs and tables.

No single clue provides the magic for a distinctive experience that will be preferred by all customers over all other alternatives. Instead, the real benefit comes from stewardship of the layering of clues in the integrated design to support the Experience Motif. Everyone knows—and is constantly reminded in the organization's educational and communication efforts—that it's the *cumulative* effect of the customer's takeaway feelings that will energize and revitalize Doylestown's future.

CFO Robert Bauer sums it up this way: "I know we've succeeded when, after experiencing the DHWC, people say 'I've never really *felt* that way about a health care experience before' versus 'I've never *seen* anything like that before.' That's how we'll know we've made a significant difference in the community's health and well-being." [2]

Where's the Conflict?

Stewarding can help surface conflicts and misalignments on many levels and in many different places in an organization. The most common areas for diligent investigation are:

- *Global Misalignment:* Conflicts with the customer's needs and desires can occur in global strategic thinking as represented in the company's reason for being, mission statement, vision, or values statement. All of these important strategic tools should be in alignment with each other and aligned with customer experience value.[1]
- *Interdisciplinary Misalignment:* Many conflicts occur when a discipline or area within a firm becomes disconnected with the customer and isn't thinking customer-back. Many Customer Relationship Management programs run off the tracks because they aren't aligned

with technology and what the technology enables the company to do for the customer; worse, what the customer *really* values wasn't aligned with the technological capabilities.[2]

- *Interdepartmental Misalignment:* Often, multiple efforts within different departments in an organization send conflicting signals to both customers and employees. That creates conflict. Have you ever received two offers from the same credit card company that seemed to be in conflict with one another, or have you been told one thing by a salesperson, only to have a customer service rep appear to come from another planet, let alone perspective? Clearly, no one is stewarding internally to make sure everyone is on the same page.

- *Program Misalignment:* The number of company programs that broadcast conflicting signals within an organization are innumerable. Such conflicting signals can create anxiety for employees and ultimately affect the customer's experience. A major car rental firm realized there was a huge difference between up-selling customers to purchase additional insurance or larger vehicles, compared with sensing and responding to customer needs and encouraging the purchase of additional insurance and larger car upgrades in that context. Upgrading based on a specific customer-driven outcome resulted in greater confidence, peace of mind, less cramped conditions—it not only increased the effectiveness of the experience, but it also enhanced how the customer felt about the company.

Disconnects occur because of a lack of clarity, communication, and understanding. Companies that have learned to leverage experience as a value proposition find that stewarding that value is a continuing concert.

---

1. I remember seeing a mission statement for a hospital that cited as its goal, "providing world-class medical care to the community," yet I couldn't get a clear, common definition of "world-class care" from any of the executives. Even more surprising was the range of answers I got from people in the organization when I asked what they thought customers wanted to feel like after a visit to the hospital. No two answers were the same from the seven executives I asked. No wonder there's misalignment and conflict.

2. Armed with CRM technology, for example, some organizations became "life-event" driven, thinking they'd establish a relationship with me. I now suffer from "birthday relationship glut"—I receive many offers around my birthday in the month of October, from restaurants to my insurance and brokerage firms. The commoditization of these birthday offers are not only mechanized and routine, they create real anxiety and stress. I now have to collect the "gift" of a free desert or appetizer, a free night's stay, a skipped loan payment, or whatever.

On a Role

A milestone in the transition from Experience Implementation to Experiential Stewardship often will be found in the evolution in the way people in the organization think about what they do. Seeing themselves as stewards of customer value creation through their performance is a significant transformational shift in their mindset. At that point, you're onto something. In fact, the people in your organization, particularly those who interact with customers, are the true owners of the experience creation. But you must be prepared to remain relentless in the clarity, focus, and commitment your organization brings to the customer experience.

An important step in making the transition up the line from commodity, product, and service to an experiential value proposition is helping people understand and truly believe that the roles they play in the customer experience are every bit as important as the functional aspects of what they do. They must be constantly encouraged to fulfill their critical roles in the context of creation of value for customers.

Long-Term Considerations

An additional aspect of stewarding is keeping clues crisp and focused. Those who attempt to analyze humor note a central and critical fact: A significant part of what makes something funny is the element of surprise. The second time you hear a joke, its impact isn't the same, is it? The humor in the situation may still bring a smile, but you already know the punch line, so the payoff isn't as powerful as it was the first time.

That raises a challenging but relevant question: Do clues lose their effectiveness over time? Do they in essence wear out? Some very well may. What makes clues click is a complete understanding of the value being created in the total experience and the impact of the clues involved on that cumulative effect. Over time, you may notice a form of experiential erosion or abrasion. As the extraordinary becomes ordinary, customers may indeed begin to take a given clue or cluster of clues for granted.

In some cases, however, you'll find ways to hone a new edge on clues that appear to be dulling over time, much in the same way that retuning a radio may bring in a station clearer or defragmenting a hard drive may help the computer run faster. In other instances, your customers—as co-creators of value—may lead you up the value scale to new clues. If you're not constantly evaluating and monitoring, things can start to pull apart without your even knowing.

Ten years ago, for example, doing business on a Web site was a relative novelty. Today, it's commonplace for many customers, yet unexplored territory for others. Consequently, customers coming to a site for the first time may react more positively to certain clues than those who are frequent visitors. From your constant monitoring efforts, you need to learn how different subsets of customers are experiencing these clues, then adapt the clue configurations on your site accordingly.

When you look at organizations that clearly had an edge but lost it over time—Howard Johnson, Dunkin' Donuts, McDonald's, even Disney—the reasons for the decline often trace back to not monitoring the experiences and Experience Clues they were providing in the context of changing environments and customer needs. In effect, they were not effective stewards of their experience value proposition. When conditions began to change—and old, comfortable assumptions became subject to some doubt—they didn't sense the shift and consequently didn't take timely action to realign their experiential connections with new, more current expectations.

By the same token, renewing focus on the customer and refurbishing the customer experience energizes old names to take on new luster. Krispy Kreme, today considered a pacesetter, languished competitively for many years—the company was founded in 1937! So, too, did Harley-Davidson, which recently celebrated its hundredth anniversary on a roll that would have been inconceivable 20 years ago.

Finally, it's important to note that there's an important difference between stewarding and stew. In a stew pot, all the ingredients tend to cook down, losing their individual flavor. The result can be truly synergistic—a pleasing combination of disparate parts. But if your customers are looking for something with a little more tang or bite to it, they won't be happy with your recipe.

Nothing in this discussion should lead you to believe that you need to compromise your own uniqueness in the name of some kind of blenderized norm. There is a significant distinction between a service model and an experience model. Not every experience has to have a smiling face, happy attitude, and gracious demeanor—in service, homogeneity of experience is a bona fide risk.

Experience management means understanding the emotional underpinnings and psychological aspects of an experience and how people relate to it. There may be no better example of this simple but essential tenet than one of my favorite restaurants.

In Boston, Durgan Park in the Quincy Market has an almost cultlike following. Yet for first-time visitors, the experience it provides can be almost disorienting in the way it turns every supposedly hallowed assumption of dining hospitality and traditional perceptions of customer service on its ear. Durgan Park's response, the wait staff isn't trained to flash a painted-on smile and attempt to evoke a counterfeit form of familiarity with a bland introduction. Actually, they're more likely to insult you.

That's right—insult you. Salty, crusty, cranky, even nasty—all of those labels and more have been applied to the restaurant's unique way of taking care of customers. Durgan Park's response is likely to be, "Guilty as charged—what's it to ya?" What's more, the connections created feel genuine, authentic, and in a strange sense, entertaining. This restaurant has been there *forever*—since the Revolutionary War, in fact. It's advertised as the restaurant your great-grandfather went to.

Uncle Pio, remember, was with the A&P—the once-great Atlantic and Pacific Tea Company—for more than 35 years. He loved that company for most of those years with a sense of "button-popping" pride. By the end, however, he almost loathed it. It's a familiar story. A once-honored company stagnates. New blood comes in. Out with the old—wholesale and general housecleaning—even getting rid of the innovators, the risk-takers, and the ones who feel more comfortable being out there with the customers than they do being stuck in a meeting with "the suits."

After dedicating his life to the A&P, Uncle Pio opted to take an early retirement. He didn't fit the new thinking (or what passed for it) at the time. He was completely frustrated by the political mess. So he cashed in his chips and left the game.

The day of his retirement interview was a dark one for him. I accompanied him, driving from Providence, Rhode Island, up to the regional office in Boston. Nothing that happened during the cursory session in the company offices brightened his spirits in the least. On his way out of the offices, he saw another manager, someone he had mentored and whose career paralleled his, and I remember him saying, "Woody, don't expect a damn thing. They'd rather spit on your grave than bring you flowers."

Uncle Pio left in a dreadful mood, as badly in need of cheering up as anyone you've probably ever known. Yet for lunch, there was only one place he would consider. Durgan Park.

So off to lunch we went. It's a day and event I'll never forget, imprinted in my mind forever. Well, certainly, you might be thinking, they recognized how down he was and softened their tone to josh him out of his bleak humor, right? No way. They piled it on. They razzed him about his tie. They chirped at him about his order. Made fun of the way he used his napkin. They dished out attitude right along with the food. The brusk demeanor of the wait staff is a hallmark clue of Durgan Park.

And it raised his spirits. There was still something experientially solid and dependable in the world. He had had to bottle up all of his feelings as he sat through his exit interview, knowing that the people now running the company to which he'd given so much had no respect and less loyalty for him. His whole business life had seemingly ended, and on the sourest of notes. It was a great release emotionally for him to be at Durgan Park, where people say what they want to say, where nothing is held back.

Stewards of True Value

Now obviously, if Perkins, Baker's Square, Denny's, or another familiar restaurant chain tried to imitate what Durgan Park does, most people would find the transformed experience annoying at best. (Some might be tempted to look for a lawyer.) Mindless copying is not the point of the story. Consistency, honesty, and authenticity are the true nature of experience value creation.

References

1. Press Ganey Associates, Inc., 404 Columbia Place, South Bend, IN 46601
2. Robert Bauer. Personal communication (November 2002).

AFTERWORD
NOW THAT YOU'RE CLUED IN, STAY TUNED IN

The knowledge of experience management and an Experience Management system is truly transformational. When you're clued in to experience disciplines and competencies, you'll never experience any experience the same way you did before. You'll see it, hear it, smell it, touch it, and be touched by it with a new and heightened awareness.

In the decades I've spent working with the concept of managing experiences, much has occurred to advance the theory and the practice. But it's very clear that this is only the beginning. I am convinced that we are entering a new era, one in which experience management skills and tools will continue to expand far beyond where they are today and the practice of Experience Value Management will become more fully leveraged.

This new era will require greater overall control, commitment and sensitivity: Hiring, education and training, marketing, facility design, incentives, measurement, and communications will all need to be aligned and synchronized to deliver on deep-seated customer needs and desires. Customers expect companies to meet their expectations every time, regardless of the channel where it takes place. Experiences will have to resonate and enhance value for customers on the Internet, over the phone, through a touch pad kiosk, in a store, office, or in person. And if you fail, the probability of defection increases significantly. No long-term loyalty and advocacy—no long-term viability and profitability. No future.

Time Starts Now

If you've decided to meet the challenges—and pursue the opportunities—of leveraging experience as a value proposition, there's no better time to start than right now. Literally everyone, from chief executive officers and chief experience officers to unit managers and team leaders, are beginning to wrestle with the common issues around customer experience as a value proposition. In small companies as well as large multinationals, the first tentative steps toward systematic management of customer experiences are being contemplated, taken, evaluated, and deemed invaluable.

On deeper reflection, I think you'll agree that the world has indeed changed. More products and services are available today than ever before. Multichannel environments have emerged. Technological advancements are unprecedented. Global markets are the rule. All of this—and more—are combining to escalate customer expectations at a time when most customers say they are less than happy with the way they are being treated. Growing numbers say they feel completely unconnected to the brands and companies with which they interact.

Experience is the common ground on which to reach them.

If you're a CEO, vice president, department head, or manager, I hope you're not just simply aware that your customers experience a countless number of clues that affect the total value they associate with your company, but also that you recognize the need to do something to begin to manage those clues with rigor. The systematic management of clues is fundamental to your future. Companies that lack it could perish, and those with it will flourish.

Measuring the Intangible

It's not unusual for executives to be concerned about how they will measure the return from "experience" initiatives because they seem soft and intangible. In reality, a focus on experience presents the opportunity to see important, often ignored correlations that can have profound bottom line consequences. This rests in the relationship between cause and effect.

CEOs and management will spend money in tough times to learn that they're falling short on delivering experiential customer value and in the process they somehow restrict their ability to do something about it. Millions of dollars will be spent on the hardware and software to manage the customer relationship without defining or creating the system that manages the experiences that truly are the basis of the relationship. There's a greater tendency to spend money on technology because it's more tangible.

Most measurements today are based on effect—customer behavior, retention, average purchase amounts, complaint resolution rates, unit sales change, profitability and so forth. Experience management presents the opportunity to understand the correlation of those "effect" measurements with new experience-driven metrics focused around "causes"—the feelings experience clues create and the customer perceptions connected to an Experience Motif (the emotional end frame) and to the resulting degree of commitment and advocacy. The essence of an Experience Management System is built around managing all of the elements in an experience—the "causes"—to create the "effects" expressed in the motif which thereby bond customers to a brand or company experience.

Experience management gives your business the means to create greater meaningful value for customers by meeting both their functional and emotional needs in a way that makes them feel what they want to feel about themselves. Feeling good about that experience, in turn, leads to feeling good about the brand or company, strengthening the bonds on which competitive success can be built and without which it may be impossible. It's all about how customers feel.

Leadership has to have skin in the game to entrench an experience management system. Once in place, it has to be bigger than any one person and able to operate in perpetuity. The Mayo brothers, Ray Kroc, the Marriotts, and Walt Disney knew that, and their legacy can be felt even today. They were committed to "creating value for customers" and making a difference in people's lives. That passion has lots of parallels with religious conviction about how we treat other people.

Serving up Feelings

About 90 minutes southwest of Washington, DC, exists a world-renowned restaurant that demonstrates the power latent of experience. The Inn at Little Washington in Washington, Virginia, was founded in 1978 by Patrick O'Connell and Reinhardt Lynch. Over the past 25 years, it has won just about every award possible. It's a regular on lists of the top 10 restaurants in America. Reservations for the 14-room Inn are sought after like hen's teeth.

It's no accident. The customer experience, particularly the emotional needs of the customer, are paramount considerations. The wait staff is trained for almost a year before interacting with or addressing guests and undergoes examinations every bit as rigorous as those given to London taxi drivers in their justifiably famed apprenticeship. New waiters aren't entitled to a full cut of the tip pool until veteran waiters have put them to a final test, firing every imaginable question at them—décor, ingredients, facts about wine, the history of the Inn, and anything else *their* on-the-job experience has shown them that a customer might care about.

Some 10 years ago, Donna Reiss reviewed the restaurant for the *Virginian-Pilot*'s Sunday Flavor section. "The secret ingredient is not an herb but an attitude," she wrote. "A former student of speech and drama who speaks with quiet precision and confidence, O'Connell prescribes fine dining as a restorative for an ailing world. With their extraordinary cuisine and opulent rooms, he and Lynch offer 'a healing experience for people who feel disenfranchised with the deterioration of culture,' says O'Connell.

"In restaurants you are transported away from the everyday world," she continued, quoting O'Connell's belief that "you can reestablish a spiritual connection. We're here to celebrate life and the beauty around you. ... You should leave feeling restored, not just fed." [1]

Yesterday's news? Not to the Travel Channel's Samantha Brown. "You've heard all the hype about this inn and I must say it's not true," she confided to viewers in August 2003. "It's even better! The owners have thought of everything to make your stay a transforming respite from the world. Even the phone ring has a soft, calming tone so as to not jar you from the fantasy land to which this inn has transported you." [2]

The entire experience is geared to what and how people want to feel—and it's monitored and measured to make sure it continues to do just that. O'Connell believes people "aren't impressed by what you know or what you can offer until they see that you care," as Tahl Raz noted in an article for *Inc. Magazine* in 2003. "And you can't possibly care in any meaningful way unless you have some insight into what people are feeling and why." [3]

One key metric is the Inn's "mood rating." When a new party arrives in the dining room, the captain assigns them a number from one to ten, which assesses the guests' apparent state of mind (seven or below indicates displeasure or unhappiness). The entire staff can see and react accordingly because the mood rating is typed into a computer, written on the dinner order, and placed on a spool in the kitchen. Whatever the circumstances, O'Connell's goal is crystal clear: "No one should leave here feeling below a nine."

To that end, the wait staff is empowered to do whatever needs to be done to raise the number: complimentary champagne, extra desserts, a tour of the kitchen, even a tableside visit from one of the owners. "Consciousness to the extreme is great customer service" in O'Connell's view. "If guests ran into terrible traffic on the way over here or are in the midst of a marital dispute, we need to consider it our problem. How else are we going to ensure that they have a sublime experience?"[1]

Good Need Not Be Lavish

Taco Bell certainly is not the Inn at Little Washington. But the two have more than food service in common. They are both keenly aware of the importance of managing the total customer experience and how customers perceive value. For that reason, Emil Brolick, Taco Bell's president and chief concept officer—whom Wall Street credits with leading a significant company turnaround—has made the customer experience the central focus for where he's taking the company in the future.

Under Brolick, Taco Bell has gone rather swiftly from the weakest to the healthiest of the fast-food chains owned by Louisville, Kentucky-based Yum! Brands, Inc. (Formerly known as Tricon Global Restaurants, Yum! Brands was spun off in 1997 by PepsiCo Inc.)

---

1. How do customers feel? I scanned numerous reviews and comments from patrons. A typical comment, posted on the epinionon.com Web site in 2000: "Outrageously Priced—And Worth Every Penny. This is the only restaurant I have ever been to where I could drop $300 and feel really, really good about myself afterward."

Hired in 2000 after spending twelve years at Wendy's as Senior Vice President for New Product Marketing, Research and Strategic Planning, Brolick put into action a risky game plan. It called for adding more expensive items—made with better ingredients—to Taco Bell's menu while working to have cleaner, nicer-looking restaurants to support the experiential upgrade. In addition, although premade food is still delivered to Taco Bell's 6,700 restaurants, new $1,450 cooking grills were installed systemwide in late 2002. Not only do they allow locations to prepare the new menu entries on site, they also allow Taco Bells to build on an awareness that the aromas of food preparation are a vital piece of the customer experience.

The move paid off quickly: In the last three months of 2001, the country's largest Mexican fast-food chain began a sales rebound. In 2002, same-store sales at Taco Bell eateries open for at least 12 months rose 7%. Through the third quarter of 2003, same-store sales continued to grow at a 1.5% clip.

Brolick, along with Pam Dumond and Mark Wilson, the leaders of Taco Bell's Branded Customer Experience team, believes that leveraging the customer experience will raise the bar for the entire industry, just as Taco Bell did back in the 1980s, when then-CEO John Martin redirected the company's efforts—and the entire industry—toward value pricing.

"Managing the customer's total experience represents the total brand value customers perceive that keeps them coming back again and again," Brolick maintains. "The more we understand that and leverage that, the greater our return will be for our stakeholders." [4]

Watch for Future Developments

In a growing number of organizations, some of which you've met in the preceding chapters, others of which you'll become aware of in the years to come, promising experience management efforts are beginning to take shape. The trails they blaze and the results they achieve will provide the grist for future discussions of the power of experience as a focal point for a business's value proposition.

Blockbuster, Inc. is one of the world's leading providers of in-home movie and game entertainment with almost $6 billion in annual world-wide revenues and 8,500 stores throughout the Americas, Europe, Asia, and Australia. Blockbuster has committed to defining, designing, and implementing an experience management system that builds strong customer commitment by creating an emotional connection. Block-buster understands that its participation in what the customers experience in seeking out entertainment that can contribute to improving customers' lives. And it's a powerful goal, according to management.

In contrast to organizations that often need to fight for top-down support, Chairman and CEO John Antioco and members of his senior management team[2] are personally championing and very actively involved in leveraging the customer experience. Antioco, who built a reputation at 7-Eleven, Circle K, Taco Bell, and Pearle Vision, joined Blockbuster in 1997 and led the financial turnaround of the company, introducing numerous marketing and operational initiatives. Under his direction, Blockbuster underwent a successful IPO in August 1999 and has completed five consecutive years of same-store sales increases. He is committed to making his legacy at Blockbuster a compelling experience that keeps customers bonded on a deep and emotional level in a way that can't be fulfilled by anyone else.

"This isn't a program but a commitment to a way of doing business, a culture and dedication to what our customers value," according to Antioco. "The value of the customer experience in our business has been underleveraged, and we have permission to participate in the emotional fulfillment of our members. That opportunity, properly honored, will provide Blockbuster with a special place in the market and in the hearts of its members and customers for many years to come." [5]

---

2. Prominent among them are Nigel Travis, President and Chief Operating Officer; Mike Roemer, Executive Vice President and Chief Operations Officer for North American operations; and Nick Shepherd, Executive Vice President and Chief Marketing and Merchandise Officer. Former Chief Marketing Officer Jim Notarnicola, Senior Vice President of Operations Ned Dickey and Director of Customer Experience Jack Keon, along with a Customer Experience Core Team, also have played significant roles.

Taking Action

An ancient Chinese proverb tells us:

> I hear and I forget.
> I see and I remember.
> I do and I understand.

Whatever you've heard, seen, and remembered about the value of customer experience, you will gain no return on the time invested unless and until you commit yourself to doing something about it. From doing will come a level of understanding that no book can aspire to create. Start to manage experiences, actively and systematically, and you'll really begin to understand what it's about in the most meaningful terms possible—the true value that's created for your customers and your company.

Farsightedness and peripheral vision versus nearsightedness and myopic vision characterize the heart of leveraging customer experience. From Howard Johnson and Disney to RBC Financial and University Hospital, you should now be able to identify the consequences of managing and not managing customer experiences. The early pioneers have shown an ability to see what others don't and a willingness to accept the challenge that experience management presents. Their trail is becoming an ever broader legacy.

Today, I find I spend less time trying to convince people that they should try to manage the value created by experience and more time showing them how to do it. Getting *clued in* is the critical first step. From that start, you too will begin to harness the kind of relentless energy that is generated by sensing clues and recognizing their meaning and importance in the eyes of your customers.

In the future, the challenge no doubt will be greater and more urgent. As more and more people and firms become clue-conscious and begin to effectively manage clues to create greater experiential value for their customers—and employees and stakeholders—the level of competition will intensify. So, too, will the consequences for those who delay getting into the game.

Don't wait. Start doing something today.

Perhaps it's my New England roots, but my favorite poet is Robert Frost. For me, the lasting impression of this great man, then 92 years old, reading one of his poems at the 1960 inauguration of John F. Kennedy, is indelible and still inspiring. Wrinkled paper in hand, sun glaring in his eyes, gray shocks of hair blowing in the frigid breeze across the Capitol steps, his raspy Yankee accent that day was as thick as cold maple syrup. It only further endeared his writings to me.

As a poet, he seemed to have an instinctive grasp of the power of clues. His work in its own way is as fully functional an experience management system as the environment Uncle Pio created in the aisles of his A&P. Frost's words are finely crafted, with a cadence and a sound all their own. Each is rich with meaning. When woven together by one as skillful as Frost, they have the extraordinary ability to drill deep into my emotional epicenter. If I close my eyes, I can still call to mind a fifth-grade teacher reciting Frost: I can see the classroom, the late morning sunlight pouring through the window, the desk where I sat; I can smell the modeling clay, sharpened pencils, crayons, and paste.

Whether it's the Kennedy inaugural or that long-ago classroom, the clued-in way Frost reaches my emotions or the warm memories of Uncle Pio teaching me lessons about business that I wasn't even conscious of learning until many years later, those vivid connections remain alive to this day. Those are experiences. And you have the opportunity to imprint experiences with similar intensity if you so choose.

My hope is that you've been bitten by the experience bug—that you've seen enough to be convinced that your organization can create competitive advantage by managing the experiences of your customers. If so, have the courage today to venture down the road less traveled. I can assure you it won't be less traveled for long.

May all your experiences be great, rich, and rewarding. And may all the experiences you create make people feel good about themselves and those who provide them.

Two roads diverged and I, I
Took the one less traveled by
And that has made all the difference. [6] ❧

■ Lou Carbone
lcarbone@expeng.com
April 2004

References

1. Donna Reiss. "Inn Style," Flavor section, *Virginian-Pilot,* page 4 (August 21, 1994).

2. Samantha Brown. "Great Hotels," Travel Channel (July 2003).

3. Tahl Raz. "A Recipe for Perfection: America's Poshest Inn Reveals Its Secrets for Satisfying the World's Toughest Customers," *Inc. Magazine,* page 1 (July 2003).

4. Emil Brolick. Personal conversation (2002).

5. John Antioco. Personal conversation (2003).

6. Robert Frost. "The Road Not Taken."

APPENDIX

Knowing there are many people looking for tools and information that will help them leverage experience as a value proposition, it's a pleasure to provide this appendix. One of my objectives in writing this book was to share insights and tools I have discovered, utilized or developed in my company's work with distinguished clients in the practice of effective experience management.

It's my belief that the presentation of this list will facilitate and speed an organization's experience management efforts, whether the tools are used alone or in combination. I also believe that this toolkit is the broadest and most distinctive available to any organization serious about pursuing experience as a value proposition. I'm certain that it will continue to expand as work in the Experience Value Management space grows. In fact, I encourage and hope, as you encounter new tools in your own experience management efforts, you will forward them to me for addition to this list to be shared with others.

Lou Carbone
Minneapolis, MN
April, 2004

Experience Management Tools

For more information on any listing included here, contact Experience Engineering, Inc. or www.expeng.com.

Adaptive Enterprise Design™

A strategic business model to help organizations understand and act on adaptive, customer-back business designs. Pioneered by Stephan H. Haeckel, it is a comprehensive framework for sensing, interpreting, and reacting more quickly to unpredictable change, including the continuous changes that affect customer value perceptions.

Haeckel's contribution to shaping the next generation of businesses is recognized as foundational.

Benefit:

Lays the foundation for becoming an adaptive enterprise and moving from a "make-and-sell" to a "sense-and-respond" organization; accomplishes this by focusing on the structure and governances necessary to be strategically driven by customer needs.

ClueScan™

A method for scanning and evaluating experience clues, in particular mechanic and humanic clues "through the customer's eyes." This technique applies to the business environment, business process, and/or behaviors in an organization as experienced by customers and employees. Often conducted with an internal team of employees to help sensitize them to the range and variety of experience clues customers encounter every day. ClueScans can also be used to evaluate competitors' experiences.

Benefit:

A comprehensive view and evaluation of positive, negative, and commodity clues that can either be elevated and expanded on or eliminated. This is often used as a starting point for experience management initiatives as well as stewarding an already implemented experience design.

Clue Ideation

A distinctive cross-functional process for creating preference-generating experience clues for an entire experience or specific subexperiences. To ensure consistency and focus, an Experience Motif and brand strategy are used as the primary design filters. Most significantly, this approach is forged around creating clues that probe the full depth and breadth of the Experience Ribbon.

Benefit:

Forces the creation of enhanced and aligned experience clues; reinforces the emotional value created for customers, and fosters a holistic perspective of experience value creation among a cross-functional team.

Cultural Archetype Studies

A market research technique that defines the psychological underpinnings of a culture by combining psychiatry, psychology, and cultural anthropology; an extension of work done by scholars such as Jung, Laing, and Levi-Strauss, and more recently popularized by Dr. G. Clotaire Rapaille and firms such as Mind Meld Consulting, Toronto, Ontario, Canada.

Benefit:

By tapping into a pool of shared "imprintings" that define the behaviors of a culture, the archetypes (or deep-seated drivers of consumer choice for the culture) are discovered. If cultural archetypes are accurately defined and addressed in experience designs and marketing efforts, they foster an authenticity that resonates more completely with the consumer.

CustCam™ Video/Audio Analysis

Pinhole video camera w/sound embedded in a wristwatch, a handbag, a coat button, tie, or eyeglasses; designed to capture one-on-one interactions with customers.

Benefit:

Creates a distinctive purview of the experience from the customer's or employee's perspective that is a fertile resource for in-depth analysis of clues. It can be used as a basis for capturing all kinds of experiences – from selling to how products and services are actually consumed. The information gathered often serves as a basis for education, training and to contrast before and after experiences.

Customer Experience Mystery Shop™

A proprietary and interactive research technique that includes videotaping a mystery shop encounter plus a comprehensive debrief in which the mystery shopper views his or her encounter on videotape; then identifies (through probing techniques) the clues that led to the feelings and emotions generated.

Benefit:

Provides a first-hand, holistic perspective of the experience and clues within it that generate conscious and unconscious reactions in a business operation.

E-Metrics™

A unique framework for measuring both the impact and performance of an individual experience clue, clue clusters, Experience Motif, and/or overall experience design as well as the value of emotional connections with regard to customer commitment and advocacy. Often embedded into the metrics an organization is already using.

Benefit:

Provides an analytical framework for understanding the cause-and-effect relationship between the emotional value (or feelings) customers have and the impact on traditional measurements such as retention, profitability, average purchase amounts, complaint resolution rates, unit sales change, etc.; provides analysis between the "causes" (clues) that ultimately create the "effect," or degree of bonding customers have to an experience.

Ethnographic Studies

A market research technique used by Procter & Gamble and others, based on an anthropological method of study; naturalistic observation and interviewing are combined to learn how consumers behave in their natural setting. Researchers actually go into households or other appropriate environments to witness the experience of using a product. This fosters a lack of inhibition for consumers about revealing aspects of their lives and consumption experiences.

Benefit:

Provides the opportunity to glean deeper insights into consumers' hearts and minds; challenges conventional thinking, which broadens the framing of customer experiences.

For a comprehensive discussion of ethnographic methods, see Jean J. Schensul and Margaret D. Le Compte (Eds.), *Ethnographer's Toolkit*. Walnut Creek, CA: AltaMira Press, 1999.

Experience Based Curriculum™

An experiential framework for education and "people skills" in an organization, based on the importance of sensitivity to customer needs, values, and humanic roles. Highlights three curriculum components to seed and foster an experiential perspective:

1. That customer value creation is experiential

2. That experiences are created in customers' minds based on clues they process consciously and unconsciously

3. That there are tools to manage clues and the resulting experiences that foster preference, loyalty, and commitment

Benefit:

An education curriculum aligned with the strategic goal of experience as a value proposition, often embedded into current education initiatives.

Experience Blueprint™

A method for pictorially capturing, articulating and cataloging a distinctive set of humanic (emitted by humans) and mechanic (emitted by the environment) clues as a basis for storytelling. Fashioned after what a set of blueprints look like for a construction project; contains graphic representations and details of each specific clue in the experience ribbon.

Benefit:

An effective way to communicate and manage experience clues generated in an experience design. It conveys the prioritization of clues in order to deliver a managed total experience and becomes a roadmap for implementation of all clues.

Experience Clueprint™

A tool often used in conjunction with an Experience Blueprint for capturing and cataloging humanic and mechanic clues with more detail and specification; includes the estimated cost of each clue, what senses are stimulated, the degree of difficulty for implementing, who owns the clue internally, as well as priority for implementation.

Benefit:

Communicates the experience design clue by clue, enabling cross-functional teams to grasp the content of the clues they "own" without losing the overall context of the total experience design.

For more information, contact www.expeng.com.

Experience Intervention Interviews™

Ten- to fifteen-minute, spontaneous customer interviews conducted immediately after a targeted transaction or business interaction. Designed to capture intuitive reactions to feelings and the relative relationship of clues experienced. The customer is probed about his or her thoughts and feelings around the experience just encountered.

Benefit:

Helps establish what the customer expected before the interaction and what the actual experience yielded, highlighting any gaps in brand and marketing communications and the actual experience being delivered.

Experience Reflection Interviews™

A proprietary customer interview process that has been influenced by Dr. Gerald Zaltman's perspectives on research techniques; designed to probe underlying emotions regarding experiences or a specific topic; follows the customer's thought patterns versus employing predictable rationale questioning.

Benefit:

Probes consumers' underlying motivations; provides deeper understanding of customer motivations, especially when combined with imagery selection and language analysis; a viable option for replacing traditional focus groups or surveys.

Experience Motif Generation™

Used to facilitate an organization in gaining consensus and articulating the emotional "end frame" it commits to deliver to customers. The process leverages input from brand and corporate strategy and core values, as well as experience audit initiatives. Participants in the Experience Motif generation session often include customers as well as a cross-section of employees and stakeholders.

Benefit:

Defines the emotional foundation of the customer experience, leveraging the uniqueness of the corporate brand. The motif then becomes the critical design fulcrum and lens for designing, managing, and aligning all customer experience clues. In addition to highly focused and aligned experience clues, there is great value in a cross-functional team being centered on defining the customer's emotional needs.

Experience Optimization Workshop™

A workshop specific to shaping an experience-driven initiative; helps identify needs, objectives, and resources to help an organization prioritize where it should begin experience-driven efforts. A work session designed to access the opportunities represented by experience management for an organization.

Benefit:

Provides clarity regarding where an organization will gain the quickest wins and most significant results in leveraging experience management.

Experience Wayfinding Systems™

Orientation is a critical element in most experiences and one that has significant emotional impact on customers. Experience Wayfinding systems are based on intuitive and psychologically influenced wayfinding that are considered from the customer's point of view and emotional impact.

Benefit:

A wayfinding system connects with customers incorporating signage and other orientation tools in support of the Experience Motif, as opposed to simply tasteful artistic design.

Humanic Narrative and Role Development™

Detailed and articulated employee roles that integrate characteristics, and story lines that reflect specific experience elements (Experience Motif, among others) and mesh with mechanic clues that have been designated.

Benefit:

Humanic roles supplement traditional job description and function with an experiential overlay, offering much more detail, including personality recommendations, desired mannerisms, phrasing, dress, etc.

Language Analysis

Patented conversation analysis software developed by Dr. Charles Cleveland that makes ultrafine distinctions in the human communication process. It does this by comparing the language of one context (or group) with another and recommending the necessary language shifts to move to the desired context. Analysis is generally conducted from customer and employee verbatims.

Benefit:

Makes it possible to measure the degree of meaningful communication between customers and a business or business division with recommendations for "high-performance" word clues and phrases to be incorporated into an experience design.

Observational Video

One or multiple stationary cameras positioned to capture experiences in business operation.

Benefit:

A roving eye that captures a "day in the life" of an operation. Enables detailed analysis of elements that provide insight into the quality of the experience: store layout, traffic patterns, body language, and interactions with merchandise and employees. Offers management the opportunity to review data multiple times as well as valuable "before and after" analysis.

Scent, Sound, and Light Management Systems

Special delivery systems that manage scent, sound, and light in highly focused ways in order to more closely synchronize with desired customer emotions. These include technologies such as scent incorporated into floor wax, business cards, and heating and ventilation systems; the use of sound parabolas to focus specific sounds or manage the absence of sound; responsive lighting systems that impact how people move through environments and experiences.

Benefit:

Provides an opportunity to define and embed sensory clues that will enhance making the desired emotional connection articulated by an organization's Experience Motif.

Sensory Motif Palette™

A collection of specifications around sensory elements that will enhance making the desired emotional connection articulated by an organization's Experience Motif. For example, the actual colors, scents, tastes, textures, or sounds that would help customers feel "strengthened, understood, and renewed."

Benefit:

Provides resources and a sensory palette for guiding ongoing clue management.

SERVQUAL Model

A framework for understanding and measuring what customers value. Pioneered by Valerie A. Zeithaml, A. Parasuraman, and Leonard L.

Berry, this four-part prescriptive model on how to improve service quality also measures the difference between customers' minimum expectations and their perceptions of those services as delivered.

Benefit:

A customer-back tool for measuring performance levels as perceived by customers.

ZMET® Metaphor Elicitation Interviews

A proprietary technique pioneered by Harvard Business School Professor Emeritus, Dr. Gerald Zaltman. Provides a thorough and integrated understanding of consumers' beliefs and emotions about a certain topic, product, or service. Designed to probe deeply to understand behaviors and attitudes of which customers are unaware.

Benefit:

Identifies the deep underlying concepts that structure people's thoughts and emotions to drive their choices and behaviors in the marketplace. The insights can be readily applied to experience design and communication strategies to resonate more completely with target audiences.

ACKNOWLEDGMENTS

Where does a person begin to acknowledge all the people who have influenced them and helped to make the seemingly impossible, possible?

I must start out where everything in my life seems to start. That is with the love that's clearly demonstrated in the innumerable sacrifices, continuous support, encouragement, and understanding I've received, not just in this project, but in the passionate pursuit of my career over the years from my lovely wife, Dorothy, my daughter, Elizabeth, and my son, Jonathan. They indeed share in the accomplishment this book represents. I sincerely and deeply appreciate the sacrifices they've made because of the countless times I've been absent for hours, days and weeks while in pursuit of my vision and work over the years. They truly make the impossible, possible. I appreciate them more that they could ever imagine or mere words could ever explain.

Next, I would like to thank those who have lived through this book with me and made what you now hold in your hands a reality. I am immeasurably indebted to them. Their commitment and intellect have been invaluable in realizing the dream of sharing the insights and excitement for the concept of experience value creation management.

In particular: Suzie Goan, director of public relations and marketing at Experience Engineering, Inc., who, through extraordinary perseverance, has lived through this project with me for more than six years and whose life (including private time and vacations) in the past 18 months has almost been consumed by this undertaking.

Gerry Strauss, retired advertising executive and my mentor who hired me and brought me to work for an advertising agency in New York City more than 25 years ago. He has continuously provided astounding perspectives throughout my career. He pushed aside countless personal hours in retirement to offer his support and insights into the processing of the material in this book.

Dick Schaaf, author and vernacular engineer, who joined the team and helped shape the expression of my life's work into this book.

Dawn Thompson, my administrative assistant, who helped shuffle and traffic manuscripts, transcribe, and juggle schedules.

And of course, there's the extraordinary encouragement and support and that came from others directly involved in this publishing project. First and foremost, Tim Moore, the publisher and executive editor for Prentice Hall, for his insight advice, understanding, and patience, which were invaluable in the realization of this book.

Also at Prentice Hall, Kathleen Caren, my production editor, and Jon Pierce, Martin Ltikowski and their marketing team; the encouragement, patience and thoughtfulness of Russ Hall, my development editor; and special thanks for the time, support and thoughtful comments from Bill Ghormley and Lewis Columbo, who served as technical editors.

A very special thanks to my colleagues and very special friends who I have been blessed to know, without whom my life would never have been the same: Steve Haeckel, Jerry Zaltman and Len Berry. Each of you are indeed a rare breed of man, whose contributions to the lives of people around you and passion for what you do are the source of inspiration for me.

I'd like to extend my deepest appreciation to my team at Experience Engineering, Inc. today and over the formative years. Each of you have made your own contribution to this body of work in so many ways, the least of which is not the sacrifice you all made taking up some of the slack in helping run the day-to-day business while this project was underway. Thanks especially to Terry Pompelia, Gil Fletcher and in particular, Nancy O'Brien, as well as those we've partnered with over the years, including Eunice Hogeveen, Betty Hutchins and Jeff Mitchell.

Special thanks must also go to Jan Homan, Molly Hudson, Jack Yurish, and Ron Masini, who at different points in my life made significant contributions to my perspectives on customer value creation which are always evident in my work and thought process.

For their roles in my life supporting my work as either "teachers," supporters and friends: Bob Faller, Lisa Faller and the team at FKQ, Ron Floto, Dave Miller, Gary Taravella, Ray Leicht, Don Werner, Ed Wax, Pete Dow, Bill McCue, Chip Eichman, Mike McPhillips, Steve Krenz, Mike McCaffrey, Mark Baszto, Craig Davis, Allen Clifford, Kim Meirrow, Michael Meirrow, Dan Gassert, Steve Joern, Bob Ernst, Tom Mercier, Jim "Mattress Mack" and Linda MacInvale, Nazir Amed, Joe Burke, Jim Markisohn, and especially Mike Long.

To George McGinnis, the legendary Disney Imagineer I had the opportunity to interview and get to know as a "cub reporter" at the Greenville Record-Argus in 1972, and William Knecht III, the most outstanding IBM Office Products Marketing Representative that I met the prior year: you changed my perspectives on experience value management forever.

Special thanks to Virginia O'Connor and the members of the American Management Sales and Marketing Council, where I first met Steve Haeckel, Bill Ghormley and a myriad of others on the council, who over the years have been the "rock" that provided the encouragement and enthusiasm that have fueled me in the development of the concepts contained in this book.

My sincerest thanks to Carolyn Pollard Neal, who as the editor of *Marketing Management* magazine, had the vision to publish the very first article Steve Haeckel and I co-authored in 1994 on "engineering experiences."

To Shaun Smith, Joe Wheeler, Bernd Schmidt, Joe Pine, Jim Gilmore, Jeannie Bliss, and Colin Shaw for their contributions in recent years to the expansion of awareness of the value of experience and all the work they've done to help others experience it.

And to all my clients and colleagues who have always taught me more than I could ever dream of teaching them, and for their support in helping me learn.

I would also like to express my deepest gratitude to the people in my life, including my late parents and grandparents and also to my extended family, cousins, and so on, who have been such a part of my life experience over the years. You have all influenced my thinking in many ways and helped me learn things I didn't even know I learned.

To each and every one of you, I say thank you.

Lou Carbone
April 2004

INDEX